Timothy Richard's Vision

Studies in Chinese Christianity

G. Wright Doyle and Carol Lee Hamrin,

Series Editors

A Project of the Global China Center

www.globalchinacenter.org

Timothy Richard's Vision
Education and Reform in China, 1880–1910

EUNICE V. JOHNSON

Edited by Carol Lee Hamrin

*With a Foreword by Ruth Hayhoe
and an Afterword by Aisi Li*

☙PICKWICK *Publications* · Eugene, Oregon

TIMOTHY RICHARD'S VISION
Education and Reform in China, 1880–1910

Studies in Chinese Christianity

Copyright © 2014 Eunice V. Johnson. All rights reserved. Except for brief quotations in critical publications or reviews, no part of this book may be reproduced in any manner without prior written permission from the publisher. Write: Permissions, Wipf and Stock Publishers, 199 W. 8th Ave., Suite 3, Eugene, OR 97401.

Pickwick Publications
An Imprint of Wipf and Stock Publishers
199 W. 8th Ave., Suite 3
Eugene, OR 97401

www.wipfandstock.com

ISBN 13: 978-1-62564-653-8

Cataloguing-in-Publication data:

Johnson, Eunice V.

Timothy Richard's vision : Education and Reform in China, 1880–1910 / Eunice V. Johnson; edited by Carol Lee Hamrin, with a foreword by Ruth Hayhoe and an afterword by Aisi Li.

Studies in Chinese Christianity

xiv + 194 pp. ; 23 cm. Includes bibliographical references and index.

ISBN 13: 978-1-62564-653-8

1. Richard, Timothy, 1845-1919. 2. 3. I. Hamrin, Carol Lee. II. Hayhoe, Ruth. III. Li, Aisi. IV. Title.

BV3427 J65 2014

Manufactured in the U.S.A.   09/09/2014

Dedicated
to the Glory of God,
in loving memory of
my parents,
and in honor of the
Shanxi University Centennial

Contents

Foreword by Ruth Hayhoe　　ix
Note on Romanization　　xii
List of Abbreviations　　xiii

1. Reintroducing a Pioneer Missionary　　1
2. Becoming a Practical Reformer, 1865–85　　7
3. Refining the Reformer, 1885–91　　30
4. Shaping China's Reform Movements, 1891–1910　　48
5. Fulfilling the Vision: The Imperial University of Shansi, 1901–10　　89
6. Giving Honor Where Honor is Due　　112

Epilogue　　127
Afterword by Aisi Li　　129
Illustrations　　133
Author's Biographical Sketch and Acknowledgments　　151
Contributors　　157
Appendices
　　1 *Chronology of Timothy Richard's Life*　　159
　　2 *Compilation of Works in Chinese by Timothy Richard*　　165
Sources of Illustrations　　172
Bibliography　　175
Index　　191

Foreword

WHAT A JOY TO see the birth of this volume by Dr. Eunice Johnson on the eminent pioneer missionary Timothy Richard (1845–1919). My connection to this book goes back to the early 1990s, when Eunice came to Toronto to consult archives relating to the British missionary who was appointed by Timothy Richard to head the Western Department of the Imperial University of Shansi (now Shanxi University) at the time of its founding. I was working on a book about the development of Chinese universities over the twentieth century and the various Western influences that interacted with Chinese patterns of higher education in the evolution of China's modern universities. There was clear evidence of influences from the French and German models in the early years, followed by the American model, and finally the Soviet model after the revolution of 1949.

One fact puzzled me, however. Although Britain had been the dominant imperial power in terms of economic influence on China, the only institution that could be said to embody elements of a British model was the Imperial University of Shansi, and only for a short time. Within a decade after its founding, it had been integrated into the province's own higher education system. When Eunice told me during our brief meeting that she was planning to write a doctoral dissertation on its missionary founder, Timothy Richard, I could only give her the strongest encouragement, recognizing that here might be a unique and important story in the history of modern Chinese higher education.

Years passed by, and occasional phone calls or e-mails let me know that she had progressed through the dissertation research and defense, and had attended the university's centenary celebrations in Taiyuan, presenting a copy of her dissertation to its current leaders. Through these years, academic responsibilities took me away from my earlier work on the history of Chinese higher education. It was only in March of 2010 when I was in a mentoring program for current doctoral students at the annual meeting of the Comparative and International Education Society in Chicago that the story of Shanxi University once again captured my attention. A Chinese doctoral student at Oxford University was assigned to my group, with a thesis entitled "Competition and Compromise between British Missionaries and Chinese Officials: The Founding of Shanxi University in 1902." She had focused her research on significant Chinese archival documentation, and explored the story of the university's founding from the perspective of Governor Cen Chunxuan (Ts'en Ch'un-hsüan), an enlightened provincial leader who wanted to see his province benefit from modern higher education but was also concerned about issues of Chinese sovereignty and Chinese control over this important sector.

The first question I asked Aisi Li was whether she had read Eunice Johnson's thesis on the role of Timothy Richard in promoting modern higher education and science in China and in the founding of Shanxi University. The answer was no, and she was eager to find an opportunity to connect with Eunice as soon as possible. My contact information enabled her to visit Eunice in Florida and compare notes from Chinese and English language archives on the founding and early development of this remarkable university. Eunice shared details of all that Richard had done in negotiating the Boxer Indemnity issues for the Protestant mission societies and his success in attracting outstanding missionaries such as Moir Duncan and William Soothill to carry forward the leadership work of the new institution. Aisi also visited the archives of the Yale Divinity School in New Haven, Connecticut, and then returned to Oxford to complete the work on her thesis.

For my part, I decided I must finally read the whole thesis and learn Eunice's side of the story, so I invited her to visit me in our retreat home in South Florida in March of 2011. We were able to spend three days together, in part talking about the vision of Timothy Richard—that establishing a modern university in every province of China would support the development of scientific reforms and enable the country to solve its deep problems of poverty and recurring famine, while also bringing them into connection with a wider world that was changing dramatically.

As Eunice and I talked and reflected on the interface between Eunice's scholarly understanding and Aisi Li's emerging doctoral thesis, it occurred to me that Oxford might invite me to serve as external examiner on this work. At that moment, I turned to Eunice and asked her if she would be willing to accompany me if I were invited to Oxford in this role. She shared with me a longstanding desire to visit Richard's grave in London in order

Foreword

to pay respects to this Christian visionary, whose work had inspired her thesis. She also wished to take there several mementos from the grave of Moir Duncan, who had died in Taiyuan in 1906 at the early age of forty-five, just four years after taking up the leadership of the university's Western Department, and had been buried in the nearby mountains. Thus emerged the idea of a pilgrimage, which is recounted in the Epilogue.

I hope readers of this volume will journey with its author, as they explore the life of a man called by God to dedicate forty-five years of his life to the uplift of China through sharing his Christian faith, alongside a profound commitment to scientific knowledge and the creation of scientific and religious literature in China as well as to the development of institutions of higher learning in every province and region of the country. Coming from a family where Welsh, not English, was the first language and educated in a theological college where he struggled for a reform of the curriculum toward valuing living languages, natural science, and world history in contrast to the curriculum oriented to classical languages and the history of Greece and Rome that was prevalent in universities of the time, he had no desire to implant a British model of the university in China. No wonder then that he happily negotiated arrangements whereby the institution he helped to found would be fully handed over to Chinese administration and leadership in less than a decade from the date of its establishment. Richard thereby fulfilled his long-held vision for a university incorporating Western learning to train Chinese officials so they could benefit not only the province but all of China.

Ruth Hayhoe
Ontario Institute for Studies in Education, University of Toronto
November 2013

Note on Romanization

CHINESE PERSONAL NAMES ARE given with surname first and, along with institutional names, are Romanized using the pinyin system currently in use in the PRC, on first usage including the Wade-Giles version in parentheses (in use during the time frame of this study). Place names also are in pinyin, with a few exceptions for names commonly known to English readers such as Peking and Canton. References retain the Romanized versions in the original source.

Abbreviations

BMS	(English) Baptist Missionary Society
BMS MSS	Timothy Richard Papers, Archives of the (English) Baptist Missionary Society, Angus Library, Regent's Park College, Oxford, England. The author used the collection of manuscripts (MSS) available in microfilm at the Historical Commission, Southern Baptist Convention, Nashville, Tennessee.
CIM	China Inland Mission (later, Overseas Missionary Fellowship or OMF)
CLS	Christian Literature Society for China, the name for SDK after 1906; used for all references to SDK or CLS in the text, but not in sources.
EAC	Educational Association of China (later, China Christian Educational Association)
OMF	Overseas Missionary Fellowship (formerly, China Inland Mission or CIM)
NLW	Timothy Richard Papers, Wyre Lewis Collection, National Library of Wales, Aberystwyth
SDK	Society for the Diffusion of Christian and General Knowledge among the Chinese, Shanghai (Christian Literature Society as of 1906)
Tls.	Tael, a Chinese monetary unit of varying value depending on the type of tael and historical period; in 1900, a tael may have been equivalent to 3s. 2d. or approximately US $0.77.

1

Reintroducing a Pioneer Missionary

THE MISSIONARY ENTERPRISE IN China has received increasing attention in recent decades, both inside and outside China, spurred by the evidence of Christian revival there. Many historians had viewed the missionaries' efforts solely in terms of cultural imperialism or colonial paternalism. While it is true the missionaries were a product of their own cultures, they did not all consciously seek to transfer their own cultures to the new context of China. Nor did they all seek to gain political advantage in China for their own countries. In fact, many endured great privation and sacrificed much, even their lives, to spreading the Christian gospel. In many situations, where they went "the gospel of good works" followed. They established schools for girls as well as boys; made available hospitals or medical services to all classes; engaged in social redemptive works, particularly for women; and created and distributed all forms of edifying literature in Chinese.

A closer examination of missionary contributions is now being undertaken by Chinese and foreigners alike. More studies are available in English and Chinese on individual missionaries or specific missionary contributions to China, such as educational institutions or technical services. Nevertheless, it remains true in the history of modern China that "Protestant missionaries are still the least studied but most significant actors in the scene."[1]

Studies on the educational contributions of the Protestant missionary enterprise in China in particular are increasing, as evidenced by a 2009

---

1. Xu, "A Southern Methodist Mission," 1, cites the Dean of American Sinologists, the late John K. Fairbank, in 1985. Recent prize-winning quantitative research underscores Fairbank's point; see Woodberry, "The Missionary Roots of Liberal Democracy."

Timothy Richard's Vision

volume on China's Christian colleges.[2] Despite the interest in individual missionary schools, there have been far fewer studies in English on the Chinese government educational institutions, even though missionaries and Chinese Christians often played an important role there. Lund's dissertation on "The Imperial University of Peking" examines its development and impact on China during the last years of the Qing (Ch'ing) dynasty.[3] Biggerstaff's survey of the earliest modern government schools chronicles the efforts made by the Chinese government prior to the Sino-Japanese War (1894–95).[4] Chapters on various government educational institutions, including Qinghua (Tsinghua) University in Beijing, can be found included in other books.[5]

In 1992, Dr. Ruth Hayhoe, an expert on Chinese higher education, affirmed the importance of the query as to why the first modern government university of the twentieth century was located in the remote inland province of Shanxi (Shansi), and what might be its connection with the 1901 higher education reform edicts. She also encouraged further investigations into the key role played by Welsh Baptist missionary Timothy Richard.[6]

Richard had administered famine relief in the province 1878–80, and remained there for the next seven years.[7] He witnessed the terrible suffering of the people as he tried to ease their plight by supplying food and money collected by Christians in China and abroad. He experienced firsthand the difficulties of transport in Shanxi in attempting to bring food to the starving. Often he had to endure resistance or maneuvers by various officials that impeded getting aid to the people. Worse, desperate famine

---

2. Bays and Widmer, *China's Christian Colleges*. See the review of the literature on Christian colleges in their Postface, 303–7.

3. Lund, "The Imperial University."

4. Biggerstaff, *The Earliest Modern Government Schools*.

5. Examples include the story of the Christian founder and successors at Qinghua University in Carol Lee Hamrin, "Tang Guo'an: Pioneering China's Rights Recovery Movement," in Hamrin and Bieler, *Salt and Light*, 13–29; Buck, "Educational Modernization," 171–212; Keenan, "Lung-men Academy," in B. Elman and Alexander Woodside, eds., *Education and Society in Late Imperial China, 1600–1900* (Berkeley: University of California Press, 1994).

6. Personal communication between the author and Dr. Hayhoe in 1992, echoed in Hayhoe, *China's Universities*, 18–19. This conversation spurred a decade of research on Richard's work in higher education in China, culminating in Eunice V. Johnson, *Educational Reform in China, 1880–1910: Timothy Richard and His Vision for Higher Education* (PhD diss., University of Florida, 2001), from which this book is adapted.

7. See Bohr, *Famine in China*.

conditions fueled the elite's animosity toward missionaries as well as grassroots anti-foreignism, prompting outbreaks of violent religious persecution that halted all Christian work. The root of these challenges he found to be ignorance, superstition, and a lack of basic understanding of the world outside China and its modern scientific principles.

Richard began to think that once Chinese officials understood the "laws of God" operating in nature, they would accept the Christian faith and seek the greatest benefit of their own people. He believed that the key to understanding these laws was education. Thus, during his time in Shanxi, Richard provided educational lectures and scientific demonstrations to the scholars and officials in Taiyuan. Out of his famine experiences and his contacts with these Chinese officials, a vision was birthed for educational reform as the principal means of Chinese "enlightenment," opening the door for the gospel as well as China's entry into the modern world.

The substance of Richard's vision went through several transformations, ultimately becoming one that encompassed all of China and its role in the world. While in Beijing in late 1895, for example, during meetings with several high-ranking officials, he offered suggestions for comprehensive reform in the economy, foreign relations, and policies for guaranteeing religious freedom, as well as recommendations for educational reform, which he viewed as the basis for all the rest. By then, he already envisioned a system of government-supported higher educational institutions located in the provincial capitals offering a curriculum of Western learning—including Christian values, to those scholars who had already achieved certain success on the Confucian education for the civil service. By 1888 this vision had expanded to include a three-tiered system with elementary as well as preparatory education for the higher educational institutions.

Through the years, some Chinese scholars and officials, who had been making their own efforts to effect change in the Confucian civil service examination system—which shaped all levels of education, became increasingly sympathetic to Richard's vision. Powerful Court reformers finally embraced it and eventually provided the necessary impetus for imperial edicts that ultimately brought about the creation of a system of modern government-supported higher educational institutions.

In 1901, at the Chinese government's initiative, Richard was invited back to Shanxi to help settle the issue of compensation for damage and loss of life by missionaries and Chinese Christians during the Boxer Uprising the year before. In late May, Richard's proposed solution resulted in a decision to fund a college of Western learning, which was later combined with a college for Chinese traditional education to become the Imperial University of Shansi (now Shanxi University) in Taiyuan.

This volume will show how Timothy Richard's work in education—both formal schooling and mass popular education through the media, libraries, and societies—served as the central component of his larger and ever-expanding vision for a modern China. He had one grand passion—the Kingdom of God worked out intellectually, spiritually, and materially, ultimately leading to peace among individuals and nations.

Richard gradually developed his vision for China and the nations as a deep thinker and committed educator, finding his primary niche as a missionary doing Christian literary work, rather than more traditional itinerant evangelism and church planting, or even teaching. Over time, he disseminated his vision through every means available—writings, translations, memoranda of advice to government, personal mentoring and cooperation with Chinese and Westerners, public speaking in China, Britain, and America, and writing thousands of letters. All this while he served in various leadership capacities (1880–1912) in the Educational Association of China, as editor (1890–91) of the reformist newspaper *Shi Bao* [Shih Pao; The Times], and as General Secretary (1891–1915) of the Society for the Diffusion of Christian and General Knowledge among the Chinese (SDK). The SDK was also known as Christian Literature Society for China (CLS), which became the official name in 1906.[8]

The chapters following this introduction are ordered chronologically to highlight key phases in Richard's life. Chapter 2 notes some parallels between Wales and China in the mid-nineteenth century and examines early formative and educational influences in Richard's life while in Wales. The early emergence in Wales of Richard's reformist bent, aimed at achieving practical results, became apparent during his first years in China. By the beginning of his first furlough to England in 1885, Richard had already begun to articulate his vision for higher education as a base for comprehensive reforms in his interactions with other missionaries and Chinese officials.

Chapter 3 looks at Richard's first efforts to secure support from the Baptist Missionary Society (BMS) for his educational project. Failing in

---

8. Hereafter in this volume, Christian Literature Society (CLS) will be used for the Society during Richard's whole tenure there. This reflects usage at the time by Richard and his missionary colleagues, reflecting the fact that the main funding arm of SDK was the CLS in Glasgow, Scotland, as well as the existence of an international network of like-named societies.

this, he returned to China determined to reproduce his vision in others. The remainder of the chapter explores the controversies in Shanxi and Shandong (Shantung) Provinces surrounding Richard's unique mission philosophy, with its focus on elites, and his insistence on the preeminent importance of his approach. Then it examines his efforts to disseminate his vision to Chinese after he (temporarily) suspended the connection with his missionary society to become editor of a reformist newspaper under the auspices of the eminent high-ranking reformer Li Hongzhang (Hungchang). The refining of the man and his vision was completed by late 1891, when Richard became General Secretary of the CLS with the renewed support of the BMS.

Chapter 4 sets forth Richard's broad-based efforts and contributions on behalf of the welfare of the Chinese people over the ensuing period of almost twenty-five years. This was the most fruitful and influential period in Richard's life as he impacted nearly all aspects of life in urban China, directly or indirectly, through his literary efforts in the CLS and his personal relationships with Chinese and Westerners. Richard's contemporaneous efforts to disseminate his educational views through the Educational Association of China (EAC) shows how the relationships among its missionary members allowed for a fruitful exchange of information and ideas and—through their many networks—more opportunities for the dissemination of his vision.

Richard's influence on his peers as well as on "young China"—a rising generation of officials who prompted the emperor to launch the Hundred Days Reform—became very evident in 1898. The most dramatic educational reforms proposed were (1) the replacement of the stilted "eight-legged" essays on the Confucian classics by required essays on current affairs in civil service examinations, and (2) the establishment of schools in the provinces that included both Chinese and Western studies in their curricula. Both reforms were based on ideas Richard had propounded since the early 1880s and likely had discussed at great length with the young reformers during their visits together 1895–98.[9]

Chapter 5 documents the culmination of Richard's vision for higher education in China in the 1901 decision on the Imperial University of Shansi. The institution's inception played a major role as inspiration and practical model when the government promulgated edicts in September

---

9. Hsü, *The Rise of Modern China*, 375.

Timothy Richard's Vision

and November 1901 to establish a national system of modern institutions of higher education teaching Western learning.

Concluding chapter 6 sums up the importance of Timothy Richard's work. Through his prolific writings, in English and Chinese, he exerted significant influence on China's elite scholars and officials, and thereby became a key figure in the modernization of late Qing China. His reform legacy extended beyond the aborted 1898 reform into the late Imperial and early Republican era and even beyond his retirement in 1915. His advice for ending China's isolation in the late nineteenth century—to send top scholars and leading family members abroad, introduce Western learning to government schools, and launch public discussion of world topics—sounds like a description of Deng Xiaoping's first actions to reopen China after the Mao era.

This book is intended to re-introduce Timothy Richard to the general reader as well as scholars interested in early modern China, the history of Chinese Christianity, and the impact of the nineteenth-century mission era on both. Amazingly, there has been no book-length overall study of Richard since 1945, the centennial of his birth. This volume, based primarily on materials in English available up to 2002—including his memoir, private notes and letters, and biographies by his contemporaries, extends an invitation to explore studies in English and Chinese, recently completed or forthcoming, related to the life and work of this remarkable man.[10]

---

10. Richard, *Forty-Five Years*. Many of the full biographies and studies use Richard's memoir as their primary source and therefore contain little new information. See the list of these sources in the Bibliography. Appendix 1 provides a chronology of Richard's life; Appendix 2 lists his major works in Chinese, in English translation.

2

Becoming a Practical Reformer, 1865–85

IN 1870 WELSH BAPTIST missionary Timothy Richard arrived in a China that was much like Wales at the beginning of the nineteenth century. Wales was an agrarian society under the rule of an alien power, struggling to maintain its identity in the face of relentless social modernization with the advent of the Industrial Revolution. Farms lay fallow as young people flocked to jobs in the city factories and coal mines in newly-developed industrial centers. New schools and ideas about schooling abounded. This modernization process seemed to sound the death knell for the old way of life in Wales.

Similarly, at the beginning of the nineteenth century, the great Middle Kingdom of China was still bowed low under an alien power. Subjugated for hundreds of years by the Manchus, the Han Chinese by mid-century saw China's power wither away as the Qing (Ch'ing) dynasty increasingly became more impotent against encroachment by the major Western powers that had forced through treaties establishing trading rights within China's borders.[1] By the late 1860s, these treaties had also guaranteed the right of Roman Catholic and Protestant missionaries to travel inland and establish centers of missionary work with churches, schools, and clinics.[2]

---

1. Historical background is from Hsü, *The Rise of Modern China*.

2. Ibid., 168–220. Pre-eminent as a world power in military might and commercial expansion, the English attempted as early as 1793 to establish trade and diplomatic relations with the Middle Kingdom. China resisted such efforts or exercised strict control over such intercourse, allowing trade only through Canton (Guangzhou). This resistance led to inevitable misunderstanding that, in turn, deteriorated into formal military clashes, which were settled by the execution of what later became known as the Unequal

Timothy Richard's Vision

EARLY YEARS

Born in 1845 in the small village of Ffaldybrenin in Caermarthenshire, Wales, to a family of blacksmiths and farmers, Timothy Richard's humble beginning gave no indication of the powerful influence he would later wield in the distant Empire of China. His parents were devout Nonconformists (outside the state Church of England) who took seriously their responsibility to provide spiritual training for their nine children, Timothy being the youngest. The children's upbringing focused on the necessity of each individual's decision to become a Christian and the importance of living out the Christian faith. Among Richard's relatives were several who had distinguished themselves in Christian ministry.[3] During the Great Welsh Revival of 1858–60, Richard was converted to faith in Jesus Christ at the age of thirteen and was baptized by the Rev. John Davies of the Salem Baptist Church in May 1859.[4] The next year he experienced a personal "call" to missionary service, though his actual entrance to foreign missionary service in China did not occur for another ten years.[5]

From an early age, Richard showed academic promise. He received formal schooling until the age of fourteen at a school associated with a Congregationalist church built in one of his father's fields. At the age of fifteen, with the encouragement of his mother and brothers, he bargained with his father to remain in school for one more year instead of coming back to the farm to help. His father agreed, and for several years he worked as a teacher while furthering his own schooling.[6]

Treaties of 1842, 1858, and 1860. The first in 1842 ended the Opium War between Britain and China. In 1858 and 1860, a second set of treaties settled a conflict resulting from a Chinese assault on a British-licensed ship. The ramifications of these "unequal treaties" were far-reaching, even into the twentieth century. See also Latourette, *The Chinese: Their History and Culture*, 344–53.

3. Richard, *Forty-five Years*, 19–20.

4. Price, *History of Caio*, 58–59.

5. Burt, "Timothy Richard: His Contribution," 292–300. Richard, *Forty-five Years*, 22, recounted that soon after his conversion and baptism, he felt moved by a sermon to go abroad as a missionary. The sermon, "To obey is better than Sacrifice" (1 Sam 15:22), failed to move his brother Joshua, who had accompanied him.

6. He was sent to study at his cousin's school in Cross Inn, some twenty miles away, where he received more schooling as well as music training in the Tonic sol-fa notation, a system that uses the initial letters of the solmization syllables [do-re-mi, etc.] to indicate the tones of the major scale, and symbols consisting of dots and lines to indicate rhythm. At the end of that year, he became the teacher in Penygroes, where during the day he taught the children and at night he taught the coal miners, some more than twice his

Soon he had to return home to help on the farm while his brother Joshua attended school. However, his oldest brother David encouraged him to apply for an advertised position of schoolmaster in an endowed school at Conwil Elvet. Surprisingly, given his youth, a mere eighteen years of age, he was selected from among sixty applicants. There he began his professional teaching career, with twenty-one students. Within eighteen months, while three nearby small village schools had to close for lack of students, enrollment in Richard's school had increased to 120 students. He also taught a weekly Bible class in the evening to the older boys, all of whom after a time became church members.

REFORM EFFORTS IN WALES 1865-69

In 1865 Timothy Richard left his teaching position to begin his preparation for Christian ministry, with the intention of becoming a foreign missionary. For the next four years, he was a student at Haverfordwest Theological College in Pembrokeshire. At the outset, he came to recognize his academic deficiencies, so he concentrated hard on his studies.[7] Theological training at that time consisted primarily of a classical curriculum studying the civilizations of Rome and Greece as well as various metaphysical and theological studies.

It was in response to this curriculum that Richard eventually began to show his reformist bent toward studies of practical use, as later recounted in his autobiography.[8] He joined a student movement "to beg that living languages" be substituted for Greek and Latin and then requested that "universal history, covering such lands as Egypt, Babylon, India, and China, should be studied instead of solely European history." These students also considered the study of science and its modern applications "more useful than barren metaphysical and theological studies . . ." Richard most

---

age. Using his wages to pay his tuition at a grammar school in Uanybyther, he was often put in charge of his classmates in the absence of their schoolmaster. For a time, he filled a vacancy as schoolmaster in New Inn and after that, supported himself with his savings while briefly attending the Normal School in Swansea.

7. Richard, letter to parents, January 13, 1866, transl. Thomas Evans, NLW, soon after he arrived at Haverfordwest, revealed a troubled heart on account of his lack of erudition. "The students who were to enter the same time as I was entering had read books which I had never read and for that reason I could not be very quiet . . . most of the things are new to me."

8. Richard, *Forty-five Years*, 25–26.

heartily joined in this move to reform the seminary's curriculum even to the point of risking expulsion. After serious consideration, the faculty surprisingly conceded to the students' demands on the condition that all theological students pass a stringent examination in Hebrew. Richard not only complied with this mandate but excelled in the examination, receiving a prize for his performance. When Richard visited the seminary fifteen years later, he probably was sad to find the curriculum had reverted to its former classical nature. Yet he knew this was a defining incident in his life, later "mention[ing] this incident because in all my after missionary life I endeavoured to seek the methods most productive of results, rather than adhere to old ones not adjusted to the changing needs of the times."

REFORM IN SHANDONG, 1870-77

Toward the end of his studies at the Seminary, Richard heard Mrs. Grattan Guinness make a passionate plea for volunteer missionaries on behalf of the China Inland Mission (CIM). Deeply attracted by the CIM's "heroic and self-sacrificing" policy, Richard offered himself for service to this mission organization but was directed to apply to the Baptist Missionary Society (BMS) of his own denomination. Even during his application interview with the BMS, Richard exhibited an early appreciation for the Chinese civilization as well as his pragmatic approach to missions when he justified his choice of North China as his mission field preference, since "as the Chinese were the most civilized of non-Christian nations, they would, when converted, help to carry the gospel to less advanced nations, and that by working in the north temperate zone Europeans could stand the climate, while the natives of North China, after becoming Christians, could convert their fellow countrymen all over the Empire."[9] This is also an early indication that Richard did not share the paternalistic approach adopted by many

9. Ibid., 29. China Inland Mission (CIM, now Overseas Missionary Fellowship or OMF) was founded by James Hudson Taylor in 1864. As a missionary society, it was unique in its self-sacrificial principles—faith in God to provide totally for all support; trust in guidance received through prayer rather than religious education before going to the mission field; and readiness to go to the interior adopting the native dress and lifestyle. Because these guiding principles were so different from those of most denominational organizations, any candidate who declared a denomination was referred to his or her own denominational mission society. This is what happened during Richard's missionary candidacy to the CIM. The Baptist Missionary Society (BMS) was founded almost 200 years earlier through the pioneering efforts of the great British Baptist missionary to India, William Carey.

Becoming a Practical Reformer, 1865–85

missionaries of his day, who were reluctant to give up control to Chinese converts. Clearly, even before being accepted as a missionary, Richard had already envisioned his responsibility to be the raising up of indigenous Christian leadership.

In 1869, Richard was accepted by the Baptist Missionary Society, and before setting out was given advice that stayed with him. One adviser admonished him to offer no opinion of things in China until he had studied them carefully; the other exhorted him "to get hold of the schoolmasters—the teachers of the land—for, by converting these, we might look to the whole nation turning to God," and to make careful study of the commands contained in Matthew 10, specifically "to seek the worthy."[10] With those words echoing in his heart, he sailed for China out of Liverpool on November 17, 1869, aboard Blue Funnel (Holt) Line's ship *Achilles*. During his four-month voyage, he assiduously applied himself to learning the 212 radicals used in the written Chinese language. He arrived in Shanghai on February 12, 1870.

The China Richard encountered had spent the last five years recovering from the fourteen-year long Taiping Rebellion, a quasi-Christian movement to establish the Kingdom of Heaven in China led by a Chinese scholar who failed the official exams and came to believe he was the younger brother of Jesus Christ. This movement had devastated sixteen of China's eighteen provinces, destroying more than 600 cities and resulting in the deaths of more than fifteen million people.[11] At that time, also, there was only one newspaper in Chinese, the official *Peking Gazette*. There were no railroads, telegraphs, or post offices. There was no official concern about public opinion, so there was little effort by the officials to maintain their popularity in the eyes of the people. The people's primary need was to maintain the favor of the local magistrate and survive. Male literacy was approximately 5 percent, but those who wrote were fewer; very few women could read. The custom of binding girls' feet was still in vogue among the Han Chinese majority, and there were no schools for girls, except as provided by the few missionaries in China.[12]

After a twelve-day stay in Shanghai, Richard left for North China, arriving three days later in Yantai (previously Chefoo) in Shandong Province.

---

10. Richard, *Fifteen Years*, 4.

11. For an overview of the Taiping Rebellion, see Hsü, *The Rise of Modern China*, 221–53.

12. Burt, "Timothy Richard: His Contribution," 295.

Timothy Richard's Vision

Yantai was one of the few treaty ports where foreigners were allowed to reside. Once there, because of the death or earlier departure of his BMS colleagues, Richard soon became the sole representative of the ten-year-old work of his missionary society. Because the responsibility of the BMS work rested squarely on Richard's shoulders alone, his experiences became his main teacher of "what courses to follow and what mistakes to avoid in the future."[13]

He did find himself, however, in the company and under the mutual influence of some remarkable pioneer missionaries from other societies. These included the Revs. Alexander Williamson of the London Missionary Society and John L. Nevius and Calvin Mateer of the American Presbyterian Mission. In a letter written in January 1878, Richard included some of his earliest statements on the need for indigenous self-support and self-propagation of Christianity, through which Chinese Christians would bear the primary responsibility for the financial support of their churches and the making of converts. These comments antedate Nevius' publication of *Missionary Method*, which first appeared in a pamphlet and then in a series of articles in the *Chinese Recorder* published in 1886 and which likely was the product of a tour of Richard's missionary centers in Shandong several years before. Richard has never received proper recognition as an originator of this famous missions methodology.[14]

---

13. Richard, *Forty-five Years*, 32; Tucker, *Notes on the Life and Work*, 7. At one time there had been five other BMS missionaries in Yantai. However, Dr. Hall had died earlier of cholera; Laughton, a seven-year veteran of China, died of typhus in June soon after Richard's arrival; and the three other men (Kloekers, Meehan, and Kingdon) had left for England before Richard's arrival. For a discussion of the missionary effort in Shandong Province by a contemporary of Richard, see Forsyth, *Shandong*. Written by a BMS missionary and published through Richard's literary outlet in Shanghai, it includes a biographical sketch and formal photograph of Richard with his government decorations (209–14).

14. Richard, letter to A. G. Jones, 18 January 1878, 7, 20–27, BMS MSS; *Forty-five Years*, 106–7; Soothill, *Timothy Richard of China*, 92–93. All unattributed references to unpublished communications are from BMS MSS.

The Rev. Alexander Williamson sailed to China in 1865 as a member of the London Mission Society, first locating in Shandong. Later he represented the National Bible Society of Scotland and in 1887 became founder of the Society for the Diffusion of Christian and General Knowledge among the Chinese (SDK) located in Shanghai. Upon his untimely death, Richard succeeded him as General Secretary. (See chapter 4.) The Rev. Hunter Corbett on a later furlough to the United States became Moderator of the Presbyterian Synod. The Rev. Calvin Mateer was viewed by Richard as "the great pioneer of scientific education in missionary work in China." Most likely it was Mateer's example of using scientific demonstrations and lectures to train young men in the workings of the

Becoming a Practical Reformer, 1865–85

In these early years, Richard was treated by the Chinese with much hostility and little curiosity. After two years, he came to realize that the established method of evangelization gained few converts or even inquirers, so he changed his approach to one he believed would be more practical. He began to follow the plan of "seeking the worthy."[15] This new approach also brought about another change when, in 1875, he assumed Chinese dress and a shaved head with an artificial queue, wondering if he "would have more visitors of the better classes" if he wore Chinese dress.[16]

These changes enabled him to move with greater ease within Chinese society and to have conversations with various individuals, such as a salt manufacturer whom Richard suspected of being a lost Nestorian Christian, Buddhist priests, military men, Islamic mullahs, young examination candidates, a prefectural treasurer, leaders of religious sects, a Taoist hermit, various literati and provincial officials, and even the high-ranking reformer Viceroy Li Hongzhang.[17] Such contacts brought him to the realization that

---

laws of God in order to become better leaders that Richard emulated a decade later in Shanxi. See Fisher, *Calvin Wilson Mateer*, 34–35. The Rev. John L. Nevius twenty years later became the American Chairman of the China Missionary Conference in Shanghai.

15. Tucker, *Notes on the Life and Work*, 7–9; Soothill, *Timothy Richard of China*, 77–79. At first, Richard engaged in all the usual itinerate street preaching and tract distribution, with few results. The paradigm shift occurred as a result of reading the sermon "Missionaries After the Apostolic School" in *The Collected Writings of Edward Irving* published in the 1860s. This sermon was based on Matthew 10:11—"Whatever town or village you enter, search for some worthy person there and stay at his house until you leave." After reading this, as recorded in Richard, *Forty-five years*, 86, he became convinced he should refocus his efforts upon those individuals who by education, religious devotion, or socioeconomic status were considered to be at a higher level or "leaders of thought" rather than in mass evangelistic efforts. Soothill's biography recorded that Richard's conviction about this approach grew such that by 1887–88, at his own expense, he mailed a copy of this sermon to "every missionary in the Far East." According to a letter Richard wrote to BMS General Secretary Alfred Baynes, 16 July 1888, he had mailed 200 copies to Japan, 500 copies to India, and 800 copies throughout China. Soothill included the text of Richard's presentation paragraph for these copies and some margin notes found in Richard's personal copy of Irving's book.

16. Richard, *Forty-five Years*, 80. This was another aspect of the policy of Hudson Taylor's CIM philosophy that Richard had found so attractive as a missionary candidate. Most likely, however, by 1890 Richard returned to using Western dress, perhaps concluding he no longer had any need to divert attention from his being a foreigner. By then he was living in the cosmopolitan city of Tianjin where social intercourse among Chinese and foreigners was more common. Moreover, it was precisely with the authority of a Westerner that he was actively promulgating his vision for the reform of Chinese education and society. There was no longer any need for "camouflage."

17. Richard, *Forty-five Years*, 76, implied in his autobiography that he first became

he needed to devise a "means to free the Chinese philosophers [scholars and officials also] from the chains of superstition by which they were bound in the theory of Yin Yang and the five elements of heaven and earth." Richard sought to accomplish this, in part, by giving his Chinese helpers lectures with demonstrations of chemistry and physics experiments with the intention of "giving them true conceptions of the laws of natural philosophy."[18] Nevertheless, he continued in his other missionary duties of street-chapel preaching, itinerant evangelism, tract distribution, and even some basic medical work. On one itineration as early as 1871, Richard and his companion John Lilley may have become the first Protestant missionaries to enter Manchuria and reach the border of Korea.

Seeing what he believed to be an unnecessary density of missionaries in coastal ports like Yantai and seeking to increase the breadth of the evangelistic effort, Richard decided to move his mission center inland. By 1875 he had settled in the prefectural capital of Weifang (previously Ch'ingchow), more than 200 miles inland.[19] Soon after Richard's arrival there, the treasurer of the prefecture sought out his company to aid in breaking his opium addiction. The treasurer was successful in overcoming this addiction and later rendered invaluable assistance to Richard. Though not a trained medical doctor, Richard did know basic medical care and some specifics for dispensing quinine and spirits of camphor for ague and cholera. In fact, he used quinine successfully to treat the wife of the superintendent of police. This same superintendent subsequently became his landlord, in spite of the violent prejudice against foreigners exhibited by a retired magistrate.

During this time, Richard again modified his approach as a result of his efforts to contact Islamic leaders. He found if he were to be "able to

---

acquainted with Li Hongzhang in 1875 when Li was in Yantai for the signing of the Chefoo Convention. Many of Li's troops contracted dysentery and ague and came to the mission hospital for treatment. Richard wrote, "I sent a present of quinine and chlorodyne to the General for distribution amongst his retinue and escort. For this he sent me a letter of thanks."

18. Richard, *Forty-five Years*, 55. As a result of conversations with various "devout seekers after the truth," Richard realized the futility of these discussions as long as their minds were in bondage to the pseudoscientific superstitions of *feng shui*. Soothill, *Timothy Richard of China*, 53, wrote that with these lectures and demonstrations, "He now took the first step which led to the foundation of the Shanxi University . . . he came back taught, or rather further enlightened as to the scholars' need of a better philosophy of God's world."

19. Richard, *Forty-five Years*, 28–29. Residence in the interior was yet another aspect that had attracted Richard as a young missionary candidate in 1869 to CIM policies.

Becoming a Practical Reformer, 1865–85

win Mohammedans [Muslims] over to Christianity it would be necessary . . . to adopt a different line of argument altogether."[20] To develop this new dialogue, he knew he needed to understand these and adherents of other religions, and he sought to do this through their literature. He found himself delving deeply into translations of the Koran and every other book he had on Islam. Also during this time, Richard immersed himself in James Legge's translation of the Confucian classics, various Buddhist and Taoist writings, as well as the most popular religious books used by other sects. From these writings, he garnered a vocabulary of religious terms already in use by the Chinese. This willingness to consider thoughtfully the validity of the literature of other religions would later cause friction between him and his missionary colleagues.

By spring 1876, more than ten provinces of North China were prostrate from drought. The suffering of the people was intense, and social disorder increased. That summer, two Shandong scholars even asked Richard to head a rebellion against the authorities who were not distributing food to the perishing people. Richard "advised them to devise constructive instead of destructive methods for improving the condition of the people." He had earlier suggested to the local prefect that the government in Peking should be memorialized to make arrangements with Korea and Japan for free trade in cereals and thus lower the price from its exorbitant level during the famine. This appears to have been the first time he presented to an official a practical remedy for a widespread problem.[21]

For the next year or two, Richard played an active role in soliciting donations from Christians in various Chinese cities as well as abroad and in distributing food and money to aid the famine-stricken in Shandong. With some of the money, he established orphanages for one hundred boys each at five different famine relief centers, a novelty in China. In these unusual orphanages, the twelve to eighteen-year-old boys were taught occupations by which they could earn their living—such as blacksmithing, carpentering, silk weaving, and cord-making. They used various new kinds of foreign tools, particularly in carpentry.

In the spring of 1877, Richard placed a proposal to avert future famine before the prefect and city magistrates in Weifang. If authorities would grant

---

20. Ibid., 86–89. Richard sought out opportunities to converse with clerics of various religions and sects, relishing these meetings as the essence of "seeking the worthy."

21. Ibid., 99–100. See Bohr, *Famine in China and the Missionary* for a definitive study of his famine relief efforts.

the land along with the houses and bear half the expense, Richard proposed he would administer the orphanages and establish affiliated schools similar to those in Peking, Shanghai, and Fuzhou.[22]

He proposed that, "these schools should be for the most intelligent of the orphans, where the pupils would be taught Western learning and English, while the less intelligent of the orphans would be instructed in new industries so as to avoid increasing the number of competitors in the old industries. When the orphans had completed their training, they would render immense service to their countrymen." Continuing his appeal, Richard argued that since the ancient sages devised "new schemes for the good of the people ... [t]herefore, in the present age of international intercourse, the mandarins should adopt new methods for their peoples' welfare."[23] His proposal, however, was never implemented.

Nonetheless, the seed of this suggestion eventually did find fertile ground. Some twenty years later, a son of this same city magistrate became involved in a reform movement that, on Richard's advice, promoted the establishment of institutions for Western learning in the eighteen provinces. Finally, the Chinese government realized the imperative necessity of Western learning and ordered the whole Empire to adopt it.[24]

Richard knew that a major obstacle in the minds of the Chinese to reform and to missionary work was the ancient concept of *feng shui* (natural harmony).[25] No burial plot was selected, house built, wall or fence erected, well dug, or road built without first consulting a teacher of *feng shui*, who

---

22. According to Bohr, 143, Richard proposed a single institution, a "government training school," but close reading of Richard's autobiography, 121, suggests that he proposed converting his five orphanages into missionary-government jointly supported schools under his supervision. The institutions in Peking, Shanghai, and Fuzhou were the Tongwen Guan (T'ung-wen kuan), special foreign languages schools and translation bureaus first established in 1862 at the suggestion of Prince Gong (Kung). About these, Hsü, *The Rise of Modern China*, 271, wrote, "the T'ung-wen kuan marked the beginning of Western education in China." Richard in a lengthy letter to his colleague A. G. Jones in Ch'ing-chow, 18 January 1878, 7, 20–27, wrote in detail about the need to provide practical training for the famine orphans.

23. Richard, *Forty-five Years*, 121.

24. Ibid., 122, 131–32. See chapter 4 for details.

25. Ibid., 123; Latourette, *The Chinese: Their History and Culture*, 585 and 651, described *feng shui*, translated literally "wind water," as a "strange system of pseudo-scientific superstition which has had so marked a hold on the Chinese mind" and which is "based upon the belief that in every locality forces exist which act on graves, buildings, cities, and towns, either for the welfare or the ill of the quick and the dead." These forces could be adjusted, mollified, or capitalized upon by reckoning with certain principles.

was often quick to become alarmed with any threatened disturbance of the *feng shui*, particularly major projects like laying railway tracks or stringing telegraph wires. Even the families of eminent scholars believed that if the feng shui of their land was disturbed "the family would produce no more scholars nor officials, but be doomed to obscurity and poverty and even sterility."[26]

Richard concluded that instruction in the natural sciences, such as astronomy, physics, and chemistry, was the best way to counteract this belief and fear. He believed the "study of science ought to be held in as much reverence as religion, for it deals with the laws of God."[27] To further this aim he drafted a scheme for a series of science textbooks to be prepared for the Chinese. Around this same time, he wrote to the BMS in London giving a description of the great suffering in Shandong Province due to the famine. He appealed to the English churches to take advantage of this opportunity to demonstrate true Christianity. He believed that China could be helped in four ways:

1. By immediate famine relief
2. By teaching the people the true principles of Christian civilization, including medicine, chemistry, mineralogy, and history
3. By the introduction of new industries
4. By the teaching of spiritual truths and the relation of progress to the worship of the true God

On behalf of himself and his assistant A. G. Jones, he asked his missionary society for an immediate grant of £1,000 to further these aims. He writes, perhaps wryly, "[It is] with great pleasure that I record the liberal spirit of the Society, shown by the immediate granting of £500."[28]

---

26. Richard, *Forty-five Years*, 81.
27. Ibid., 123–24.
28. Ibid., 124. A. G. Jones left a successful business in Ireland in November 1876, responding to a personal call from God to go to the mission field in China. As members of the BMS, Jones and Richard worked together during the early years of famine relief in Shandong. Later, they amicably separated with Richard moving to Shanxi to administer famine relief there. Even from Shanxi, however, Richard would send pastoral letters, sometimes quite voluminous, to Jones advising this less experienced colleague on various matters. An example is Richard's 34-page letter to Jones dated 18 January 1878, which Richard requested be forwarded to Baynes as a report to the Home Mission Committee.

Even though Richard had only been in China seven years, he had become proficient enough in the oral and written language to engage in philosophical discussions as well as translation work. His earlier study of Chinese religious and philosophical thought proved invaluable because it gave him a vocabulary of religious terms that was intelligible to the Chinese. This enabled him to prepare a catechism in Chinese that avoided the use of unfamiliar foreign terms and appealed to the conscience of the Chinese. He also translated a Religious Tract Society book entitled *The Philosophy of the Plan of Salvation*, Francis de Sales's *Devout Life*, and the first part of Jeremy Taylor's *Holy Living*.[29] Since these were translations of religious and philosophical treatises, these were directed toward the educated or those whom Richard saw as the "worthy," the devout seekers of the truth.

REFORM IN SHANXI, 1877–85

In the midst of his work in Shandong, Richard received a letter from the Famine Relief Committee in Shanghai expressing their appreciation for the manner with which he had been distributing the relief fund they had collected. They then informed him that the famine was even more severe in the inland province of Shanxi and asked if he would go there to administer famine relief. After talking and praying with his colleague and the native pastor, Richard knew he was to go. He wrote later he "was so profoundly impressed with the deep feeling that God was giving [them] an opportunity of exercising influence over many millions of people."[30] With a passport issued by Li Hongzhang, then viceroy of Zhili (covering most of North China), to assure his safe passage into the interior, Richard began the 500-mile trip to Shanxi in the company of two Chinese Christians, who later became fainthearted and parted company with him once they began to see the terrible sights resulting from the Shanxi famine. Richard eventually arrived in the provincial capital of Taiyuan where he found himself the sole representative of the Protestant faith in a community that already had a Roman Catholic bishop and a dozen priests, remnants of a Jesuit effort begun more than 200 years before.[31]

29. Ibid., 86.
30. Evans, *Timothy Richard*, 65.
31. According to Stauffer, *The Christian Occupation of China*, the first Protestant missionaries to visit the province were Alexander Williamson and Jonathan Lees in 1869–70. In April 1871, Joshua Turner and Francis James of the China Inland Mission

Becoming a Practical Reformer, 1865–85

Soon after his arrival, he met with Governor Zeng Guochuan (Tseng Kuo-ch'üan), brother of the illustrious Zeng Guofan (Tseng Kuo-fan), suppressor of the Taiping Rebellion, and uncle of the Marquis Zeng Jize (Tseng Chi-tse), then Chinese Minister to London. The governor greeted him with suspicion and later attempted to capitalize on the long-standing tensions between the Roman Catholics and Protestants by insisting that Richard give the money to the priests to distribute. In the end, however, Richard was able to enlist the cooperation, not only of the priests in some basic information-gathering tasks about the extent of the famine, but also of various provincial officials in establishing the famine relief strategy. He also recommended to the governor three urgent measures to aid in famine relief: encouraging migration to Manchuria or any other place where inexpensive grain could be obtained; establishment of public works, such as the construction of railways, that would not only give the people wage-earning opportunities but also aid in the transport of grains and food stuffs, thereby preventing the recurrence of the famine; and, lastly, imposition of a famine relief tax on those provinces not suffering from famine.[32]

The Chinese officials did not welcome the idea of railways, for fear of disturbing the *feng shui* and bringing a large number of foreigners into the area. Another recommendation Richard made, later discovered by the succeeding governor in the provincial archives, was to establish a college of Western learning in Taiyuan. The officials were also reluctant to follow this advice, so no such school was established until 1901, again on the recommendation of Richard.[33] Over the next two years, however, Richard succeeded in distributing more than $65,000 in famine relief funds collected both in China and abroad. Nonetheless, an estimated fifteen to twenty million people still perished in the famine.[34]

---

arrived in the province to begin a permanent work there, but both fell ill to typhoid fever. They moved to another location outside of Taiyuan to convalesce and by November 28, 1877, had regained their strength sufficiently to return to their home base in Wuchang (now Wuhan). They left Taiyuan just two days before Richard's arrival on November 30, 1877. Turner returned in March 1878 with companions and relief funds. See Broomhall, *Assault on the Nine*, 87–90.

32. Timothy Richard to William Muirhead, 28 December 1877. In this letter, Richard suggested that the proclamation Zeng issued for the care of the famine orphans throughout the province was in response to his proposal to Zeng for their care made two or three days earlier.

33. See Chapter 5 for a detailed study of the founding of this institution, the Imperial University of Shansi in Taiyuan.

34. Richard, *Forty-five Years*, 134. See Bohr, *Famine in China*, for a thorough

Timothy Richard's Vision

In 1878 Richard went back to Yantai in Shandong to marry a missionary with whom he had corresponded; they immediately returned to Shanxi to continue famine relief work. His new wife, Mary Martin Richard, founded an orphanage for boys in Taiyuan soon after their return; meanwhile, Richard began to consider more carefully how to approach the believers of the various philosophies and religious sects who lived in Shanxi.[35] He had deep respect for and was inspired by the efforts of Matteo Ricci, an Italian Jesuit who, after arriving in China in 1582, "had written Christian books which brought converts from amongst the highest circles in the land, and also a large number of followers from among the masses." He came to realize he needed to prepare special Christian literature that would appeal specifically to adherents of these various beliefs. To prepare himself for this task, he gathered a set of Roman Catholic, Greek Orthodox, and the few existent Protestant books in Chinese.[36]

---

examination of Richard's famine relief efforts in both Shandong and Shanxi Provinces. Richard's letters from Taiyuan 1877–78 regularly appeared in *The Celestial Kingdom*, a publication in England on China. These letters were replete with horrific examples of the desperate situation of the famine-stricken people of Shanxi Province. Letters of this same period from Richard to BMS home secretary Alfred Baynes contained urgent pleas to the BMS to send more personnel to assist Richard, the only member of his mission in Shanxi engaged in famine relief. By late 1878, however, there were members of other missions permanently residing in Taiyuan, mostly from CIM.

35. Richard, *Forty-five Years*, 141. When Richard was commissioned by the BMS to go to China as a missionary, the committee requested he remain unmarried for ten years once he arrived in China. Richard reported in *Forty-five Years*, 29, his reply that he would do what was practically the best for his work. As it was, eight years later in a letter to Baynes, 20 April 1878, Richard revealed his plan to go to Shandong in the autumn to marry Mary Martin, a missionary based in Yantai with the United Presbyterian Church of Scotland. Richard in a letter to his mother, 3 July 1879, transl. Thomas Evans, NLW, described Mary's many skills and attributes, and his letters to Mary throughout the years of their marriage until her death in 1903 reveal a husband passionately devoted to his wife. Others who knew her well believed her to be uniquely suited for Richard in every aspect. See the obituary "The death of Mrs. Timothy Richard," *North China Herald and Supreme Court & Consular Gazette*, July 17, 1903, 133. Richard's letters to his mother, 31 March, 3 July, and 11 December 1879, transl. Thomas Evans, NLW, indicated that Mary had a school of 29 orphan children under her care, teaching them to read and sing. In a letter to his mother, 17 January 1880, transl. Thomas Evans, NLW, however, Richard wrote that they intended to give up the school since "another missionary who has just come here is hoping to open a school to about 60 children. We intend to send the thirty with us to him."

36. Richard, *Forty-five Years*, 144–45. The Protestant books available in Chinese for distribution to "intelligent Chinese" were the following: Ernst Faber's *Western Civilization* and *Commentary on Mark*, A. G. Williamson's *Natural Theology*, Y. J. Allen's *Statesmen's*

Since Russia and China were threatening hostilities about this same time, Richard also wrote a pamphlet in Chinese on peace, which he then had circulated among the government officials in Peking. In August 1880, he travelled to Peking to present a memorial to these high officials on peace. The anti-foreign war party there was offended by his pamphlet and labeled a traitor anyone who sought peace. On his way back to Taiyuan, he stopped in Tianjin where he was invited to call upon Viceroy Li Hongzhang. During that visit, Li expressed his gratitude for Richard's efforts to avert the suffering of his people during the recent famine. There was some discussion about missionary work during which Li implied that the Chinese became converts to Christianity only because they received payment for services. Richard states in his autobiography that Li "also pointed out that there were no Christians among the educated classes of the land. This made me consider more than ever the importance of influencing the leaders, and I returned to Shanxi resolved to lecture to the officials and scholars."[37]

Upon returning to Taiyuan, Richard began to study the causes for human suffering not only in China but the world. He concluded that Western civilization "sought to discover the workings of God in Nature, and to apply the laws of Nature for the service of mankind." The root of this world view was Richard's trust in the Judeo-Christian religious belief that God gave man dominion over all things. In man's effort to exercise this dominion, he developed many inventions that enabled him to extend its exercise. Eastern civilization, on the other hand, sees man to be inextricably linked to the passive acceptance of his fate as he is frequently found to be at the mercy of the natural elements. Richard hoped by revealing the natural laws in operation in scientific experiments that he could remove some of the fearful superstitions held by some officials. Then they would be more inclined to undertake the reforms necessary to prevent a recurrence of the devastating famine and provide means to relieve the poverty of the people.[38]

Richard began to consider the idea of presenting scientific lectures like those he had used to enlighten his Chinese assistants several years earlier

---

Year Book, W.A. P. Martin's *Christian Evidences and Allegories*, and a tract by a Chinese Christian entitled "The Mirror of Conscience."

37. Richard, *Forty-five Years*, 151–52. Perhaps another reason for calling on Li was to explain his intention behind the pamphlet *He Yilun*, the pamphlet he wrote on peace.

38. Ibid., 158. This belief is based on the Creation contained in the first chapter of the book of Genesis, which recounts that God gave Adam and Eve dominion over the earth, commanding them to subdue it, a view contrary to Chinese culture in which humans are at the mercy of the natural elements and fate.

in Shandong. He made plans to give monthly lectures and demonstrations on various scientific topics. He was "convinced that if [he] could lecture to the officials and scholars and interest them in these miracles of science, [he] would be able to point out to them ways in which they could utilize the forces of God in Nature for the benefit of their fellow-countrymen. . . . Besides the officials of the province, and the students of the Chinese colleges, there were a few hundreds of expectant officials who, later, would be given posts in other parts of the Empire, and through whom beneficial results might accrue to other provinces."[39]

In preparation for these lectures, he gathered, at great personal expense, a library of books on astronomy, electricity, chemistry, geology, natural history, engineering, medicine, workshop tools, and industries as well as work on comparative religion, theology from various denominational perspectives, histories of various nations, biographies, and Asian religions and literature. He even ordered a set of the *Encyclopaedia Britannica*. He gathered a vast array of scientific equipment to aid in demonstrating various scientific experiments. He procured a telescope, microscope, hand dynamo, Wimshurst machine, induction coil, various galvanic batteries, a galvanometer, Geissler tubes, a voltmeter, electrometer, pocket sextant, pocket aneroids, a sewing machine, and a complete photographic outfit. He purchased magic lanterns with slides about astronomy, natural history, and natural science.[40]

Over the next three years, Richard used these materials to respond to requests for lectures from local officials and scholars on various topics including these:

1. The astronomical miracle discovered by Copernicus

2. The miracles of chemistry

---

39. Ibid., 159–60.

40. Ibid, 160. Richard wrote that this magic lantern, the earliest slide projector, "worked by oxy-hydrogen, spirits of wine, and acetylene." He ordered this equipment with the expectation that the BMS would see their value and pay the invoiced total of £200. Mary Richard to James Martin, 5 December 1882, however, reported that the Society had just written to say that "at present they can't go in for such expenses . . . Strange that they don't see the necessity to meet the enquiring turn that the Literati & ruling class have just taken—yes & to meet it in a Christian spirit. If they don't look sharp we will have infidels teaching this people Western Science as in Japan." Mary Richard to James Martin, 5 May 1880; Timothy Richard to James Martin, 18 October 1880, indicate that this expense was ultimately borne by Richard through a legacy left him by the death of an unmarried uncle who considered Richard his favorite.

3. The miracles of mechanics, such as the lathe and other tools, leading to the sewing-machine and bicycle, etc.
4. The miracles of steam, bringing incalculable blessings to every country that adopted them, as seen in railways and steamers and factories
5. The miracles of electricity as seen in the dynamo, utilized for light and power transmission
6. The miracles of light, as seen in the magic lantern and photography
7. The miracles of medicine and surgery

After delivering each lecture, Richard found himself besieged with many questions by members of the audience who remained behind. He also learned early on that he needed to respect the social convention of rank differences among officials. On one occasion when he had given no thought to this point and invited both high and low-ranking officials, he found that the questions did not flow as freely. Thereafter, he "was careful to invite only those of the same rank together in order that they might feel free and sociable."[41]

As a result of these lectures, more officials and students began to visit him in his office. One such frequent visitor was an official who later became the prefect at Ningwu. Soon after assuming office, this prefect called on Richard, who asked him about the reforms he was initiating in his area. The prefect described the new school he had established in which modern science was taught. He indicated that he himself was examining the students and rewarding them for their studies. Prefect Wang also recounted how he had recently given a scientific explanation for phenomena that had previously been attributed to various superstitious beliefs. All these were likely the results of Richard's lectures and their conversations about foreign learning. Moreover, Richard rented an apartment in his compound to a leading literary scholar of the province, who had been selected by the government

---

41. Richard, *Forty-five Years*, 160–63. On this occasion he had invited some *dao dai* (tao tai, officials overseeing about thirty counties), *zhi fu* (chi fu, prefects over about ten counties), and county magistrates to listen together to the same lecture. One official who usually was filled with questions remained silent the entire evening. When questioned later privately the reason for his silence, he "replied that he had not dared to speak in the presence of so many of his superiors." Both Richard, 161, and Soothill, *Timothy Richard of China*, 123, record an incident reflecting one official's appreciation for these lectures. A disagreement had arisen between the Manchu and Chinese officials over a newly constructed theater. According to Richard, a prefect had "strongly urged" the governor to give it to Richard for his lectures.

to edit a new edition of the Shanxi Province *Topographical Cyclopaedia*.⁴² Eventually, the number of visitors to Richard's home became so great and their visits so long that his study and translation work began to suffer. He remedied this by renting additional office space on another street where he could work on these without interruption.

During these few years just prior to his first furlough to England, Richard's contacts with officials had expanded to include even those in high government positions. Soon after the end of the famine around 1880, he was invited to accompany provincial officials to meet Zuo Zongtang (Tso Tsung-t'ang), the liberator of the border area Ili from the Russians and viceroy of Shaanxi and Gansu Provinces, as he passed near Taiyuan on a journey to Peking. In a private meeting, Richard presented Zuo a chart of the comparative history of the world he had recently completed. Zuo discussed at great length with Richard not only the chart but also the relationship between the missionaries and the Chinese government as well as the many reforms he himself had initiated in Gansu.⁴³

Richard developed a relationship with another great official, Zhang Zhidong (Chang Chih-tung), when he became the successor of Shanxi's governor. Outstanding in his brilliance and anti-foreign stance, Zhang nevertheless distinguished himself in his determination to find a way to alleviate some of the famine-causing conditions in Shanxi. While searching the provincial archives in 1882, he found the recommendations Richard had written in 1880 and presented to the former governor. These included building railways, opening mines, establishing industries, and founding a college for modern education.⁴⁴ Zhang later sent a deputation of three

42. Richard, *Forty-five Years*, 163–66.

43. Ibid., 166–67. Richard considered it noteworthy enough to put in his autobiography that when Zuo became Viceroy in Nanjing several years later, he "commanded the district magistrates to see to the suitable establishment of Christian Missions in Nanking." This attitude reflected a change from the former obstructionist official policy in operation for many years, and Richard implied their meeting that day may have softened Zuo's attitude somewhat toward Christianity.

44. This may have been the yet un-located pamphlet "Chin-shih yiao-wu" (Present Needs or, in an alternate translation, Urgent Affairs of Recent Times), referred to by Bohr, *Famine in China*, 148–61, which was serialized earlier under the same title in the *Review of the Times* in "twelve weekly installments between November 1881 and January 1882." Richard referred to this item in the preface for *Xi de* ("Warning Bell from the West") written in 1895. An English translation of this preface is available in Kikuchi, "Timothy Richard's Influence," 113–14, along with an incomplete translation of an essay by Richard from *Xi de* on the material and educational superiority of Western powers. The reform recommendations Richard made in 1880 obviously antedated Cheng Kuan-ying's reform

leading officials to Richard to issue his first of two requests that he leave missionary work and enter the governor's service to carry out these ideas. Richard respectfully declined these offers as he believed the missionary to be "engaged in work of still greater importance."[45] However, Richard did help him by completing land surveys of potential flood areas and obtaining cost estimates on mining machinery; furthermore, he stated he would be glad to refer foreign technical experts to him to help in implementing his reforms. Very soon thereafter, before he had time to implement his planned reforms in Shanxi, Zhang was transferred to become viceroy first at Canton (Guangzhou), then Wuchang, where he founded a steel works, built a railway, established industries, and founded modern colleges, such as Richard had suggested to him.[46]

In 1882 Richard was called back to Shandong Province for a year to oversee the BMS churches there while his colleague A. G. Jones returned to England for a year to try to persuade the China Missions Committee to send more missionaries. While in Shandong, Richard planted three important seeds that later bore fruit for modern education in Shandong. The first was the conversations he had while he lodged with an enthusiastic missionary named Whitewright. They engaged in many lively late night discussions about Richard's educational work in Shanxi. Richard later recorded in his autobiography that Whitewright opened a museum in Weifang in 1887, where he gave a course of lectures to students. In 1904 he moved to the capital of Shandong, and built what he called the Jinan Institute (but was

---

ideas relating to schools and Western learning, particularly the study of law and politics, contained in his "Words of Warning to a Prosperous Age (People?)" published in 1892. An English review of this book is available in *Chinese Recorder* 30 (April 1899), 195–98. Even though caustically anti-foreign and possessing hatred for Christianity, Cheng cited Richard as one of four missionary authors "worthy of commendation." The degree to which Richard's writings may have influenced the reformist thought of this anti-foreign compradore is yet to be researched.

45. Richard, *Forty-five Years*, 173. Nevertheless, Mary Richard, a letter to her father, 2 November 1882, 9, alluded to the confidence the officials had in Richard, writing that Taiyuan was "full of officials & Mr. Richard is the only one [missionary] who can (for some years at least) have dealings with them."

46. Richard, *Forty-five Years*, 172–73. Mary Richard, letter to her sister Mary Jane, 18 May 1882, 4, mentions a survey. Mary Richard, letter to her sister Mary Jane, 29 August 1882, gave another reason why Zhang's reforms were not initiated in Shanxi. "I fear that [foreign improvement] is set on one side for some time at least, as the Treasurer says he can't grant funds for any such purpose at present. They say he was piqued at not being taken into counsel from the first on the matter."

called by others the Missionary Museum).⁴⁷ Most likely this is the antecedent of the present day Jinan Institute of Technology.

The second seed was the magic lantern show Richard gave to the local magistrate, his secretaries, local gentry, and minor officials. This was the first they had seen, and Richard wrote later that this demonstration favorably disposed them to the missionaries and removed these officials' resistance to allowing the missionaries to obtain a house.⁴⁸ Moreover, this demonstration influenced these officials and gentry later to attend Whitewright's lectures and to allow him to establish an educational center for Western learning in the environs.

The third seed he planted affected that year's Triennial Confucian Examinations. Richard organized an effort to offer monetary prizes for the best essays on religious subjects. Perhaps this was one of the earliest modern efforts, though unofficial, to expand the topics for essays by examination candidates beyond the required Confucian literature.⁴⁹

In March 1884, several months after returning to Shanxi, Richard received a letter from the China Committee of the BMS in London requesting that he go to Peking to discuss the matter of religious liberty with the newly

---

47. Richard, *Forty-five Years*, 180. Evans, *Timothy Richard*, 90, states that "Whitewright gratefully acknowledged his deep indebtedness to him [Richard], and confessed that but for Richard's influence his famous Missionary Museum (or Institute), opened in 1887 in [Weifang] and then, in 1904, transferred to [Jinan], might never have come into existence." By the time Richard published his autobiography in 1916, he claimed the Institute had close to a thousand visitors a day and had received more than a half million visitors since its inception. He described it as "by far the most remarkable Institute in the world." Richard clearly implied the establishment of this museum and its lecture series was the direct result of these discussions of his educational work in Taiyuan with Whitewright in the early 1880's.

48. Timothy Richard, letter to Baynes, 2 February 1884.

49. Mary Richard, letter to James Martin, 14 June 1882. Kuo, "The Chinese System," 62, describes several levels of the civil service examinations. The preliminary examinations were given at the prefecture and district levels. If a scholar were successful at these levels, the next level was the triennial provincial examination. The successful passing of this examination elevated the man and his family in social status and access to power and wealth. There were at least two other levels, the National and the Palace Examinations held in Peking, each offering differing rewards and status. These examinations were based almost exclusively on Confucian literature. Some twenty years earlier, Chinese officials had begun to recommend revising the content, but no official reform had occurred. Richard's effort had nothing to do with the official examination. The contest merely attempted to introduce Western learning and Christianity to an elite corps of scholars hoping to engender a more positive attitude toward native and foreign Christians and Western learning.

appointed British Minister and Chinese government officials. Chinese officials generally had demonstrated great hostility toward anything labeled Christian since the end of the disastrous pseudo-Christian Taiping Rebellion. They circulated unfavorable propaganda, provoking persecution and numerous outbreaks of violence against foreign missionaries and Chinese Christians.

By May, Richard and Francis H. James, his colleague from Shandong, were in Peking where they discussed the issue at length with other missionaries, the new British Minister to China, Sir Harry Parkes, and Sir Robert Hart, the highly respected inspector general of the Imperial Chinese Customs. A petition for religious tolerance was drafted and delivered to Parkes for presentation to the Chinese government. By detailing specific incidents of treaty violations, they hoped to secure better protection for the native Christians and foreign missionaries alike. Meanwhile, the BMS had also written Lord Granville, who in turn forwarded "definite proposals" to Parkes, of which the missionaries knew nothing but a general account. As a result, Richard "felt we were not placed in a very advantageous position" with Parkes.[50]

It is not clear whether a memorial was ever presented to the Throne, and even if so, the twenty-some weeks of effort certainly did not succeed in ending hostilities against Christians. Over the next twenty years, at least 300 missionaries and uncounted thousands of native Christians would lose their lives. Richard was to revisit this issue with the Chinese government many times before leaving China.

While in Peking, however, Richard succeeded in groundbreaking work toward union among the missionary societies. His assiduous efforts led to the founding of the Evangelical Alliance for which he served as secretary, presaging even broader mission union efforts forty years later.

He also took advantage of his visits with Sir Robert Hart to discuss at length their past reform proposals for the benefit of China, including Richard's proposals to the two Shanxi governors, Viceroy Li, and the Foreign Office "that the introduction of modern education would save China from foreign wars and indemnities," as well as his proposal that Hart himself back the idea that "a Commission consisting of a number of leading scholars of the Empire should go abroad and report on the educational systems

---

50. Richard, *Forty-five Years*, 185–93; Richard, letters to Baynes, 8 March 1884 and 31 May 1884; Timothy Richard and Francis H. James, letter to Sir Harry Parkes, 5 May 1884; Mary Richard, letter to brother and sisters, 4 August 1884.

of the world . . ."[51] Richard told Hart that while it would take at least twenty years for such efforts to have beneficial results, he believed it to be a necessary expenditure of time as China prepared herself to enter the family of nations.

During this same visit to Peking, Richard also published a lengthy article in a missionary journal to articulate his views. "Christian Persecutions in China—their nature, causes, remedies" contained Richard's earliest recommendation for the establishment of a system of modern higher educational institutions to be located in each provincial capital, a recommendation hitherto articulated by very few, if any, Chinese or foreigners. Of several specific remedies, he included six specific means of enlightening Chinese officials as to the true nature of the Christian works in progress in China. The second set addressed the preparation missionaries should undertake before entering work during this critical moment in the development of China. Finally, he touched on three means to facilitate cooperation between Chinese and foreigners.[52]

By this time, Richard's proposed program had become the key issue in his correspondence with the Home Mission Committee in London, as well as the focus of his energies. Richard believed that education of the Chinese by better-educated missionaries would engender friendly relations between the Chinese officials and all Christians. As a result of his experiences during the famine and the resulting years of more receptivity by government officials, Richard became convinced of China's need for a multitude of well-educated missionaries who could provide the specialized education and literature needed for the uplift of all of China. To some extent, this was also a reaction to Richard's experience with missionary colleagues, most of whom in Taiyuan were members of the CIM, a British mission society that did not require advanced education in preparation for missionary service. As a result, many CIM missionaries, while devoted in their Christian faith, lacked a scientific understanding of the modern world, in contrast to well-educated missionaries Richard had worked with when first arriving in

---

51. Richard, *Forty-five Years*, 191.

52. Richard, "Christian Persecutions in China," 246–47. Richard stated that Marquis Zeng earlier had recommended the establishment of an "International College . . . where missionaries and Chinese officials may mix freely and be mutually benefitted." Perhaps this came to fruition with the establishment of the International Institute in Peking by Gilbert Reid. However, in this 1884 article, Richard recommended "to have not one but twenty Chinese-supported Colleges in the provinces," a concept antedating by more than a decade the memorials to the Court by Kang Youwei in 1895. See chapter 4 for details.

Becoming a Practical Reformer, 1865–85

China, many of whom were also committed to educating Chinese. Resentment and friction between the two groups would grow as Richard became more adamant about the wisdom of his approach.

After a five-month absence in Peking, Richard returned to Taiyuan to continue his lectures to the officials there, and he set about to reorganize the missionary operations in Shanxi in order to ensure a more scientific approach. His native evangelists would itinerate for three weeks, then return to Taiyuan for a week of rest and study, to include topics in geography, history, Christian endeavors, Church history, and Christian biography, as well as aspects of indigenous religion.[53]

At a conference of the Shanxi missionaries in August, he presented four means of accomplishing a permanent systematic work in the main mission centers, which by now he envisioned as eventually extending throughout China, with Taiyuan serving as the model. First was "establishing colleges in ten of the leading provinces, where a hundred Chinese graduates would be given a three years' course in Western learning," starting in Taiyuan. Second, to aid in this training, Richard saw the need for appropriate literature of a Christian nature "to enlighten China on all topics of real benefit to her." Third, he proposed to establish a Christian Literature Society (CLS) to publish and distribute this literature. While he found some of his colleagues were sympathetic to his vision, their number was not sufficient to fulfil the task. So fourth, Richard proposed an increase in the number of missionaries committed to this purpose in Shanxi.[54]

As Richard later wrote, by the "autumn of 1884, I felt that I had come to the end of a chapter in my work in China." At this point, he saw the need to lay his new scheme of work before his mission society in London to obtain the financial support and personnel necessary to realize these goals. In early 1885, Richard, his wife and four daughters, sailed for England for a well-deserved furlough, his first in almost fifteen years of continuous service. By now his vision for missionary service had expanded to changing the whole of China.

53. Richard, letter to Baynes, 2 February 1884, outlines the training program he developed for his native evangelists, including "A new branch of study with them was that of the Sacred Books of one of the Secret Societies of China—probably not studied by any other Evangelist in China." This welding of various social sciences and geography with the study of an aspect of the indigenous culture may be viewed as another of Richard's earliest efforts to introduce Western learning among the "worthy," the seekers of truth, who were usually the more educated Chinese. On Richard's introduction of a new scientific approach to missions, see Johnson, "Timothy Richard's Theory."

54. Richard, "Christian Persecutions in China," 246–47.

3

Refining the Reformer, 1885–91

DURING HIS FIRST FIFTEEN years in China, Timothy Richard's missionary work had evolved through several approaches. After engaging in the traditional evangelistic work directed to the general populace, he decided to assume Chinese apparel, and to seek out the more educated Chinese with whom he could discuss religious and philosophical issues. During the famine of 1876–79, Richard added yet another dimension to his missionary service—practical social work. Reflections on this experience were to prove a major turning point in his life.

LESSONS FROM FAMINE RELIEF

During relief operations, Richard had experienced much resistance on the part of the officials to providing for the needs of the people. Besides their fear of a loss of power and control, another factor was their ignorance of both practical knowledge and the benefits that could accrue to them from peaceful relations with representatives of Western nations, most particularly the resident missionaries. Richard had become convinced that education in practical Western learning was the key to change. Chinese leaders could develop an understanding of the laws of God working in the forces of nature and then learn how to use these forces for the benefit of their people. The ultimate purpose of this Western learning, however, was to open these leaders to the Christian faith.

In Shanxi, he singlehandedly began this process of enlightening the scholars and officials with lectures and demonstrations of scientific Western learning. Soon he came to realize that the benefit to them and the province could be multiplied with some sort of institutional setting. At first, Richard tried establishing a reading room or library staffed by an educated missionary where scholar-officials could come to read, discuss, and discover the newest information and inventions from Western countries. By 1882, however, Richard knew this setting would be insufficient to meet the need, and formed the idea of a college staffed by several educated missionaries where the student selection and learning process was more formalized. In 1884 this plan received the backing of his Shanxi missionary colleagues.

SEEKING SUPPORT FOR A NEW APPROACH

Richard was enthusiastic about their support, and by the time he left for his first furlough in 1885, his idea had expanded to become a passionate vision that included all the provinces in China with a college in Taiyuan as the model. One of the primary reasons he chose to return to England at this time was to solicit the support of his Home Mission leaders to spearhead a movement to provide a united financial backing for his educational strategy.[1] As he prepared his presentation, he stressed the many benefits that could accrue from such an effort. First, the officials would gain scientific information through Western learning that could avert future famines. Second, instruction in modern Western learning by missionaries could open the scholars, and ultimately all the people, to the Christian faith and engender peaceful relations between Chinese and missionaries. Third, employment of the scientific principles undergirding Western learning would lead to the modernization and reform of China, enabling the most popu-

---

1. Richard, *Forty-five Years*, 197–98. He recorded that this was to be the first time he articulated his plan to the home board's China Committee, although he had presented a similar plan first to his colleagues several months before in Taiyuan. He did not expect the BMS to provide total support for this or any institution. He merely wanted the BMS to marshal the support of all the mission societies, regardless of denomination. He believed there were philanthropists who would also be eager to back such an effort. Timothy Richard, notes, 26 February? 1886, indicated that another purpose of the furlough was the education of the Richard children. While all four girls were schooled by their mother at home in China, Timothy and Mary decided they should be given the advantages of an English education. The two oldest, Mary and Ella, were enrolled at the Seven Oaks Boarding School; Florrie and Maggie returned to China with their parents. See also Mary Richard, letter to brother, 26 April 1886; Mary Richard, letter to sister Mary Jane, 7 August 1886; Mary Richard to Mary Jane, 22 September 1886. All such unattributed references to unpublished communications are from BMS MSS.

lous country in the world to enter trade and international diplomacy with Western nations as a peer. Fourth, the uniting of effort among the mission societies would remove needless duplication and competition, enabling a more efficient use of missionary funds and personnel.

In 1885 in London Richard carefully presented his plan in person to the leaders of the Baptist Missionary Society (BMS), expressing his wish for "all the missionary societies [in Great Britain] to unite in establishing a high class missionary college in each provincial capital, beginning with the maritime provinces, in the hope of influencing the leaders of the Empire to accept Christianity."[2] The scheme also called for a united effort by British mission societies to provide "highly qualified missionaries" (preferably and predominantly men with degrees but also including women) to establish a "high-class Training Institution-not inferior to our University Colleges" in each of the eighteen provincial capitals. These were to train the Chinese scholars as evangelists through a Christian curriculum emphasizing modern science, geography, and modern world history—the essence of Western learning.[3]

The BMS printed *A Scheme for Mission Work in China* for distribution among members of the Committee for China, which rejected it because the "scheme was far too great for their funds." They did agree, however, to send six additional men, "and these specifically qualified so that they may [be] engaged in the best way possible." After this rejection, Richard reemphasized, but to no avail, "the importance of opening colleges in the provincial capitals for the *training of accomplished native missionaries* [emphasis, mine] who would be given, besides theological work, courses of study in the various branches of knowledge taught in Western Universities."[4]

The scheme was subsequently referred to the General Committee for final consideration. Furthermore, it appears that Richard, "to save time," sent copies of the scheme to other mission societies while he was awaiting the final decision by the BMS. Richard expected to get its decision about this educational scheme as early as its May 7 meeting, but by May 15 the Committee still had "not given Mr. Richard what he wanted; kind words & promises bounded by ifs but nothing more definite." Finally, the

---

2. Richard, *Forty-five Years*, 198; Richard, letter to "Brother and Sister," 26 February 1886.

3. Richard, "Outline," 4–5.

4. Richard, *A Scheme for Mission Work*; Richard to brother and sister, 26 February and 26 April? 1886; Richard, *Forty-five Years*, 198–99.

BMS General Committee insisted that the scheme was beyond its financial means; Richard was bitterly disappointed by what he regarded as their short-sightedness. "After this I began to realize that God would have me bear my cross alone, and that I must fit myself more fully for influencing the leaders of China."[5]

In all fairness to the BMS, this amount was in fact beyond its financial capacities. Such a scheme for even the 13 maritime provinces would have cost approximately one million Tls. [approximately $730,000 total or $56,000 per institution] the first year alone, and Richard was talking about all eighteen provinces. However, he was not asking them to finance the entire endeavor, but only that the BMS coordinate a united effort by all British mission societies active in China, along with some British philanthropists, to endow the institutions. Since Richard even then was a staunch advocate of self-support, most likely he expected outside support to end after a fixed period of time at which point the Chinese government would take over the total support. These germinal concepts would come to fruition in the start-up by Richard of the Imperial University of Shansi in 1901. Like many visionaries, Richard was twenty years ahead of his time.

Upon the official opening of classes, Richard wrote a letter to the BMS on stationery with the university letterhead, pointedly recalling the Committee's lack of support many years earlier:

> The University proposed by me to the BMS in 1885–86 is now already opened at the expense of the Chinese government and your missionary Rev. Moir Duncan is the Principal of the whole Foreign Department ... When I suggested the same scheme kindly printed by Mr. Baynes that a similar Educational Institution be started in the capital of each of the 18 provinces, Max Muller remarked to me that youth would often plant trees that would grow to the sky but Heaven takes care that they don't![6]

The remainder of Richard's furlough in England was spent in gathering and dispersing information pertinent to education of the Chinese in Western learning. To fit himself further for the task of educating the scholars in Shanxi, Richard took science courses at South Kensington. In June

---

5. See Anon. [Mary Richard? dictated by Timothy Richard], handwritten "Note," n.d. [1885?]; Mary Richard to Mary Jane, 15 May 1886; Richard, *Forty-five Years*, 199; Richard, *Wanted: Good Samaritans*. Most probably, the note accompanied this pamphlet Richard had written and printed for the purpose of informing other mission societies in preparation for the union effort.

6. Richard, letter to the BMS Home Secretary Alfred Baynes, July 10, 1902.

1886, Richard went to Berlin and Paris to seek information about the best educational systems on the Continent. While in Berlin, the minister of education angrily refused to provide him any information; however, another senior education official, who was a Christian, "most readily gave [him] all the information" he wanted. In Paris, the minister of education was out of town, however, and Richard reported he got no information other than that they wanted to remove the name of God from their schoolbooks.[7]

Richard used the remainder of his furlough to share information about his work in China with different English churches and religious organizations, and was able to report that "several are impressed with the importance of the work considerably." One gentleman was willing to give £1,000 while another had "taken the matter up rather enthusiastically and says that he can't see why the Denomination cannot raise £20,000." While Richard was encouraged somewhat by the interest shown, he felt the overall response was far less than the need. By September 1886, the Richards were aboard the S.S. Oxus on their way back to China, with Richard deep in anguish over the Committee's refusal of support, yet undaunted in his vision. A fellow passenger was Marquis Zeng, who would later become a supporter of these new educational ideas.[8]

STRIFE AMONG COLLEAGUES

The Richards reached China early in November and were back safely ensconced at their home in Taiyuan just after New Year's 1887. They had been away nearly two years, of which eight months were spent aboard ships. By then, a few reinforcements from the BMS had arrived, but Richard believed the number was still too few for the need. Apparently, Shandong was getting the larger number of reinforcements for a work that covered only eight counties; whereas, Christian tracts had been distributed in all 108 counties in Shanxi, two-thirds of them under Richard's superintendence. Richard,

---

7. Mary Richard to Mary Jane, 1 March 1886; Richard, *Forty-five Years*, 199–200. Mary wrote that his physics course was being much interrupted by various meetings. Timothy indicated he took a course in electrical engineering.

8. Richard to "Brother?" 11 March 1886; to "Brother and Sister," 16 September 1886. These speaking engagements included the BMS General Conference, Rev. Spurgeon's Cathedral, the Religious Tract Society, a united missions meeting of Baptists and Congregationalists, as well as individual churches in Watford, Hastings, Cardiff, and Edinburgh, to name just a few. Early in the voyage, Richard commented, in passing, about Marquis Zeng's early disembarking but gave no indication whether they had any discussions.

therefore, felt it only right that the greater number of reinforcements should be sent to Shanxi as the newer developing field had greater breadth. Therefore, soon after his return to Taiyuan, he spearheaded a resolution signed by all six Shanxi BMS missionaries requesting the Home Committee to send fourteen more missionaries to Shanxi.[9]

When Richard had first arrived in China, he had been just like most of the other missionaries in his primary concern for "saving souls" and belief that the only source of truth was the Bible. Within five years, however, he had experienced a paradigm shift that pressed him to begin to "seek the worthy." He gave a sympathetic reading to the literature of the indigenous religions and philosophies and began to approach the educated Chinese or the leaders of the indigenous faiths rather than the illiterate populace. Both were considered contrary to orthodox practice. Some of his more conservative missionary colleagues, both members of China Inland Mission and those from his own BMS with fewer years' experience in China, decided these practices were equivalent to heresy.[10] By the time of his furlough in 1885–86, however, he was the senior missionary in Taiyuan, perhaps the oldest and best-educated, as well. Most likely, others did not feel at liberty to chastise him.

The tensions came to a head soon after his return from England. Richard likely attempted to continue his missionary work in the same vein as he had before, but by this time the CIM had sent more missionaries, and the BMS had sent young inexperienced reinforcements whose theology and methodology echoed that of the CIM. Therefore, Richard and those in sympathy with his thinking and approach now found themselves in the minority.

Unknown to Richard, some of these newer colleagues not only did not endorse his methodology but also had already actively opposed it by writing accusatory letters back to the BMS General Secretary; one such letter

---

9. Richard to Committee of the BMS, 4 March 1887; Timothy Richard et al. to Committee of the BMS, 12 May 1887, 4; see also Richard, Sowerby, and Turner, "Statement of Facts."

10. Richard, *Forty-five Years*, 204–6. See Pfister, *Rethinking Missions*; Cohen, *Missionary Approaches*, 29–62; Wright, "J. Hudson Taylor"; and Broomhall, *Assault on the Nine*, 287–93. The first three are academic studies; the latter study is authored by a CIM missionary who is the great-nephew of Hudson Taylor, founder of the China Inland Mission, now the Overseas Missionary Fellowship. Richard's letters to the BMS home secretary 1887–88 were replete with his defense of his mission methodology. It would seem to be vindication of both Richard's and Taylor's approaches that both are considered valid today.

"inadvertently" appeared in the August 1886 issue of *Missionary Herald*, published by the BMS. This issue came out while the Richards were en route to China, so Richard had not seen it. His autobiography revealed that what irked him most at first was not so much their criticism as their unwillingness to wait to discuss their criticisms with him before sending letters "reporting" on him. One major target was the catechism he had written for new believers, imposing his views of the appropriate practice and study for six different levels of affiliation with the mission. Those who entertained achieving the fourth level of being a minister and beyond were expected to engage in a study program that included various forms of Western culture—in addition to parallel forms of Chinese learning and Christian subjects. These were his ideas for training native evangelists.[11]

As their opposition grew more vitriolic, Richard chose to stop attending the meetings of the Local Missionary Committee even though he was its secretary. Richard also wrote a lengthy, detailed letter to Mr. Baynes, perhaps as a belated response to the published letter and his colleagues' letters. He subsequently sent another voluminous letter to the Committee of the BMS, also detailing his position. In it, Richard recounted a controversy three years earlier regarding his Chinese translation of the life of a devout Roman Catholic, intimating some points of disagreement were long-standing. In this same letter to the Committee, Richard asked them "to judge whether you think I am still worthy of your support or not."[12]

Finally, Richard felt it behooved him to leave Shanxi Province in the interest of unity within the missionary community. He declared his willingness to accept an invitation to go to Peking to do translation work with the former missionary Dr. Edkins or to relocate to a coastal city. Years later, Richard characteristically wrote very little in his autobiography about this

---

11. Richard, "Translation of Order of Study." On close inspection, the curriculum appears to be the embryonic form of the study program that Richard had hoped to initiate in the college of Western learning that he proposed in his union educational scheme to the BMS. Specific Western subjects included European mental and moral philosophy, geography, geology, physics, chemistry, mathematics, astronomy, Western medicine, Western history, and music for worship. A question arises as to why active opposition to Richard took so long to surface and mobilize. While there had always been a smoldering difference of opinion between the CIM and Richard, perhaps the arrival of BMS reinforcements during Richard's absence spurred the offensive.

12. Mary Richard, letter to sister, 14 April 1887; Richard to Committee of the BMS, 3 March 1887 and to Baynes and BMS Committee, 12 May 1887, 8, 15. The very fact that he wrote a sympathetic biography of a Roman Catholic was offensive to more fundamentalist colleagues.

conflict (only two paragraphs). But there continued to be attacks against his theological and methodological stance from members of the Shanxi BMS missionary community more than three years after he had left.[13]

During this time of internal conflict, Richard gave little attention to implementing his educational scheme since it had now become one of the central issues in the controversy within the missionary community. However, he did continue to have personal conversations with various scholars, Buddhists lamas, and officials in the government. Moreover, in the first five months after his return to Taiyuan, Richard delivered eight lectures to provincial officials.[14]

Mary disclosed in a letter that by then there were eighteen adults and eight children in their missionary community—"too many for one city don't you think?" By autumn 1887, Richard chose to leave Shanxi Province, his home base for nearly ten years, because it was clear to him that as colleagues they "could never work harmoniously together. To remain would induce permanent strife, which would be fatal to missionary work."[15]

A TIME OF TRANSITION

He and Mary went to Peking for a short time, but by November they found themselves in Tianjin where Richard was offered a salaried position (£600 per annum) to do translation work at the Arsenal, a military school and translation bureau run by the Chinese government. He declined this offer because he still "could not contemplate breaking with missionary work."[16]

---

13. Mary Richard to Mary Jane, 23 June 1887, said they expected this move to be approved and take place in August 1887. Richard to Baynes, 26 December 1887, 1–4, gives Richard's view of what was occurring prior to his departure. The fact that the attacks continued even after Richard left Shanxi until he assumed his position in Shanghai almost four years later, suggests that the conflict had degenerated to a personal level. Those critics he named in his correspondence were the younger missionaries who had just been sent to China as his reinforcements. It must be kept in mind that Richard himself, as a zealous young missionary candidate, had been attracted to the conservative, self-sacrificial principles that characterized the CIM. After his first ten years in China, however, he concluded he could most efficiently gain the most beneficial results for China with an educational or literary approach. There were few similarly-minded men in China at that time. See Richard, *Forty-five Years*, 204–5; Broomhall, *Assault on the Nine*, 289–93.

14. Richard to Committee of the BMS, 12 May 1887, 9; Richard to T. R. Glover, 26 May 1887.

15. Mary Richard to Mary Jane, 4? January 1887?; Richard, *Forty-five Years*, 205.

16. Richard, *Forty-five Years*, 206. He had been offered government employment

They returned to Peking to await a reply from the BMS to their request to establish a BMS work in Peking. Richard took advantage of this time to write the pamphlet *Modern Education in Seven Nations*, which he distributed among the leading Chinese officials there. It "suggested that the Government should commence educational reforms by setting apart a million Tls. annually for it."[17] Richard finally did receive the Society's reply, which stated that no new work would be opened in Peking but that he should return to his first field of endeavor in Shandong. By now, however, Richard was so firmly convinced of his calling to reach elites and the value of his educational program that in his reply he insisted that he be permitted to found a college for Western learning in Shandong once he relocated there. Again he awaited the BMS General Committee's decision about his future work.[18]

The Committee's answer, in a letter dated September 26, was received some time before Christmas. It revisited all sorts of issues encompassed by the controversy in Shanxi, much to Richard's distress, and insisted that Richard go posthaste to Shandong, where earlier his colleagues had resolved that he would need to adhere to established BMS practice as elucidated in the local Committee policy. So Richard repeated his need for autonomy and the liberty to engage in his kind of missionary work.

For the first time Richard boldly placed partial responsibility for his difficulties on the doorstep of the BMS in London. He suggested that the home society exercise more supervisory discipline over the younger, inexperienced missionaries in Shanxi who continued to send letters about him. He requested London to send a deputation to China to study their missionaries' efforts there. He noted that he was leaving soon to go to Shandong

---

before, in 1882 by Governor Zhang Zhidong of Shanxi Province. Richard had declined the offer then because he thought missionary work to be even more important. Other missionaries had accepted government employment in educational or translation work. John Fryer (formerly of the London Missionary Society) did translation work at the Arsenal in Shanghai, and W.A.P. Martin (formerly of the American Presbyterian Mission) was appointed by the Chinese government in 1864 the first president or dean of the Western Studies Division of Tong Wen Guan in Peking.

17. Evans, *Timothy Richard*, 102.

18. Mary Richard to Mary Jane, 16 December 1887, stated that should the BMS not approve her husband's scheme to start the Christian college in Shandong, he planned to remain in Peking, where he had access to government officials and would teach English in the mornings. This would provide the needed income "should the Society grudge supporting him here." Anticipating this, Richard had already posted a placard that resulted in inquiries from two Japanese and several Chinese.

with his former Shandong colleague A. G. Jones, to discuss further his possible placement there.

After five weeks in Shandong, in early 1888 Richard submitted a report to the Home Secretary concerning the outcome of his visit. "Now they will write you of the new conditions which they offer. They do not ask the former pledges. They wish me to start a small newspaper, and to start an Institution for the educated and leading classes in [Jinan]. They suggest (a) the appointment of one European and two Chinese to assist me; (b) that funds to get suitable teaching appliances and apparatus be got from private individuals in England."[19]

For the next two years, Richard and Baynes exchanged numerous letters thrashing out not only the past controversy in Shanxi but the current issues involved in Richard's joining his colleagues in Shandong. Because the Shanxi colleagues were continuing to question his orthodoxy, Richard did not want to have to endure this same questioning of his methods by less experienced colleagues in Shandong. Therefore, he hinged his placement in Shandong on an absolute demand for autonomy within a divided field of labor, of which his responsibility would be the educational and literary work within a two-county area, which included the provincial capital. This would give him the needed liberty to establish the college and run the newspaper. His colleagues in Shandong seemed supportive of his plan, but work of this nature was a drastic departure from the BMS's adherence to the traditional modes of missionary work and might well meet with disapproval by the donating public.

Richard's time in Peking meanwhile was quite productive in terms of translation work, presenting papers, and developing relationships with like-minded missionaries and various Chinese leaders. These provided an intellectual breath of fresh air. Richard presented a long paper on "The Influence of Buddhism on China" to the Peking Oriental Society on January 25, 1888, and Mary Richard felt it "delightful" that her husband's opinions were listened to with respect, contrary to the "contempt of the narrow school in Taiyuan."[20]

Central to his scholarly work was the pamphlet on modern education, mentioned above, in which he described the educational systems or methods of seven leading nations of the world, emphasizing four methods

19. Ibid.; Richard to Baynes, 26 December 1887, 11; 25 January 1888; 12 March 1888; and 21 May 1891.
20. Mary Richard to Mary Jane, 21 January 1888, 4.

of education—the historical, the comparative, the general, and the particular. He posited an inextricable relationship between specific knowledge or education and the progress of a nation.

Richard distributed this pamphlet "among the leading statesmen in Peking and personally presented it to Li Hongzhang in Tianjin." It was probably during this visit with Li that Richard presented him the proposal that the Chinese government commence educational reform by setting apart for it a million Tls. annually. Richard made clear in this interview that this was "seed money" with a hundred-fold return sure to be realized, but only after twenty years. To that, Li responded China could not wait that long.[21]

Also during this time, the Richards renewed acquaintance with Marquis Zeng, who had been aboard their ship returning to China. The marquis, a former minister to London and Paris, also was the son of the famous statesman Zeng Guofan. On one occasion, Richard helped supply information to him about railways in England, which had been requested by the emperor's father, and there began their friendship. Mary Richard later taught English to his youngest son. Marquis Zeng had developed an enduring interest in European education and made a recommendation for an institution in Peking where Chinese and foreigners could freely meet. But he felt inhibited from actively promoting educational reform once he returned to China, due to accusations by the conservative political faction that he was unduly influenced by foreigners. On various occasions Richard was invited to meet with Marquis Zeng in Peking, and in 1888, Richard presented Zeng a copy of his scheme for modern education in China. "He [Zeng] approved of it most enthusiastically, and urged me to circulate the treatise amongst the highest officials, as he was convinced that the only hope for China lay in education."[22]

Meanwhile Richard and Mary started "a high class school in which the pupils were to pay for their education."[23] Among those enrolled were

---

21. Richard, *Forty-five Years*, 206–7. Richard recounted: "Many years after, I met a Hanlin [scholar] who was in charge of a Chinese provincial college, and who had read my pamphlet on education. He told me that he had striven to carry out in his institution the former methods I had pointed out."

22. Ibid., 208–9; Mary Richard to Mary Jane, 26 November 1887.

23. Richard to Baynes, 13 March 1888. Richard's letter is unclear whether "class" here referred to social or academic level, but most likely it referred to academic level. He wrote that his wife Mary provided the instruction when he traveled to Shandong at Baynes's request, and that Mary also had "another school of a dozen poor orphan boys where she assists in teaching daily."

three Japanese and one Chinese who was studying mathematics." Richard took further advantage of this hiatus in his assigned missionary work to visit Japan in the spring of 1888 to study mission methods used there. He concluded with enthusiasm that the "educational work I was urging on the BMS was being carried out in Japan with great success."[24]

On his return to China, however, Richard heard from the BMS leaders that "though they would sanction my work among the literati and officials, they could not support any educational institution, as they considered that the Churches would not approve of such a use of their Mission funds."[25] Once again greatly disappointed with the refusal of the BMS to support educational endeavors, Richard considered withdrawing from the Society. When his former Shandong colleague A. G. Jones received word of what Richard was considering, he telegraphed him convincing him to wait on this decision until they could visit Shandong together. In September 1888 they did go to Shandong together, where Richard personally presented to his missionary colleagues not only his vision for a Christian college but also his need for autonomy within a field in which there was to be an equitable division of labor. The outcome remained uncertain, and the Richards moved to Tianjin in May 1889.

In the meantime, famine again raged in Shandong. Richard chose to return almost immediately in June, first to lend his experience to the relief efforts, then later to attend a local missionary conference. For the first time, he contracted the dreaded "famine fever" that usually followed in the wake of famine and for a time was imminently in danger of his life. Though still convalescing from this attack, he attended the conference where his "scheme of educational work was agreed to by the Shandong colleagues, and a letter was sent to the BMS with the signatures of them all, twelve in number," indicating they would welcome his arrival in October. Still in a weakened condition, during the first meeting of the conference Richard succumbed to "neural prostration" or perhaps "malarial paralysis," a common sequel to "famine fever." This caused him great pain and the incapacitation of his right arm for a time, delaying his return to Tianjin. His wife, also reported to be ill at the time, was "ordered" to go to enjoy the sea air at Yantai "for a change." She had not been informed of the gravity of his illness

24. Richard, *Forty-five Years*, 211–12.

25. Ibid., 212. Since the BMS was totally supported by voluntary contributions from members of the Baptist churches in Great Britain, it was absolutely necessary to have the full backing of the home churches. Yet what Richard was proposing was a radical departure from what the contributing public considered to be the domain of the missionary.

until he arrived to join her at the coast to convalesce, being carried there on a litter at night. Letters written from Yantai informed the BMS of his illness and inability to return to Shandong due to his medical condition. Richard needed assistance writing, so Mary served as his able secretary.[26]

By early October 1889, the Richards had returned to Tianjin to await the BMS's response to their news and the Shandong request. Richard was recovering very slowly, and the medical doctor supervising his care said "it would be madness" for Richard to think of relocating at that time.[27] Sometime later in October, Richard received a reply from the BMS in London that "the Committee once more rejected the scheme of a Christian college." As one protesting member of the Committee disclosed, this was the first time in at least twenty years the Committee had denied a unanimous request from the mission field.[28] The emotional shock most probably slowed Richard's recovery, and perhaps he even suffered a relapse, as his wife continued to have to do most of his writing, even six months later. The infrequent letters to London during his continued convalescence continued to indicate a willingness to go to Shandong if certain conditions were assured.[29]

At this juncture, Richard again pondered what to do next. He knew he could never again work under a forced co-pastorate system as he had experienced in Shanxi. He knew he worked best autonomously, as by necessity he had done most of his first years in China, and that he was to use a different method in his missions work than most other missionaries. He could no longer in good conscience engage in the traditional methods but was called to reach the educated, employing educational and literary means. He believed if the leaders were converted to Christianity, then the welfare of the masses would be improved—intellectually, socially, politically, materially, morally, and spiritually.

26. Ibid., 213. Famine fever may refer to many diseases that spread in famine conditions, most often epidemic louse-borne typhus. Richard (dictated to Mary Richard) to Alfred Baynes, 23 July 1889, while convalescing in Yantai, called his relapse condition "nervous(?) Prostration" while Richard, *Forty-five Years*, 213, called it "malarial paralysis." This was the first letter written by Mary Richard as dictated by Richard during his extended convalescence, according to Soothill, *Timothy Richard of China*, 166.

27. Timothy Richard to Baynes, 4 October 1889, indicated that though he had "fully hoped to be able to move to [Jinan] about this time, he had been medically advised against it." He was continuing his literary work.

28. Richard, *Forty-five Years*, 213–14. That was the third time since 1885 that the BMS had refused to endorse Richard's scheme to establish a college for the education of the Chinese in Western learning.

29. Richard to Baynes, 18 March 1890.

During this time of recovery and reflection, Richard engaged in literary work, writing a series of articles serialized in the *Chinese Recorder* and later put in book form, exploring the various benefits of Christianity—material, intellectual, political, social, moral, and spiritual. He had been prompted to write these in response to a question posed by Viceroy Li—"But what is the good of Christianity?" He submitted for publication in Shandong a four-volume work with two other volumes in process.[30] Some of his evangelistic efforts bore fruit as well. In a March 1890 letter written by his wife, Richard disclosed that "a devout man" who had come to them as an inquirer some months before was baptized, and the first thing this literary man did after his baptism "was to write a Tract giving his reasons for having become a Christian."[31]

In his autobiography, however, Richard wrote nothing about his activities during this time except to disclose that in May 1890 he presented the paper "The Relation of Christian Missions to the Chinese Government" to the Second General Missionary Conference in Shanghai (the first was held in 1877, but he had been unable to attend due to famine relief work).[32] Richard "prophesied" in this paper that if the government did not do something to quell the negative propaganda coming out against Christians, then a new wave of persecution would occur. Some colleagues believed this too gloomy a picture, but nevertheless appointed a committee to study the matter and draft a memorial to present to the Throne. Richard and six others were appointed to this committee, but before a memorial could be drawn up, a number of violent outbreaks did occur in the Yangtze (Yangzi) River valley. Richard quickly went to Wuchang (Wuhan) to prevail upon Viceroy Zhang Zhidong, a former governor of Shanxi on whom Richard previously had a significant influence, to intervene, but Zhang received him coolly,

---

30. Richard to Baynes, 7 April 1890. Richard did not give the titles of these works, but probably one was the Chinese language book form of the series of English language articles appearing in the *Chinese Recorder*. See "The Historical Evidences of Christianity for China: the Material (ff'd by Intellectual, Political, Social, and Present) Benefits," *Chinese Recorder* 21 (April, May, October 1890), 22 (January, April, May, October, November 1891).

31. Richard to Baynes, 18 March 1890. This literary man's name is not given, but "[A]ll who know him consider him a choice man." Neither this conversion nor the man's tract is mentioned in Richard's autobiography, which calls into question either Richard's memory or, more likely, the sincerity of the man's intentions for baptism. Richard's habit was not to write details of events that caused him great disappointment; he did not hesitate to mention the name of one Japanese convert. Richard, *Forty-five Years*, 207, 213-16.

32. Richard, "Relation of Christian Missions," 401-15.

doing nothing. Richard then returned to Tianjin where he made the same request of Li Hongzhang, again with no evident action taken. Much later a memorial was drawn up and presented by this Committee, but violent acts continued to be perpetrated against Christians for many years.

In a letter following the May conference in Shanghai, Richard disclosed to Baynes that he "felt very loathe to continue to draw my salary to do work in which I was but partially supported." In this same communication, Richard also wrote that he "must write a report of [his] state of health and of the important steps" he had just taken in consequence of his health. He again had been medically advised not to relocate to Shandong to take up the strenuous missionary work there. He then disclosed he had received and accepted an offer to become editor of an experimental Chinese newspaper in Tianjin beginning immediately, in July 1890. Viceroy Li and some personal friends had offered Richard the opportunity to become editor of a very influential daily paper in Chinese, called *The Times* (Shi Bao). "The appointment was most providential." He stated it would enable him to engage in "one part of the work appointed me by the Society to do in [Jinan] and would reach four Provinces instead of one—and that including Shansi and Peking—this without any cost to the Society, not even my salary."[33]

EXPLORING A NEW PROFESSION

After prayer and consulting with missionaries, Richard was convinced that it would be better for him as a Christian to fill the editorship than a non-Christian. Furthermore, he probably was hopeful this would present an amicable resolution to the long-standing issues in Shanxi and Shandong. With the acceptance of this position, Richard left the fold of the BMS, something he had long resisted doing because of his deep commitment to serving as a Christian missionary, and one he hoped would be temporary. He stated this was to be only until his health would be "more fully restored and until the way be opened for fuller work in connection with the Society."[34]

33. Richard (dictated to Mary Richard), 26 June 1890; Richard, *Forty-five Years*, 215. The *Shi Bao* was a daily Chinese language newspaper started by Gustav Detring on behalf of Li Hongzhang; however, it was Li who "personally invited Timothy Richard in 1890 to become the editor." Li knew the power of the press and often used the foreign and domestic press in China as well as America and Europe to promote reform. The *Shi Bao* "was represented to foreign advertisers as having an extensive circulation among high Chinese officials," according to Britton, *The Chinese Periodical Press*, 77–78.

34. Richard (dictated to Mary Richard) to Baynes, 26 June 1890. With this statement,

Richard, in truth, as editor of *The Times* was offered a different kind of "pulpit" from which to preach "good news." Through the agency of this newspaper, he had greater autonomy and freedom to proclaim his reformist ideas for the benefit of the Chinese. These were ideas that he held dear, yet few Chinese, even though in agreement, were at liberty to expound because of official conservatism. Most likely, Li was one of those officials under constraint and thus sought to exploit Richard's zeal for reform at this time to blast open the logjam of Chinese conservatism.

For approximately one year, then, Richard wrote on many subjects bearing on reform in China, introducing not only new ideas for reform but also a new form of journalism. Rather than a dull recital of official decrees from the Court, Richard sought to educate his readership. He utilized comparative diagrams on various subjects—education, trade, railways, population. and the like for various nations—with the purpose in mind of moving Chinese officials toward a greater awareness of their country's needs and of the means by which they might meet them and with what benefits. Richard believed "these diagrams proved probably one of the greatest forces in compelling intelligent Chinese to advocate reform."[35] He also included information such as he had presented to the officials and scholars in Taiyuan during the early 1880s. When persecution broke out against missionaries, Richard "wrote 6 Leaders [headlined articles] upon the subject, some of them double the usual length, giving a full account of Missions work throughout the Empire and throughout the world besides giving frequent [shorter] reports of Mission work" in China. In a letter to the BMS in London, Richard clearly implied that his articles may have prompted the emperor to issue an edict calling upon all the viceroys and governors to suppress these riots immediately by punishing their leaders and protecting Christians.[36]

His Japanese readers were most appreciative of the articles he wrote on the reforms taking place in Japan. When the heir apparent of Russia, later to become czar, was to come to China to break ground for the building of the Trans-Siberian Railroad, he first went to Japan but "encountered difficulties" during his visit there. Richard sought to allay the fears of the

---

Richard formally severed his position and salary with the BMS. He requested, however, that he be allowed to pay "for the education of my daughters through the Society. I shall pay the equivalent to *your* [emphasis mine] Mission in China." Note his use of the non-inclusive possessive adjective "your" by which it can be inferred that he no longer considered himself a representative of the BMS.

35. Richard, *Forty-five Years*, 215.
36. Richard to Baynes, 4 July 1891, 3-4.

Chinese as well as the Japanese by writing many articles for *The Times* about the protocol of royal visits among European countries as fostering peace and goodwill.[37]

The newspaper gained the attention of Chinese elites as Richard had hoped. The statesman Zhang Zhidong "wired to me from Wuchang for copies to be sent direct to him. Moreover, 5 other Daily Papers conducted by Chinamen [sic]—2 in Shanghai, 2 in Hong Kong and 1 in Canton—after the first month or two began to copy our Leaders in theirs." By "the second moon of the year they copied among them no less than 15 of our Leaders!"[38] Within a year, however, just when the readership seemed to be expanding, the financial support for publishing the newspaper ceased and the newspaper folded. At the end of June 1891, with this unexpected development, Richard found himself once again at a crossroads.[39]

Soon thereafter Richard was invited to become General Secretary of the Society for the Diffusion of Christian and General Knowledge among the Chinese (SDK, hereafter called the Christian Literary Society or CLS, its later name), an event he viewed as providential. With the untimely death

---

37. Mary Richard, Diary, 12 May 1891; Richard, *Forty-five Years*, 215.

38. Richard, *Forty-five Years*, 215; Richard to Baynes, 21 May 1891. Zhang's request from Wuchang indicates that Richard's readership went beyond the four-province area adjacent to Peking. Zhang continued to respect Richard's ideas as he had in the early 1880s when he was governor of Shanxi. Mary Richard to "Brother and Sister," n.d. wrote that Richard had "started a 'Weekly' besides the Daily! It contains all the Leaders & the main News of the Dailies... The circulation of the Paper is gradually increasing. Someone suggested lately that the Reporters of news in the Provinces shd [sic] be paid in Papers instead of money... If he has not already adopted it, Timothy means to do so."

39. Britton, *The Chinese Periodical Press*, 78, implied that Richard's departure to become secretary of the SDK hastened the suspension of the *Shi Bao*. Whereas Soothill, *Timothy Richard of China*, 170, claimed the newspaper lost its financial support, and that this antedated Richard's acceptance of the SDK position. Britton stated that the "*Shi Bao* was suspended when 'The Chinese Times' [a weekly English language newspaper] ended on the retirement of Alexander Michie [its editor, the *London Times* author and correspondent]." But his timing appears to have been in error. Not only was Soothill an "insider" as a close colleague of Richard, but also his view is supported by Mary Richard, Diary, 20 and 21 April, 30 June 1891: "Heard to-day that the Company [the large import-export firm Jardine & Mathison, Ltd.] have decided to give up the *Shi Bao* end of June... Planning to telegraph to Glover in Hong Kong asking what they sanction in the event the Co. giving up the Paper... They talk of giving compensation as they are giving up the Paper one year sooner than they engaged Mr. R.[Richard] for." Richard had, in fact, a two-year agreement with the *Shi Bao*; moreover, it appears that Richard was considering reconnecting with the BMS to serve as a missionary after the *Shi Bao* editorship ended. Mary wrote in June, "Mr. R. joined us—free from his Editorship a missionary once more."

in 1890 of his friend the Rev. Dr. A. G. Williamson, the position of general secretary had become vacant. The CLS Executive Committee and its President, the eminent Sir Robert Hart, head of the Imperial Chinese Customs Service, were very familiar with Richard's writings and apparently felt assured that he had both the sympathies and competencies equal to the task. Meanwhile, "[h]aving experienced the widespread influence of a newspaper, I [Richard] was convinced of the value of literary work in China."[40]

The Society was in no financial position to offer a salary, but Richard had no other financial support. He accepted the position, provided that he receive certain assurances of support from the BMS, as his predecessor's mission board had done before.[41] The BMS eventually did agree, perhaps reluctantly, to support Richard for three years.

By the time he relocated to Shanghai in 1891, Richard had endured almost five years in the refiner's crucible of conflict and uncertainty. The issues that had precipitated his departure from Shanxi in 1887 had continued to shadow him. His home committee had continued to insist that he engage in traditional missionary work, but, after almost twenty years in China, Richard believed he knew better what methods worked best. In any case, he believed that his talents, honed as editor of *The Times*, could best be used in the literary and educational arenas. Ironically, as general secretary of the CLS, with the support of the BMS, he could break free from their traditional approach to missions.

40. Richard, *Forty-five Years*, 217. Mary Richard, Diary, 4 June 1891, suggests there may have been some political pressure to close the *Shi Bao*; she wrote, "*Shi Bao* has greatly displeased Brennan[sic] our Eng. Consul." Richard's writings were generating an increasing national consciousness, and maybe the British consul was concerned that this would, in turn, destabilize the positions of the foreign powers in China.

41. Richard, *Forty-five Years*, 216-17. By the time this call to SDK was offered, the first BMS deputation had come to China with Dr. Richard Glover and the Rev. W. Morris as its members. Richard perceived that the BMS deputation "naturally assumed that the chief cause of my separation from the Mission lay in me, and proceeded as if to make peace between me and my fellow-missionaries." When the deputation met with the missionaries in Shandong, they found he had no differences with any of them. Another important factor at this juncture was the visit to China of Dr. Murdoch of the Christian Literature Society of India. He met with the BMS deputation, telling them his own CLS in Scotland supported him, and had also supported the late Dr. Williamson. He urged the BMS to do the same for Richard. At last, Dr. Murdoch and the deputation placed the matter before the BMS, which finally committed to support Richard for three years. Richard's autobiography is silent about Dr. Murdoch's intervention, but he included Murdoch's printed appeal to the BMS Home Committee two years later in the *Sixth Annual Report of the Society for the Diffusion of Christian & General Knowledge among the Chinese* (Shanghai, 1893).

4

Shaping China's Reform Movements, 1891–1910

TIMOTHY RICHARD RELOCATED TO Shanghai in 1891 to accept the position of General Secretary of the Society for the Diffusion of Christian and General Knowledge among the Chinese (SDK) and entered what was to become the most fruitful and influential period of his life. His tenure as head of the Society lasted for some twenty-four years until his retirement in 1915, and during these years, he would use this role and the various offices he held in the Education Association of China (EAC) as the means to disseminate his vision for a modern China. For most of this time, he exerted a powerful influence on the direction of elite Chinese thought and politics, both directly and indirectly, through a host of publications.

Richard, by early training and experience in Wales, as well as personality and talent, was an educator in the broadest sense of the word. In the 1880s he struggled to fit into the traditional missionary mold of Bible preaching and teaching along with humanitarian work. But in Shanghai in the 1890s, he would find his niche in Christian writing, translation, and publishing circles. By the end of the century, in addition to work on textbooks and popular media, the educator had expanded to briefing and mentoring national officials and scholars, as well as advising and lobbying the Imperial Court through petitions at a momentous time in Chinese history. In all this, he was no longer alone but the vortex of a broad and deep network of like-minded reformers. His legacy would include a key role in the establishment of a modern system of higher education as means

Shaping China's Reform Movements, 1891–1910

to fulfilling his vision for bringing China into the modern world through Christian auspices.

TURBULENT TIMES

The years 1895–1906 brought far-reaching institutional changes in China. These changes would affect not only education but also industry, the government, and the military. The complete and humiliating military defeat of China by the tiny "inferior" nation of Japan in 1894 led to soul-searching at the apex of society. The "Self Strengthening" Movement championed earlier, which hoped to adopt Western military technology to protect the empire, was discredited as not only ineffective but insufficient. How and where to make changes in a society steeped in a conservative Confucian ideology that engendered inertia was perplexing to high government officials, such as Viceroys Li Hongzhang and Zhang Zhidong. Japan's further victory over Russia—a Western power—in 1905 made this reform wing among Chinese officials even more eager to learn the secret of Meiji Japan's strength. After thought, some Chinese concluded that the answer lay in emulating broader training in Western learning, which Chinese students experienced when they went to Japan, especially when they returned to China with not only a new kind of knowledge but also the energy of a new spirit of nationalism.

Since the early 1880s Richard had been presenting broad-ranging recommendations for change to officials whom he met in Shandong or Shanxi, including Li and Zhang—key leaders of the reform wing—concerning the institutional reforms he envisioned China would need for the country to experience economic progress and domestic security. He did not believe that developing China's strength would require only the development of railways or a modern military; he had concluded that only officials educated in practical Western learning—including the Christian religion—could bring progress to society and equality for China on the stage of international diplomacy.

Richard had discussed with these leaders on more than one occasion the need to make this Western learning available within a Chinese institutional setting. In the mid-1880s, Zhang had invited Richard to become his adviser.[1] In 1891 in Tianjin, Richard urged on Viceroy Li the need for

---

1. Prior to becoming governor of Shanxi, Zhang Zhidong had little interest in Western learning beyond military weaponry. Then he encountered, in the provincial archives, Richard's recommendations for reform. He invited Richard to serve as his adviser. While

the Chinese government to invest up to 1 million Tls. annually toward the establishment of a national system of higher education institutions.² At the time, neither Richard's sending society, the Baptist Missionary Society (BMS), nor the Chinese government was convinced, and both withheld their backing. However, his short tenure in 1890 as editor of a reformist newspaper had further convinced Richard of the power of the written word, so he set about through the SDK publications and contacts to "convert" the minds of Chinese elites. Richard knew he was uniquely suited to carry on this work. Richard was also keenly aware that this would provide him the necessary platform from which to exert an even greater influence on the thinking of educated Chinese for the ultimate benefit of China. He would continually bring before his readers the need for a system of government colleges offering Western learning.

THE CHRISTIAN LITERATURE SOCIETY PLATFORM

The SDK (in Chinese, Guang Xuehui/Kuang Hsüeh Hui) has enjoyed an illustrious reputation in China. [Hereafter, Christian Literature Society (CLS), its later name after 1906 and the more common name used for a world-wide network of such societies, will be used for the SDK.] The earliest years of the Society, however, were not propitious. Its antecedent, the Chinese Book and Tract Society, was first established in Glasgow, Scotland, in 1884 but dissolved itself by 1887. Soon thereafter, with a transfer of equipment, the Rev. Alexander Williamson—a colleague and friend of Richard's from Shandong days—founded the CLS in China. He stated

---

he graciously declined the invitation in order to continue his missionary work, Richard had other communications with Zhang during his tenure. Zhang's endorsement of *education* (emphasis mine) primarily as a means of stabilizing the Qing dynasty and enhancing Chinese power can be traced to his time in Shanxi where he was exposed to Richard's educational ideas. He thereafter inaugurated various practical solutions to meet China's present needs, most important being founding schools of Western learning. *The North China Herald Supreme Court & Consular Gazette* (hereafter, *North China Herald*), August 22, 1884, published a translation of a proclamation issued by Zhang in Shanxi in May 1884. It called for men familiar with astronomy, mathematics, foreign languages, weaponry, mining, foreign and domestic law, and world travel and men with practical knowledge of machinery and navigation to come forward to establish a "bureau giving special attention to such matters." He closed by stating, "In these troublous times strange and curious learning must be encouraged, for it is of urgent importance."

2. Mary Richard, Diary, 17 June 1891. All such unattributed references to unpublished communications are from BMS MSS.

its object to be the circulation of literature based on Christian principles throughout China, her colonies, and dependencies—literature written from a Chinese standpoint, with knowledge of native modes of thought and adapted to instruct and elevate the people, especially through the more intelligent and ruling classes. (Richard offered a similar proposal for a CLS in Shanxi in 1884.)[3]

In 1889 the CLS began publishing Dr. Young J. Allen's monthly periodical *Review of the Times* (Wanguo gongbao/Wan-kuo kung-pao) and Mr. D. S. Murray's *A Chinese Boy's Own Paper*. Allen had founded the *Review* in 1868 as *Church News* and then as *Globe* until he suspended operations in 1883. But the promise of new life in 1889 was short-lived; the CLS fell on hard times in 1890 and sold its printing facilities to the National Bible Society of Scotland for its use elsewhere.

After Williamson's death in August that year, some members of the Society's Board of Directors sensed the value of the Society and sought to continue its work. Mr. C. S. Addis (later, Sir Charles Addis), then of the Hong Kong and Shanghai Bank, became its acting secretary. Richard's name was likely suggested to fill the general secretary's position by Sir Robert Hart, president of the Society, a friend familiar with his ideas and writings.

Richard took up his new post in October 1891, but probably not without some reservations on the part of the BMS, which had reluctantly agreed to support him for three years. Richard also noted at that time he was the only member of a missionary society in China entirely set apart for literary work. He indicated the direction and impact the Society should one day have in his 1891 annual report, his first as its general secretary, in which he refers to the ignorance of the literati as the root of many of the causes of China's famines. He wrote, "there is a growing feeling that the best way of helping China is to give such kind of enlightenment as this Society attempts to give. We cannot even *dream* [emphasis, his] of establishing modern schools throughout the Empire; this will be the province of the Chinese Government after it somewhat understands its own needs and how to meet them."[4]

Clearly, the CLS's purpose in Richard's eyes was the removal of the ignorance he had seen demonstrated by various Chinese officials during

3. Richard, *Forty-five Years*, 218–19.
4. Ibid., 219–21. The other missionaries with the CLS were involved only on a part-time basis, with Dr. Young J. Allen employed as the principal of the Anglo-Chinese College in Shanghai, and Dr. Ernst Faber, a student of the Chinese classics, employed full-time as a translator at the Arsenal in Fuzhou.

his famine relief efforts of the late 1870s. He saw the ultimate responsibility of the Society to be to make Chinese officials aware of their need for Western learning and to promote the enlightenment of the tiny elite of scholar-officials so that they would be convinced of the usefulness of modern education to meet China's needs. This was no easy task, and Richard was not naive enough to believe the ideas presented in the CLS publications would reach every mandarin, official, or scholar. However, he believed the chief mandarins, together with the high examiners, educational inspectors of counties, professors of colleges, and a small percentage of the literati, with some of the ladies and children of their families, might be reached. (This number was estimated at 44,036.)[5]

To accomplish this purpose, Richard as general secretary expanded and revised the publications available through the CLS. The Society earlier had published only two Chinese language magazines, and its property was valued at only $1,000. The style and focus of *Review of the Times* changed with the launch of the *The Missionary Review* [Zhong Xi jiaohui bao/Chung-hsi chiao-hui pao]. The former became more secular in content and aimed at the Chinese elites; the latter continued the reporting on missionary and church news worldwide. Richard also launched a new focus—translating and publishing Western language literature—beginning with his project to translate Robert Mackenzie's *The Nineteenth Century: A History*. The author shared Richard's faith in steady human progress through science, and even more important to Richard, he posited that Western civilization's real strength came through possessing Judeo-Christian theological underpinnings. This book, one of Richard's most influential works, was published in 1894 with his personal introduction addressing China's situation in the immediate aftermath of the Sino-Japanese war. The volume was sent throughout the empire to leading government officials, eventually sold more than a million copies (many of them pirated editions), and by the end of the decade even made its way into the Forbidden City where it was read to the emperor by his tutor Sun Jia'nai.[6]

---

5. Ibid., 221.

6. Richard, *Forty-five Years*, 256, cites his interview with Sun on October 12, 1895. Mary Richard, Diary, 16 March 1891, indicates that the couple was reading this book together in Tianjin in March 1891. Within two years, he was translating it into Chinese.

Robert Mackenzie, *The Nineteenth Century: A History*, 15th ed. (London: Thomas Nelson & Sons, 1909), was first published in London in 1880, and the Library of Congress lists that edition with only seventy-two pages as published by G. Munro, New York. Another source noted the book was first published in 1889, and this would be the first

To attract the interest of a varied readership, Richard developed a seven-point plan for the CLS. The first was to provide "periodicals of a high-class order" in which "some subjects would be treated systematically, somewhat after the manner of Cassell's 'Popular Educator.'" The second, and perhaps most far-reaching, was to provide "a series of books and pamphlets . . . to show the bearing of educational and religious development in industries and trade and in every department of national progress." The third was a unique incentive—to offer prizes "for the best papers by Chinese on various subjects connected with the enlightenment and progress of the nation." The fourth was to stimulate interest "in useful information" among the Chinese in venues such as "lectures, museums, [and] reading rooms." As its fifth means, Richard envisioned opening depots for the sale of CLS publications in the provincial capitals where the civil service examinations were administered. A sixth point was "to secure the cooperation of the Chinese in all efforts and to get them to form societies for the advancement of learning."[7] The seventh and final method in the plan clearly illustrated Richard's intention, as the Society's general secretary, to broaden the scope of the Society's influence. "We intend to have advertisements of our Society's aims and purposes put out at every examination. As the best schoolmasters of every distant village attend these examinations, we hope in this way to make our influence felt in every nook and corner of the Empire." Not only did the CLS widely distribute publicity stating its aims, but it also targeted examination candidates with specially prepared materials.[8]

---

edition of 472 pages published by Thomas Nelson Sons, a Baptist affiliate, with offices in both New York and London. By means of its translation, Richard sought to guide thinking Chinese to understand the reasons and remedies for China's weakness in the face of aggression by Japan, since it espoused Western progress and lauded the achievements of Western science, enlightenment, and democracy. The English editions came to include a section about Richard's sending agency, the Baptist Missionary Society.

7. Richard, *Forty-five Years*, 221–23. In 1894 Mr. Thomas Hanbury, a member of the Society, donated 600 Tls. toward prizes for essays from civil service examination candidates on subjects dealing with reform or foreign relations. In 1891, there were eighteen examination centers. By 1893, in time for the special examinations convened to commemorate the empress dowager's sixtieth birthday, the CLS had established depots in Peking, Shenyang (Mukden), Tianjin, Xi'an, Nanjing, and Yantai (Chefoo). With the early reform movement of 1895–98, reform societies or study groups were established in various provincial capitals to explore ideas for institutional reform.

8. Ibid., 222. At the spring 1892 triennial examinations for *Juren* (MA) in Peking, free copies of Richard's *Four Great Problems* were circulated. In autumn 1893, more than 60,000 CLS publications, including Faber's *Civilization*, were distributed among candidates.

Timothy Richard's Vision

Since the magnitude of this plan was beyond the capability of one man, Richard devised another plan to "increase and intensify" interest in the CLS within the foreign community in China, particularly among the missionaries, as well as to enlist their assistance. He wrote to a "number of leading missionaries in China," requesting that they submit suggestions for topics needing translation for the Chinese. An open letter of invitation through the *Chinese Recorder,* in which Richard also published a summary of his goals, added momentum. The four main topics on which Richard sought to enlighten China were these:

1. "How to support her people"
2. "How to give peace to her people"
3. "How to make her people good"
4. "How to educate her people"[9]

The result of casting this wide net was a list of about seventy topics and more than twenty volunteers to write articles on various subjects. Authors mainly included educational missionaries and also members of the Chinese Imperial Maritime Customs and the diplomatic community. Provincial Executive Committees for the Society (with both foreigners and Chinese) were established to generate and distribute literature and solicit financial patronage.[10]

By the end of the first three years of his appointment, Richard had enunciated a clear vision for the direction of the Society and had developed a strong base of support. His efforts reflect his usual ethic of hard work and prolific writing. Just in the first year 1891, he had already undertaken to distribute free literature at the triennial examination in Peking, for which he prepared the tract "Four Great Problems," while his book *Historical*

---

9. Richard, "Scheme for the General Enlightenment of China," 1892, 131–32; and "Letter to the Editor of *The Chinese Recorder*—S.D.K," 1892, 237–38. The open letter solicited articles from readers demonstrating "the importance and economic value of modern subjects of education and true religion." By that time, he had already received commitments for articles on such topics as the post office, immortality, light, sound, machinery, agricultural chemistry, rulers and princes and statesmen traveling abroad, the press, national uniform taxation, the "new birth" in Christianity, sulphuric acid, and modern education. He encouraged more than one article on the same topic but from different standpoints.

10. Ibid., 221–22. The duties of the provincial Executive Committees included writing at least one article a month for the CLS magazines, awarding prizes for essays written by examination candidates, sending or selling CLS literature to expectant officials and professors, and raising financial support from sympathetic foreigners and Chinese.

Evidences was prepared for presentation "to the highest authorities in most of the eighteen provinces." During the next two years, 1892–93, Richard single-handedly did the work of the Society as Allen was in the United States and the other active contributor, Dr. Edkins, was in Europe, leaving Richard to edit the monthly *Review of the Times* and *The Missionary Review*. During the same year in which he began to translate Mackenzie's history of the nineteenth century, Richard also strengthened the board of directors and executive committee by adding influential religious, political, and business leaders (none being Chinese or women).[11]

In the *Sixth Annual Report*, Richard related correspondence he had received that demonstrated appreciation by the Chinese for CLS literature. When the newest CLS book depot first opened in Xi'an, violent opposition forced the missionary in charge to "fly for his life. That was only two months ago . . . Very recently that same missionary ventured back into the city. A mandarin there offered a house to him free of charge if he would stay there and continue his work, saying: 'If you will remain here it will be a god-send to our place.'" Richard also reported there were increased orders for the *Review of the Times* from Formosa (Taiwan) and Shandong, which further demonstrated "the appreciation of the value of this periodical." Allen, the editor of the *Review*, stated that one of the most important and encouraging facts he observed after recently returning from more than a year's furlough was the "naturalization" of ideas: "The Chinese are beginning now to accept our teaching, adopt our ideas and adapt them to their own use . . ." He further remarked that the CLS was contributing to that purpose which, in turn, would affect all nations. "The healthful development of this country would add greatly to the blessings and benefits of the world . . ."[12]

Several proposals were also made at this Annual Meeting regarding distribution to high mandarins of Dr. Ernst Faber's *Civilization* and the sponsorship of an essay contest endowed by Thomas Hanbury (later knighted) for a prize of 100 Tls. for the best essay on one of five questions presented at each of five examination centers, plus expenses. The

---

11. *Sixth Annual Report of the SDK, 1893*, 6, 13, 17, 220, 222. On the lists of the "Office-Bearers," one for 1892–93 and the other for 1893–94, eight Ordinary Directors were added to the former. Two new men were added to the Executive Committee—British Consul-General G. Jamieson and the Rev. Paul Kranz, an independent missionary who later became acting secretary of the CLS during Richard's absences in September 1895–February 1896 and again in 1896–97. The total amount received in subscriptions and donations in the year ending October 31, 1893, was $478.35.

12. Ibid., 16, 17, 20.

questions covered a wide range of topics dealing with modernization, such as the benefits of a postal office, railways, silver coinage, mechanization of industries, the Imperial Maritime Customs, suppression of opium cultivation and trade, as well as how to improve international relations. A final proposal approved was by Mary Richard for the printing of the *Women and Children's Series for China*.[13]

In March 1894 Richard published through the CLS a circular entitled "How to Multiply Trade in China," which linked economic development with educational reform. The Educational Department of the *Chinese Recorder*, the public organ for the Educational Association of China (discussed below in this chapter), extracted a portion of the circular and published it as a scheme for the reform of education.[14] This plan had three major points on the funding, examination, and control of modern education in China. Richard recommended the establishment of a Board of Modern Education placed under the direct control of the Foreign Affairs Office (Zongli Yamen) and Robert Hart, head of Chinese Customs. They would be responsible "to develop the vast resources of the empire and to further the best interests of China in every possible way by means of modern education." He then recommended that edicts be issued to replace some of the existing topics in education and the examinations, e.g., to replace traditional poetry with Western knowledge—universal history, physical sciences, political economy, commerce and industries, and mathematics. He also recommended that this Board of Modern Education appoint the examiners on Western subjects and that degrees should distinguish between those who attained proficiency in traditional subjects or in Western learning.

A unique facet of this scheme was its funding base. First, Richard proposed in 1894 that "one per cent of the foreign Customs' revenue [be] set apart for modern education." Second, he recommended that China use "the surplus American indemnity returned to the Chinese government" for education. This money could be invested in the Chinese government

---

13. Ibid., 21. Richard, *Forty-five Years*, 222. According to Soothill, *Timothy Richard of China*, 178, Hanbury was a prominent CLS donor who bequeathed to the Society funds sufficient to buy land and an additional 25,000 Tls. to construct buildings to house the CLS permanently.

14. Richard, *How to Multiply Trade in China*, 1894. This scheme was published as "A Practical Plan for Education," 1894, 255. The idea eventually came to fruition in 1904 when a Director of Education and a Bureau of Educational Affairs were established in Peking, and in December the next year became a separate Board of Education to administer the embryonic school system. See Bailey, *Reform the People*, 31, 37.

railways (perhaps at 5 percent interest), and then the interest could be totally devoted to modern education. Two aspects make this unique: that Richard himself would propose that the means of funding this reform proposal be based on Customs revenue, and that one of the means of funding dealt with the reversion of indemnity funds. The first bears the stamp of Sir Robert Hart, inspector general of the Imperial Chinese Customs (and CLS president), but the second seems unique to Richard. Unfortunately, this scheme never had a chance to be implemented or even debated as war was declared between China and Japan on August 1, 1894. Nevertheless, this was the first occasion Richard (or, perhaps, anyone) presented the possibility of using indemnity funds for educational purposes, as would occur after 1900.[15]

By 1894 Richard had begun to reap the rewards of his labor. Financial support was forthcoming from both Chinese and Westerners. The viceroy at Wuhan, Zhang Zhidong, sent a donation of a thousand Tls. He made his largest donation of $3,000 several years later, in 1901, to express his delight for receiving the three-volume set *Ancient and Medieval History of the World*, authored by the Rev. J. Lambert Rees, a missionary on loan to the CLS from the American Protestant Episcopal Mission. Also, a high-ranking official in Shandong not only sent in donations, but later as governor of Zhejiang also "induced the officials and gentry there to send annual orders for books to the CLS of the value of sixteen hundred Tls."[16]

Further evidence of the impact of CLS publications is suggested by the nature of some of the newer questions on the provincial examinations. Some "high officials . . . instead of basing their questions on Chinese literature as

---

15. This was the first time that Richard suggested concrete sources by which the Chinese could fund their modern schools. It is not clear where the surplus American indemnity funds came from; Richard did not specify. Possibilities include indemnities imposed on China for the loss of life and property either during the Tientsin Massacre of 1870 (when American churches were burned) or during the violent outbreaks in the early 1890s recounted in Hsü, *The Rise of Modern China*, 301. The most likely possibility, however, is the indemnity fund for losses sustained in 1844–58. By 1884 all claims had been paid, and there remained a surplus in excess of $200 thousand with its earnings of another $340 thousand. See Senate Committee on Foreign Relations, Chinese Indemnity Fund, 48th Congress, 2nd Session, 1885, S. Rept. 1190, 3.

16. Richard, *Forty-five Years*, 223. Shanghai Daodai Nie Qiqiu's son later became a leading member of the Shanghai YMCA (Young Men's Christian Association), and Nie's wife became a Christian in 1914.

was the rule in all past time, put a number of questions that the candidates could not have answered unless they had read Mr. Rees' *History*."[17]

With an increase of readership came growth in CLS membership, to sixty-nine members by 1897, including five Chinese and three women, a radical departure from earlier members, which were exclusively Western men who were government officials from Western countries, businessmen, and educational missionaries, primarily from the United States and Great Britain. Since Shanghai had become inundated with foreign commercial endeavors, this was understandable, and many of Richard's articles of the mid-1890s continued to address the economic benefits that would accrue to China if certain reforms were instituted.[18]

ADVISING THE COURT

China's defeat by Japan in 1895 marked a turning point in Chinese people's thinking about their nation and its place in the world. It also inaugurated a new period of influence for Timothy Richard and the CLS. In spring 1895, perhaps soon after the May settlement of the Sino-Japanese war, Richard's translation of *The Nineteenth Century: A History* by Mackenzie was published. It caused quite a stir in Chinese officialdom. As a result of this and other literature he published through the CLS around the same time, Richard's reputation as a disinterested and wise adviser continued to grow among the Chinese officials. Viceroy Zhang Zhidong of Wuchang invited Richard to meet with him in February 1895 for the first of three interviews that year to discuss China's precarious situation as demonstrated in her humiliating defeat by Japan. Richard proposed that peace with Japan was necessary before any reform could take place in China, and that "thorough reform rested upon right education." Since Richard believed this education would take twenty years to prepare China's leaders, he made a remarkable proposal that in the meantime, a protectorate of foreign powers be established to initiate reforms and to "settle all the foreign relations of China for

---

17. Ibid., 228.

18. *Tenth Annual Report of the SDK, 1897* (hereafter referred to as *Tenth Annual Report*). See Richard, "How to Multiply Trade in China," condensed, 1894; and Richard, "God's Various Methods of Blessing Mankind," 1894, 272–82, as examples of his economic focus.

a definite term of years." At the end of that term, this protectorate would devolve its authority and control to China's then-trained leadership.[19]

That same spring of 1895, a number of elite scholars who were in Peking for the national civil service examinations had begun to meet to discuss measures to strengthen China after her recent humiliating defeat. A memorial was drawn up by the scholar Kang Youwei [K'ang Yu-wei] and signed by more than 1,300 other scholars to be presented to the Throne, requesting that the emperor immediately take steps for reform. This was the first such mass action on behalf of Westernizing reform; the steps they advocated were similar to those discussed in publications of the CLS.[20]

Subsequently, Kang and his friends created the Reform Society (Jiang Xuehui or Higher Learning Society). Its secretary in charge of journalistic work was Kang's protégé Liang Qichao (Ch'i-ch'ao), also from Guangdong, and its membership included Hanlin Academy scholars, official censors, and under-secretaries of the Grand Council. Richard noted that the Reform Movement had the "full sympathy" of Weng Tonghe, then de facto "prime minister" of China, and Sun Jia'nai, one of the emperor's tutors, and received "great encouragement" from the British Minister, Sir Nicholas O'Connor. Richard wrote that he, Dr. Gilbert Reid (American Presbyterian missionary to the higher classes in Peking), and Mr. William Pethick (an American who was one of Li Hongzhang's foreign secretaries) frequently dined with members of the Reform Club.[21]

---

19. Richard, *Forty-five Years*, 235–37. These interviews preceded the 1898 publication of Zhang's seminal book *Ch'üan-hs'üeh p'ien* (Exhortation to Learning), translated into English by S. I. Woodbridge as *China's Only Hope: An Appeal By Her Greatest Viceroy, Chang Chi-tung, With the Sanction of the Present Emperor Kwang Si* [Guang Xu]. Zhang's book has interesting points both of convergence and divergence with Richard's thought on educational reform. Richard's seeming political imperialism in promoting a protectorate may stem from his view of teaching as mentoring (the Lancasterian system). The use of the "more experienced in world affairs" to teach the "less experienced" Chinese, then, would seem entirely in order to Richard. This protectorate was intended for a limited time for a specific purpose. Chapter 5 shows how Richard put this principle into practice in his administration of the Imperial University of Shansi.

20. For a more complete discussion of the Reform Movement, see Cameron, *The Reform Movement in China*; Kwang, *A Mosaic of the Hundred Days*; Lo, *K'ang Yu-wei*.

21. Lo, *K'ang Yu-wei*, 252, 255, 266–68, included by name the following members (besides Kang and Liang) of the Reform Society: Chang Yin-huan (Zhang Yinhuan), former Chinese minister to the United States of America and chief peace envoy to Japan; Wen ting-shih (Wen Dingshi), from Kiangsi Province, a Hanlin scholar and tutor to the ladies of the Court; T'an Tze-t'ung (Tan Sitong), son of the governor of Hopei (Hebei) Province and later martyr in the 1898 Reform Movement; Ch'in Chih (Qin Zhi), of Kiangsi, who

Timothy Richard's Vision

Then, on August 17, 1895, the first issue of the reformers' independent newspaper came out, which not only reprinted many of the articles from the *Review of the Times,* but assumed its name *Wanguo gongbao* as well until Richard persuaded the reformers to change it; it became *Sino-Foreign News* [Zhong-Wai Jiwen]. Soon, other scholars formed a Junior Reform Society in Shanghai, with branches in several other major cities. These men brought their regulations for Richard to revise as well as to discuss "how they could help to enlighten their country." One member even suggested "the Chinese Government should make ours the organ of the Government, and publish ten thousand copies regularly."[22]

Richard's original mandate to visit Peking in September 1895 was for another purpose—to prepare an appeal on religious tolerance (the "Mission Memorial") for presentation to the emperor on behalf of all the Protestant missionaries.[23] Inadvertently, he became involved in internal Chinese politics. On October 17, less than a month after arriving, Richard met with Kang Youwei for the first time; Kang said "he hoped to co-operate with us [the CLS] in the work of regenerating China."[24] Liang Qichao offered

---

wrote out Richard's reform scheme for Weng T'ung-ho (Weng Tonghe); Yuan Shih-k'ai (Yuan Shikai), general of the Chihli Army and later president of the Republic of China, 1914–16; Wang Chao (Wang Zhao), Liu Kwang-ti (Liu Guangdi), Yang Tze-wei (Yang Ziwei), Yang Shih-shen (Yang Shishen, a censor and Hanlin scholar), K'ang Kwang-in (Kang Guangyin, K'ang Yu-wei's brother), and Lin Shio (sic), a descendant of Commissioner Lin of the Opium Wars fame. Of the last six, three were under-secretaries of the Grand Council and all but Wang later became martyrs to the 1898 Reform Movement. The Hanlin Academy was comprised of Confucian scholars who had received the highest honors at the Palace Examination in Peking and thus were destined to receive high political appointments. Miyazaki, *China's Examination Hell,* 100, viewed the Academy more as "a secretariat under the emperor's supervision that compiled books and drafted decrees . . . and further served as a source of young officials who could be sent to the provinces as the need arose," rather than as an academic institution. Normally, several hundred candidates were in this pool of available talent.

22. Richard, *Forty-five Years,* 245, 254–55. Kang and the others knew that the *Review of the Times* had been in circulation for several years without official opposition, and they apparently hoped for the same lack of official censorship for their newspaper. That their newspaper was printed with the help of the official *Peking Gazette* indicated to Richard "a slight change of attitude was seen on the part of the Government."

23. "Memorial to the Chinese Emperor on Christian Missions (Translation)," *The Peking and Tientsin Times* March 7, 1896; "Memorial to the Chinese Emperor on Christian Missions (Translation)," *Chinese Recorder,* April 1896, 177–83. The translation and an article entitled "The Missionary Memorial," giving its history, may be found in the BMS MSS collection.

24. Richard, *Forty-five Years,* 254.

to serve as Richard's Chinese secretary, which he did while in Peking. His tasks would have included preparing the memorial in Court Mandarin.

For his original purpose, Richard had meetings with several high government officials and many scholars, including three different visits with Li Hongzhang. In their first meeting, Li made several comments related to education, revealing that "high Ministers in Peking spoke of Western education as 'Kwei-tze hsuoh' [guizi xue, 'devil's learning'] and spent all their time on Chinese learning alone," which Li believed to be of "no practical use." Li also indicated that definitely the "Government would not grant posts to those qualified in Western learning," presumably in response to Richard's suggestion. Li recommended that Richard request a meeting with Prince Gong (Kung), brother of Emperor Xian Feng (Hsien Feng), whom Li knew had read his translation of *The Nineteenth Century: A History*.

In a conversation later the same month, Li indicated that the Hanlin College was in the grip of extreme conservatism. The head of the college "would not allow the Hanlins to study foreign books, and that he was always cursing foreign learning and religion," which made Hanlin scholars and other reformers powerless to effect or even recommend reform of any kind. During their second meeting that September, Richard presented Li himself with three suggestions related to education: (1) that one hundred Hanlin and ten of the Imperial family be sent abroad; (2) that foreign or Western learning be given to all *Xiucai* [equivalent to BA degree holders]; (3) that "lectures on world topics be given regularly in Peking."[25]

On Li's recommendation, and with a letter of introduction, Richard met on October 26 with Weng Tonghe, then prime minister, whom some believed was "practically Emperor of China." Only one staff member of the Foreign Affairs Office was present. The primary purpose was to discuss the issue of religious liberty. Since Richard thought ignorance and superstition among the officials was the root of religious persecution, particularly against the Christians, he requested the government to grant religious liberty to all faiths. Then, to eradicate the root of persecution, Richard suggested that other reforms were also necessary, most importantly those related to the

25. Ibid., 245–46, contain Richard's account of these meetings with officials. This last suggestion to Li was similar to the concept he had employed in Shanxi Province from 1880–84 and hints that Richard was seeking official sanction of his lectures to the Reform Club. Richard's idea of making this Western learning available to the scholars was an idea he had first presented to Zhang Zhidong in 1882 while governor of Shanxi. The Rev. Gilbert Reid eventually founded the International Institute first in Peking, then later in Shanghai, for this purpose.

enlightenment of officials. At the close of their meeting, Weng requested that Richard "prepare a statement of what I [Richard] considered were the needful reforms for China at that juncture."

The comprehensive reforms Richard subsequently submitted to Weng as most needful were subsumed under four general headings: educational reform, economic reform, internal and international peace, and spiritual regeneration. Of course, he included establishment of a Board of Education to oversee the introduction of "modern schools and colleges throughout the Empire." Richard learned that Weng showed the plan to the emperor, who approved it.[26]

Richard and Weng met at the end of February 1896 for the last time before Richard's furlough to England. This time, Weng visited him personally in the home where Richard was staying, "an unprecedented act, for no Prime Minister of China had ever called at a missionary's house before." Besides apologizing for the non-appearance of the edict sanctioning the requests of the Missionary Memorial, Weng's second object was to "ask if I would aid in the Reform Club which the Government talked of resuscitating. I refused to have any connection with it if it would be of no practical service to China." Richard indirectly was expressing his concern about the speed and the content of the radical reform program, as well as distancing himself from the Chinese reformers. Richard from the beginning had always stated that practical change was needed and that it should gradually take place over at least a twenty-year period.[27]

---

26. Ibid., 246–48, 252, 256, 259 give Richard's account of interactions with Weng. Page 256 states, "To carry out these great measures I proposed—

1. Two foreign advisors to the Throne.
2. A Cabinet of eight Ministers, one half of Manchu and Chinese, and the other half of foreign officials who would know about the progress of the world.
3. The immediate reform of currency and the establishment of finance on a sound basis.
4. The immediate building of railways and the opening of mines and factories.
5. The establishment of a Board of Education to introduce modern schools and colleges throughout the empire.
6. The establishment of an intelligent Press with experienced foreign journalists to assist Chinese editors for the enlightenment of the people.
7. The building up of an adequate army and navy for the country's defence."

27. Ibid., 259. Soothill, *Timothy Richard of China*, 224, wrote that "Richard had no desire to be mixed up in merely political affairs. He asked to be excused, unless the club were meant to be a real power for the service of China, that is, not a centre for intrigue."

Richard also met with Prince Gong (Kung), the president of the Tsungli Yamen and a member of the imperial family. While Li would not give Richard an official letter of introduction, he revised Richard's letter requesting an appointment. During the meeting, with the other seven members present, the prince accused Christians of various crimes he believed worthy of the punishment they were receiving at the hands of the people. Richard's request that the prince "appoint a Commission of Inquiry into all the alleged charges against the Christians" and his hope for an imperial edict on religious liberty both came to naught. But Richard believed he had been able "to enlighten the members, whose ideas had been vague in the extreme, as to the object and value of foreign Missions," and Li Hongzao, one of the members present and a tutor to the emperor, reassured him that his "visit here will do good."[28]

Another of the emperor's tutors, Sun Jia'nai, also received Richard several times during his stay in Peking. In October, Sun told Richard he had been reading from his translation of Mackenzie's *Nineteenth Century* to the emperor every day for two months. So impressed was the young emperor with the CLS and other Western literature that he sent orders to purchase as many missionary writings as could be found, buying a total of 129, including the Bible, which he began studying.[29] Sun on three separate occasions offered Richard the position of president of the Imperial University in Peking, but he declined the offers, recommending another.[30]

Richard returned to Shanghai in February 1896 to prepare for his second furlough in twenty-six years. For two years, the factional strife in the

---

28. Richard, *Forty-five Years*, 349. Li also thanked Richard for the gift of his translation of Mackenzie's *Nineteenth Century: A History*. For some time, Christian missionaries had been falsely accused of kidnaping Chinese children, gouging out their eyes, and killing them. They were also accused of all kinds of immoral behavior, especially since single female missionaries traveled freely in their work on unbound feet. These fears and prejudices were deeply lodged and frequently fed by rumor and salacious literature.

29. Graybill, *The Educational Reform in China*, 46. Headland, "Missionary Influence in Chinese Reform," 26–27, wrote as an eyewitness telling of the emperor's penchant for Western clocks and gadgetry. After the Boxer Uprising in 1900 when he visited the emperor's still-vacated room, he found that it was "filled with clocks of all kinds." This same source passed along hearsay about the emperor's interest in Christianity. He was reported to be reading the Gospel of Luke in the New Testament, and "not long after that it was reported that [Emperor Guang Xü] had decided to become a Christian."

30. Richard, *Forty-five Years*, 257. Richard does not give his reason for declining the offers, but Soothill, *Timothy Richard of China*, 222, described Richard's reason: "... he felt he could do better work for China in an independent position rather than as a servant of the Government."

capital resulted in waves of reform and reaction. Even before Richard had left Peking, the reformers were being censured by government officials. The attacks became so virulent that Kang and Liang were advised to leave the capital, and in time, the formal organization and newspaper they had maintained were suspended. Yet by the summer of 1898, Kang and Liang both received appointments to official posts in Peking—Kang as a secretary of the Foreign Affairs Bureau and Liang in charge of the translation bureau.[31]

On Richard's voyage from Shanghai, he found that Li Hongzhang, on his way to the coronation of the czar in Russia, was a fellow passenger, and they enjoyed several conversations, although Li expressed surprise that Richard was traveling second class "considering the important part [Richard] had taken in Missions and in Chinese Reform." Richard had a stopover in India, and took advantage of the opportunity to tour mission educational work there. He was particularly interested in and encouraged by the work of Dr. Miller's Christian College in Madras, because Miller too had experienced a "storm of opposition to educational work" by his colleagues. In Europe, Richard was delighted to reunite with his wife, who had left Shanghai over a year earlier with their two youngest daughters to further their education in Europe. In England, he saw his two oldest daughters for the first time in ten years.[32]

Richard finally arrived in England in the summer of 1896. For his report to the BMS Home Committee, Richard presented them a box filled with his Chinese publications, bound annual editions of the *Review of the Times* and *The Missionary Review*, items from *The Times*, as well as an edition of the New Testament presented (by Mary with other women missionaries) to the empress dowager, along with appropriate explanations that served as ample evidence of his diligence since his previous furlough ten years earlier. During the rest of his time on furlough, Richard focused on securing qualified personnel for translation or literary work with the CLS and informing various business and government leaders in London about "China's awakening."[33]

---

31. Lo, *K'ang Yu-wei*, 110.

32. Richard. *Forty-five Years*, 286–89; Richard, letter to his wife, 1 December 1894; Richard to "My Beloved and most longed for wife," 13 March 1896.

33. Richard's report and presentation to the BMS Home Committee indicate that he was still functioning and being paid under the auspices of the BMS even beyond the initial three-year period. His presentations were published in *The Crisis in China and How to Meet It*, 1897, and *Prospectus of a Society for Aiding China*, 1897.

On February 17, 1897, he delivered an address on "The Crisis in China" to the Association of Secretaries [of mission organizations] to "lay the matter [the need for personnel solely devoted to literary work] before the Committee of each Missionary Society." The substance of this address was published by the BMS and several months later by the *Chinese Recorder* after his return to China.[34]

HIGH TIDE OF REFORM

In 1897 while Richard was still on furlough, Young J. Allen, editor of the CLS' *Review of the Times*, published the monumental eight-volume Chinese work *The History of the War Between China and Japan* in which Allen analyzed the recent conflict with Japan. Supplements included one with four volumes of the telegrams issued and received by Li Hongzhang during the war, and the other was a two-volume work entitled *The Importance of Educational Reforms*. These and Richard's translation of Mackenzie's *Nineteenth Century*, according to the newspaper *North China Herald*, sent shockwaves throughout the Chinese Empire.[35]

Copies of both sets were sent to the emperor and high officials, just as they were seeking an explanation for China's defeat and the source of Japan's power. These publications, probably more than any others, firmly established the reputation of the CLS in the eyes of the Chinese government officials. These books also helped revitalize the dormant Reform Movement. On Richard's return to China near the end of 1897, he observed a sudden increase in newspapers, from nineteen to seventy, in three years. Dr. Young J. Allen had been invited to take charge of a new university to be established in Shanghai, which he declined, but he did respond to a request from General Director of the Railways Sheng Xuanhuai to draw up a code of rules for a national system of modern education, by preparing a detailed manuscript based mainly on the system established by the British Government in India.[36]

34. After Richard's presentations were circulated in 1897, efforts were made to secure the cooperation of British and American Societies. According to Richard in a postscript to the article in the *Chinese Recorder* in 1898, "[A]t present there are three British Societies, three American and one German Society co-operating."

35. "Book Review—*History of the War between China and Japan*," *North China Herald*, May 15, 1896, 754–55; *Tenth Annual Report*, 7.

36. Richard, *Forty-five Years*, 260–61. It appears that Richard's observations from his tour of these schools in India during his last furlough may have influenced Allen's

Timothy Richard's Vision

The Chinese reformers also became more active. Liang Qichao, Kang Youwei's chief disciple and Richard's former Chinese secretary in Peking, had started the Chinese newspaper *The Chinese Progress* in Shanghai, which now served as the organ for the Reform party. Richard would later indicate there was a renewed affiliation with Liang around this time.[37] The new newspaper enjoyed strong support from other scholars as well as Viceroy Zhang Zhidong. In the meantime, Liang had become president of a Reform College in the provincial capital of Hunan, Changsha, a province known in the recent past for its strong anti-foreign and anti-Christian activities. A Chinese Girls' School, for which Mary Richard served as a consultant, was founded in Shanghai by the head of the Chinese Telegraph Administration and other Reformers.[38]

These were all hopeful signs to Richard that the Chinese were losing their antipathy toward learning from foreigners. Encouraged, in his *Tenth Annual Report* for 1897, he spoke prophetically—yet evincing an optimism tempered with broad experience and knowledge of China. He suggested that within four years Western learning would flourish and that Chinese professors in the natural sciences would "compete with their European

---

preparation of this code. It has not yet been determined to what extent Allen's manuscript may have had any influence on Sheng's future educational endeavors. See Feuerwerker, *China's Early Industrialization*, 69–71, 211 64n and 65n.

37. *Twenty-fifth Annual Report of CLS*, 9. Richard, when discussing activities of CLS personnel, reported that Liang Qichao, who like Kang Yuwei "had a price put on his head for advocating reform, acted for a short time as Chinese Secretary in our Society, and became the most brilliant journalist in the whole Empire." In 1918, when Liang stopped in England on his way to the Peace Conference in Versailles, Liang called on Richard before visiting any others, explaining "how valuable [Richard's] influence & help had been to China at the time of the Reform Movement." See "Notes on His Visit—Liang Chi Chao (sic)," handwritten ms, n.d., NLW.

38. Richard, *Forty-five Years,* 261–66. Soon after his 1891 arrival in Shanghai, Richard approached the Municipal Council, which was responsible for the International Concessions in the city. He requested that it reconsider the issue brought up the year before by Mr. Addis, of the Hong Kong and Shanghai Bank, concerning the provision of public schools for the Chinese. Richard and Mr. D. C. Jensen, a member of the Council, gathered information about "what was done for native education in other foreign lands." Jensen then laid their scheme of grants-in-aid to Chinese students before the Council, but due to his untimely death, the issue was dropped for several years. Richard, along with the Revs. F. L. H. Potts and J. C. Ferguson, took up the issue again with the Municipal Council in 1899. Eventually, the Chinese themselves contributed 37,000 Tls. for buildings. By November 1906 this school was in operation with almost 300 students attending. The girls' school was founded several years later. See "The Public School for Chinese," *North China Herald*, November 30, 1906, 495–96.

and American colleagues in enriching the world by new discoveries." He also noted that there were colleges of Western learning that had already been founded by viceroys and leading officials "with public money." The very next year the Imperial University of Peking and feeder colleges in the provinces were founded by imperial edict. The university was, in fact, the transformed language college, with a curriculum broadened to include more areas of Western learning. The feeder colleges never appeared, due to official and popular opposition. Only the later educational edicts in 1901 actually began the process of establishing a full system of educational institutions by 1906.[39]

Richard's 1897 report went on to note that Chinese of the better classes were becoming interested in learning English and studying the natural sciences. Other signs of change were the use of electricity to light the examination halls in the capital of Hunan, formerly one of the most anti-foreign provinces, and inclusion of a question on the civil service examination in Jiangxi Province that compared the floods mentioned in the Confucian classics and in the Old Testament, with the Bible given as a reference. Richard was very explicit in his report that he was not propagating the trappings of modern civilization alone but was seeking to guide public opinion in China to an understanding of the need for "the application of the healing powers of the Gospel to the social miseries of a great nation; it is a benevolent work, exemplifying the love of Christ, on the grandest scale . . . [which] needs most of all character and conscience, purity in the family life, integrity in the official life, and in order to get these, she needs a religious New Birth—she needs Christianity."

The year 1897 had been demanding and successful as far as CLS publications went. The *Review of the Times*, with thirty-six double-sided pages, continued to be published on a monthly basis with an average of 3,300 copies. *The Missionary Review* usually had twenty-eight double pages, and 550 copies were distributed every month. This was also the year of publication for Allen's volumes on the Sino-Japanese War, a reprint of Richard's translation of Mackenzie, and Richard's *Essays for the Times* and *Reform Papers*. The catalogue for the CLS contained over 100 publications. Growth in demand over four years was reflected in an increase of total sales for the

39. *Tenth Annual Report of CLS*, 1, 4. Precursors he mentioned were the colleges founded by Li Hongzhang in Tianjin, the most prominent being Beiyang University (1895); Zhang Zhidong's colleges in Canton, Nanking, and Wuchang (1887–97); and Sheng Xuanhuai's Nanyang College in Shanghai (1897). See Kuo, "The Chinese System of Public Education," 69–70; Ayers, *Chang Chih-tung*, 104–33.

two magazines and books from only $817.97 in 1893 to $5,899.92 in 1896, with an estimated total for 1897 expected to exceed $15,000.82.[40] Moreover, more than 120,000 copies of various CLS publications were distributed at provincial examination centers.[41]

Appreciation for the work of the CLS also came through letters and increased membership. The new emperor of Korea, a regular reader of the *Review of the Times*, testified to the trustworthiness of Allen's book. Richard reported that "people of the middle classes and the general public" also expressed their appreciation for Allen's book, as did scholars in Shandong and Zhejiang Provinces. Cai Erkang, Richard's secretary and translator who also assisted Allen, was offered editorship of the progressive *Hunan Journal of Science* and a position as instructor in a new college of Western learning being established in the province. Li Hongzhang, Zhang Zhidong, and Sheng Xuanhuai all invited Allen and Cai to serve in other capacities.[42]

It is said that imitation is the sincerest form of flattery, and with books, this imitation can take the form of piracy. Because of the great demand for Allen's and Richard's most recent books, there were many attempts to pirate or reprint them. The CLS brought offenders before the Mixed Court in Shanghai and fined them. Richard was concerned enough to seek legal action for two reasons: The Chinese were selective in what they reprinted, leaving out Christian teaching and any criticisms of bad customs in China; and there was a significant loss of income to the CLS. Nevertheless, this too is clear evidence of the high regard in which the CLS, and in particular Drs. Allen and Richard, were held. At the Annual Meeting in December 1897, Richard reminded those in attendance that the aim of the Society was to provide literature "for all classes of people in China . . . *especially the middle classes*" [Emphasis his]. This suggests a broader target than the tiny scholar-official elite. Clearly, Richard saw that the literature of the Society

---

40. Ibid., 5, 9, 14.

41. Ibid., 15–17. The books or pamphlets distributed included Richard's *Reform Papers, Modern Education in 7 Foreign Nations*, and *Hope for the People* and Allen's pamphlet on "Examination and Importance of Educational Reforms," as well as back issues of the *Review of the Times*. The centers were in Chengdu, Sichuan; Xi'an, Shaanxi; Taiyuan, Shanxi; Peking; Shenyang, Heilongjiang; Jinan, Shandong; Kaifeng, Henan; Wuhan, Hubei; Hangzhou, Zhejiang; and Fuzhou, Fujian.

42. Ibid., 10–12, note. Allen declined to take charge of a university, believing, as Richard had almost twenty years earlier, that he had more important work to do that benefitted the whole of China.

was to be a shaper of public opinion and, conceivably, in the future would become "the most influential leader of the thoughts of China."[43]

The year 1898 for the Reformers was one that began in high hopes but ended in despair.[44] In February the Reform Society in Shanghai published a *New Collection of Tracts of the Times*. Liang Qichao wrote forty-four essays, and Kang Youwei, thirty-eight; among the foreigners whose writings were included, Richard stood out with thirty-one essays.[45]

After seven memorials to the emperor in fewer than ten years, Kang finally had captured the ear of the emperor in support of the program to move beyond "self-strengthening" and establish a modern constitutional monarchy in China, following the Meiji model. In June, Kang was appointed secretary to the Foreign Office and consulted with Richard and others on measures of reform.[46] Between June 11 and September 20, the young Emperor Guangxu issued at least forty edicts on education, govern-

---

43. *Tenth Annual Report of CLS*, 13–14. This is the first time Richard acknowledged that there was a middle class (he actually says classes), and he seems to shift the focus to those more receptive to new ideas and Western learning than the officials. See p. 23 for "Fine inflicted on Chinese for breach of Copyright, received from Chinese Magistrate . . . $100.00." According to Soothill, *Timothy Richard of China*, 183–84, in Hangzhou there were six pirated editions, even a deluxe edition for the rich. It was "estimated that no less than a million pirated copies were in circulation throughout China." Copies of this book sold for $2 in Shanghai but sold for $6 by others in Xi'an, representing a significant income loss, but still the "sale of the Society's publications now produced an income twice that of all its subscriptions from abroad, thus enabling free grants of literature to be made where needed."

44. For in-depth perspectives on the Hundred Days' Reform, see Cameron, *The Reform Movement in China*; Kwong, *A Mosaic of the Hundred Days*, 1984); Compilation Group, *The Reform of 1898* (Beijing: 128 Foreign Language Press, n.d.).

45. Richard, "New China and Its Leaders," 1898, 415–17, elaborated: The first twenty-volume *King Shih Wen* (*New Collection of Tracts of the Times*) was published in 1826 with "essays from the most distinguished men in the [Chinese] empire on all questions of public interest during the 60 previous years." Another was published in 1886 "containing the most important documents since 1826." In 1898 the "reform party published what they call the *New King Shih Wen*, also in 20 vols., and uniform with the former two works." This new edition contained 580 essays and documents by 135 attributable authors and many others anonymously written. Only ten authors had from eight to forty-four essays or documents each: Liang Ch'i-ch'ao (forty-four essays), K'ang Yu-wei (thirty-eight essays), Timothy Richard (thirty-one essays), Hwang Tsun-huen (twenty-eight documents), Hsueh Fu-ching (twenty-five documents), an under-secretary of the Cabinet in Peking (eighteen documents), Kung Sze-chin (seventeen essays), the editor of the *New Learning* newspaper (thirteen articles), Ma Kien-ching (eleven documents), and one of the editors of *Chinese Progress* (eight articles).

46. Richard, *Forty-five Years*, 263.

mental administration, industry, and international cultural exchange. One of the earliest edicts (issued June 12), guaranteeing the protection of missionaries, another establishing the Imperial University at Peking, as well as those dealing with railway construction and with agricultural, industrial, and commercial development reflected the probable influence of Richard's ideas.[47]

Richard was invited by Kang Youwei to go to Peking to serve as one of the emperor's advisers. He arrived there in mid-September, but by then the conservative element within the Imperial Court had convinced the empress dowager to resume control—on the very day of Richard's scheduled appointment. The situation quickly deteriorated for the reformers with orders for their arrests issued. On September 21, Kang and Liang fled Peking for their lives, but six others were arrested and summarily executed on September 28.

All the reform edicts were rescinded except one establishing the Imperial University of Peking and another establishing colleges in the provincial capitals; neither was fully implemented. Most of those individuals identified with this Reform Movement then became known as bandits and rebels, with a price on their heads. Richard did what he could to rescue members

---

47. Hsu, *The Rise of Modern China*, 375. The educational edicts are listed below in chronological order:

June 11: Establishment of an Imperial University in Peking
June 23: Replacement of the eight-legged essays in the civil service examinations by essays on current affairs
July 10: Establishment of modern schools in the provinces devoted to the pursuit of both Chinese and Western studies; transformation of large private academies (*shuyuan*) in the provincial capitals into colleges, of those in the prefectural capitals into high schools, and those in the districts into elementary schools
July 13: Opening of a special examination in political economics
July 26: Publication of an official newspaper
August 6: Establishment of a school for overseas subjects
August 9: Establishment of the Imperial University of Peking, 2nd edict
September 8: Creation of a medical school under the Imperial University

Bastid, *Educational Reform*, 12, emphasized that this was the first known attempt to set up a truly modern system of education that would put examinations under supervision of the schools and devote a large part of the school curriculum to the teaching of sciences, technology, arts, and Western law. Bastid also concluded that Liang was the source of the memorial submitted by Li Duanfen (Liang's father-in-law) detailing the new system. Cameron, *The Reform Movement in China*, 65–87, included a chapter on educational reform. The opening page states, "Few did more in the cause of educational reform along Western lines than the veteran educator and friend of Chinese reformers, Dr. Timothy Richard."

of the Reform Club, even helping Kang and Liang escape to Japan, while he remained in China.[48]

THE ROLE OF THE EDUCATIONAL ASSOCIATION OF CHINA

During a quarter century in Shanghai, Timothy Richard was no longer alone in his approach to Christian ministry. In fact, he developed a web of overlapping networks of influential political, business, and religious leaders, both Westerners and Chinese. One such network was the interdenominational Educational Association of China. The records of its triennial meetings reveal Richard's growing impact both upon and through the EAC.

The School and Textbook Series Committee, the antecedent of the EAC, had been formed at the first general conference of Protestant missionaries in China in 1877 and charged with the task of writing a series of elementary school textbooks to be used in the mission schools. After several meetings, this was expanded to include an advanced series as well. By 1890 it became clear that there was a need to coordinate efforts among the missionary educators, and so the EAC was officially organized during the 1890 General Conference of the Protestant Missionaries of China.[49]

First the School and Textbook Series Committee and then the EAC were able to generate considerable interest in education among the missionaries, leading to an increase in mission schools opened and articles written, many of which were printed in the EAC outlet, the *Chinese Recorder*.[50] Only three articles on education appeared in the *Chinese Recorder* 1868–77, while thirty-two appeared 1877–90. The EAC Constitution and By-Laws declared, "The object of this Association shall be the promotion of educational interests in China, and the fraternal cooperation of all those engaged in teaching."[51] Some Chinese government officials also began to

---

48. Richard, *Forty-five Years*, 263. M. Richard (Mary Richard?), "The Martyrs of 'Young China,'" 285–88, included unique photographs and stated that several of these martyrs and others of the reformers were "Christians in all but name, even to the point that several of the survivors had either applied for Christian baptism or become earnest inquirers."

49. Wang, "The Educational Association of China," 6–18.

50. See Chen, "The Educational Work of Missionaries in China," for one of the earliest Chinese scholarly works to examine missionary education.

51. Kranz, "List of Educational Articles," 228–33; *Second Triennial Meeting of EAC*, 3.

evince a greater interest in "modern education," particularly higher education. Prior to 1877, two institutions had been founded specifically for training in foreign languages; two others had curricula with other subjects such as mathematics, law, and history. After 1877, at least five other schools of a technical or military nature were established.[52]

Richard began his association as early as 1880 as an agent of the Textbook Committee. Although his exact role is unknown, one critical need in writing textbooks would be to develop standardization in terminology, an abiding interest of Richard's. It is reasonable to assume that he shared the religious terms he had collected since the early 1870s.[53] Regrettably, rivalry and differences in methodological considerations deterred the School and Textbook Series Committee from completing its tasks as charged.[54] Nevertheless, during those early years of his association with the committee, Richard established enduring friendships with many missionaries who were like-minded concerning the value of the literary and educational missionary approaches with the Chinese.

Richard's more active role with the EAC began after his 1891 relocation to Shanghai to become general secretary of the SDK/CLS. At the first triennial meeting in 1894, he delivered the opening address, entitled "The Principles of Education," in which he discussed education in China from a comparative slant.[55] One point of note was his recommendation for a three-tier educational system. This antedated by eight years—and very likely influenced—the three-tiered system recommended in Yuan Shikai's memorial to the Throne in 1901, which was adopted by the imperial edict of November 25 and designated as the model for the first national school system for China in the twentieth century.[56] Richard's system was to be sequential, that is to

52. Wang, "The Educational Association of China," 19-20.

53. Richard's interest in terminology was first demonstrated in Shandong when he formulated a list of religious terms used by the Chinese and employed them in his catechism to instruct Christian inquirers. This interest intensified, out of necessity, once he became devoted to literary endeavors through the CLS. See Richard and MacGillivray, *A Dictionary of Philosophical Terms*, 1913.

54. Wang, "The Educational Association of China," 12-14. They did publish forty different wall charts and completed forty-one different works.

55. [First] *Triennial Meeting of the EAC*, xi, 1-2, 8-12. These records noted that Richard had become a member of the EAC in 1891. He was one of three men appointed at the 1893 meeting to the Committee on Revision of the Constitution and By-Laws. The records, 16, 24, 38, 39, 55, also contained Richard's comments on several papers presented for discussion.

56. Bailey, *Reform the People*, 28. While Yuan was governor in Shandong, he sought

say, "[g]iving 5 years of Western Christian education on top of 10 years [of] Chinese study . . . [which was] more adapted to Chinese life and mode of thought . . ." Providing Western learning to those students who had already received their first degree in Chinese studies would assure they were firmly grounded in their own culture. Clearly, Richard's system did not intend to make the students Western, but to provide them an understanding of the laws of God and other Western knowledge to benefit their own people—a persistent theme with Richard since 1880.[57]

Through this early work with the EAC, Richard continued to have numerous and extended contacts with other missionary educators, including the Revs. J. C. Ferguson, W. M. Hayes, Calvin Mateer, F. L. H. Potts, and D. Z. Sheffield. Ferguson and Hayes would become his two vice presidents in 1899. All these men would play key roles in educational institutions in China within a decade.[58]

Richard was not present for the Second Triennial Meeting of the EAC held in Shanghai May 6-9, 1896.[59] At the time, he still was in Peking, preparing the memorial to present to the Throne regarding the protection of Christian missions from persecution. Soon thereafter he was on furlough until the fall of 1897.

During these years of political ferment, the missionary community demonstrated a growing interest in educational approaches to work in China, as reflected in the increase in EAC membership and the number of articles on education printed in leading missionary journals.[60] Membership grew from seventy-three members in 1891 to 189 in 1899, with two Chinese now listed.[61] By the time of the Third Triennial Meeting in May

---

the assistance of W. M. Hayes in drawing up these regulations. By that time, Richard and Hayes had more than ten years of mutual effort through the EAC. See note 58. Therefore, it is most probable that Richard's stamp was on those regulations, though indirectly.

57. *Triennial Meeting*, 10.

58. J. C. Ferguson assisted in the founding of Nanyang University in 1897; W. M. Hayes in the founding of Jinan College in 1901; Calvin Mateer founded Dongzhou (Tungchow) College in 1877, which later became Shandong Christian College; F. L. H. Potts expanded the founding vision for St. John's University from 1888; D. Z. Sheffield founded North China College in 1889. Ferguson and Hayes both were presidents of government, not mission institutions.

59. *Second Triennial Meeting of EAC*, 6, 19, mentions his name in the membership list, and as one of ten men elected to the Educational Reform Committee.

60. See note 51, Kranz citation.

61. Richard, "Educational Problems in China," 1899, 47. For information about his appointment, see Richard, *Forty-five Years*, 263-64.

1899, interest and attendance surpassed the earlier two, possibly because of the missionary interest and personal involvement of some in the Reform Movement.[62]

At the meeting, Richard offered his views on "Educational Problems in China," and was elected president of the EAC for the next triennium (1899–1902), marking a choice to bring the Association into the new millennium with renewed vision.[63] Under his leadership, two joint committees for education matters, made up of himself and other leaders from the EAC and the CLS, were formed.[64] They issued a mandate to make recommendations to the Chinese government "in regard to a Public school system for China . . . and other educational reforms," and Richard was appointed to go to Peking that summer "in order that the Government might be induced to approve of an educational scheme for China."[65]

The exact nature of this educational scheme was not disclosed in the written record, but most likely it was the examination and study scheme

---

62. "Educational Association of China," *Chinese Recorder* 30 (June 1899), 289, mentions how missionaries Timothy Richard and Gilbert Reid were directly and actively involved with the Chinese reformers.

63. *Third Triennial Meeting*, 7; Richard, to Baynes, 29 May 1899, emphasized the "great disproportion between the efforts of British and American Missionaries in the Educational line," indirectly chastising the BMS.

64. *Third Triennial Meeting*, 8, 38, 48; "Educational Association of China," *Chinese Recorder* 30 (June 1899), 292. It seems clear that Richard was behind these joint efforts. The Revs. A. P. Parker, D. Z. Sheffield, and E. F. Gedye were appointed to a "Committee to prepare Courses of Study and Plan for General Examination Board, etc." which was "to form a joint committee with the following gentlemen appointed by the Society for the Diffusion of Christian and General Knowledge among the Chinese: Rev. Timothy Richard, Rev. J. C. Ferguson, and Rev. F. L. Hawks Potts. Richard and the other members of this joint committee (minus Ferguson) were also appointed to a "Committee on Educational Reform." Significantly, four of the six members were residents of Shanghai who then made up the majority and could easily constitute a quorum for decision-making. These men generally were like-minded in their ideas about educational reform. This EAC committee made three recommendations: that it cooperate with a CLS committee to develop a scheme for preparing and examining students in Western learning throughout the empire; that this joint committee be authorized to make recommendations to the Chinese government; and that action be expedited with the full authority of the EAC until the next Triennial Meeting. *Second Triennial Meeting of the EAC*, 19, indicates that in 1896, an earlier Educational Reform Committee had been named: C. W. Mateer, A. G. Jones, Y. J. Allen, H. V. Noyes, Gilbert Reid, E. Faber, D. Z. Sheffield, G. B. Smyth, G. Owens, and Timothy Richard. This committee apparently never issued a report, and perhaps it never convened.

65. Richard, *Forty-five Years*, 293.

developed earlier by the CLS.[66] This scheme was a bold attempt to launch the instruction and examination of students in Western learning, a kind of transitional teacher training program. Those so trained could earn mandarin rank, as well as being qualified to be instructors of Western learning in the government colleges that Richard saw on the horizon. The creation of textbooks and the examination process would be by missionaries, so that the Christian underpinning and missionary control of the modern system of higher education could be guaranteed. Richard was the natural representative of the mission community as head of both the EAC and the CLS and as a seasoned missionary accustomed to dealing with government officials after twenty-nine years in China.

Once in Peking, however, Richard learned that the timing was not right for this major initiative. Sir Robert Hart, director of the Imperial Chinese Custom and president of the CLS, advised Richard not to approach any high government officials about the issue, as it would be "useless," since all suggestions for reform were immediately being vetoed. Nevertheless, Richard did meet or correspond with some officials privately.[67]

The mission community, nonetheless, was prepared by this exercise in strategy and by its preparations of educational materials for whenever the next opportunity might arise. At the Third Triennial Meeting in 1899, the EAC's Publication Committee reported on its mandate to publish and keep on hand sufficient stock of all levels and titles to supply the necessary books for schools in China. There were at least thirty different book titles and thirty different wall charts and maps available. For an educational system accustomed to rote memorization in its learning, the availability of illustrations for use in the education of the Chinese students was in itself a reform in methodology.[68]

The first Executive Committee meeting during Richard's tenure as president convened May 25, 1899. Attending was a representative of Macmillan & Co. of London. It was decided at this meeting that six different books published by Macmillan for the study of English be approved and

66. See "Examination Scheme," *Chinese Recorder* 31 (August 1900), 420-23.

67. Richard, *Forty-five Years*, 293; Hsü, *The Rise of Modern China*, 370. Richard recorded that he did see a "few officials" privately, but the only ones we know by name are Li Hongzhang with Zhou Fu present. He corresponded with others, namely with Rong Lu, a Manchu general and president of the Board of War as well as a "confidant" of the empress dowager, and Kang Yi, the grand councilor.

68. "Educational Association of China," *Chinese Recorder* 30 (June 1899), 297-98, lists the titles.

recommended to the schools of China. The committee also approved publication of a bilingual geography text, a bilingual series of readers in science, and bilingual editions of the first four books of the *New Orient Readers*.

Richard also convened an Executive Committee meeting on December 12, 1899. At that time the financial status of the EAC was precarious, with the chairman of the committee reporting it was $1,649.39 in the arrears (which was remedied by year's end). The explanation given was the "reactionary policy of the Peking government," indicating that the demise of the Hundred Days' Reform led to a drop in demand.[69]

In May 1900, an Executive Committee meeting was held but with only four members present; Richard was absent due to his attending an Ecumenical Conference on missions in New York. The Executive Committee did not convene from May 1900 until fall 1901 due to the upheaval resulting from the Boxer Uprising. In the years to follow, however, the influence of the EAC network of missionary educators on a renewed wave of reform would show how well it had been prepared by Richard to advise and lobby the Imperial Court.

THE BOXER WAR RESURRECTS REFORM

As Richard returned to Shanghai in late 1898 after the empress dowager's takeover, with hopes for reform dashed for the indefinite future, he received some much-needed encouragement. His pleas to the missionary societies of Europe and America for highly qualified personnel to assist him in literary efforts at the CLS began to bear fruit as reinforcements started arriving. Early in 1899, the Rev W. A. Cornaby of the English Wesleyan Mission joined the CLS staff to edit *The Missionary Review*. In May, Richard received word that the Rev. Donald MacGillivray, of the Canadian Presbyterian Mission in Henan, was being sent to the CLS. By March the next year, the Church Missionary Society had reassigned the Rev. W. G. Walshe to the CLS "for the purpose of taking a share in this great enterprise."[70]

These long-awaited reinforcements came just in time, since Richard had been invited to present a paper on Christian Literature at the New York

---

69. "Educational Association of China," *Chinese Recorder* 31 (January 1900), 39–40.

70. Richard, "Reinforcements for the Christian Literature Society for China," 1900, 159–60. MacGillivray would step into Richard's position as general secretary of the CLS upon his retirement in 1915.

Ecumenical Conference on missions in May 1900.[71] While attending the sessions—the first to focus on the value of literary work by missionaries, Richard took advantage of the opportunity to talk with many American business and government leaders as well as other missions leaders. He spoke prophetically about his conviction that there would soon be a cataclysmic outbreak of persecution of Christians in China unless there was a united effort to avert the danger. Most were sympathetic but unable, or unwilling, to take action based solely on the opinion of one man.

By the time he reached Japan en route to China, the violence he had foreseen had indeed already erupted in the form of the Boxer Uprising.[72] The Boxers (*Yihe chuan,* "harmonious fists") was a spiritual sect whose members practiced a form of physical exercise said to make them invincible to foreign weapons. This anti-foreign grassroots-level uprising began in Shandong in the summer of 1900, soon gained the patronage of reactionary members of the Court, and spread to Shanxi. International outrage resulted after the killing of more than 100 missionaries and uncounted thousands of Chinese Christians. Most shocking was the beheading of several dozen missionaries by armed soldiers, directed by the fiercely anti-foreign Shanxi Governor Yu Hsien, in his official courtyard in Taiyuan. This action signaled approval for the subsequent deaths of hundreds in Shanxi alone.[73]

When Richard's ship arrived in Yokohama on July 2nd, he gradually became aware of the gravity of the situation in China as he read first of the murder of the German minister in Peking and then the "narrow escape of the Shantung missionaries." He sought to prod the British government to send telegrams to the Chinese viceroys and provincial governors informing them that they would be held accountable for the well-being of the

---

71. Richard, "Christian Literature," 1900, 597–603. Richard, *Christian Literature: Its Extent and Value* (1900?) was a pamphlet made available for distribution at the New York Ecumenical Conference on missions. The first two sections only, those on extent and value, were printed in "Literature as an Evangelistic Agency," Ecumenical Missionary Conference, *Vol. II* (New York: American Tract Society, 1900), 74–76. Those parts in Richard's presentation dealing specifically with China were omitted from this written record.

72. For a more complete record of these events, see Cohen, *History in Three Keys*; Elliott, *Who Died for Civilization?*; Esherick, *The Origins of the Boxer Uprising*; Purcell, *The Boxer Uprising*; and Tan, *The Boxer Catastrophe*.

73. n.a., "Dr. Timothy Richard and Shansi University," *The Missionary Review of the World* 24 (July 1911), 551, stated, "In 1900, 137 Protestant missionaries were killed in Shansi by order of the Governor Yu Hsien." For a listing of the names of victims from throughout China, though incomplete, see *Boxer Rising*, 115–18.

Timothy Richard's Vision

foreigners within their borders.[74] Soon after his return to China on July 7, Richard took an active role in trying to secure the safety of missionaries throughout China as well as receive credible information about their welfare. By the end of July, he was sufficiently alarmed about the situation to send his wife ahead of himself to Japan as there had been rumors of Boxer violence in Shanghai. The Richards remained in Japan until mid-September at which time they returned to Shanghai.

By then, eye-witness accounts of the massacres revealing the magnitude of the violence were becoming available.[75] However, it was not until Allied military forces from eight nations occupied Peking that the massacres ceased and the Boxer Movement was quelled.[76] By that time, Peking was in ruins and the Court had fled to Xi'an in exile.[77]

Once safely there, perhaps the empress dowager realized that to retain power after this defeat, she needed to restore the confidence of both the international community and the more progressive Chinese officials. In January 1901, even before the settlement of the international issues related to the Boxer Uprising or the return of the Court to Peking, the empress dowager issued an edict from exile in Xi'an in the name of the emperor, acknowledging the Court's responsibility for the crisis and requesting memorials that would recommend reforms.[78] Whether this was a sincere *mea culpa* or merely a desperate measure to forestall any further military action

---

74. Richard to Baynes, July 1901.

75. Edwards, *Fire and Sword in Shansi*; Forsyth, *The China Martyrs of 1900*; and Woodberry, *Through Blood-Stained Shansi* record some eyewitness accounts of the violence.

76. Edwards, *Fire and Sword in Shansi*, 122. After the Allied forces entered and ransacked Beijing, Chinese officials were concerned that they would head to Shanxi next; the governor who had personally perpetrated the mass violence in front of his court was transferred. The new governor, Cen Chunxuan (Ts'en Ch'un-hsüan), perhaps in hopes of forestalling the army's entry, "within four days of the taking of the passes by the Germans," quickly telegraphed Richard and requested his assistance in negotiating indemnity issues.

77. Wu, *The Flight of an Empress*. According to Edwards, *Fire and Sword in Shansi*, 111, the empress dowager and the entire retinue on their way to Xi'an stayed for some days in Taiyuan, the very city where more than fifty missionaries and their families were killed. Perhaps it was at this time the governor was transferred elsewhere.

78. For English translation of this imperial edict, see Reynolds, *China*, 201–4; Hart, "These from the Land of Sinim," 296–99.

was unclear; Richard probably was not alone in doubting the sincerity of the Court in either new reform efforts or the protection of the foreigners.[79]

Nevertheless, with this edict the tide gates of reform were again opened, which led to drastic institutional changes within the government. This upsurge proved not to be of short duration like the Hundred Days' Reform; reform edicts continued to appear under imperial sanction until 1906, a period of almost five years.[80] By then the tide of reform could not be stemmed but continued to rise until in 1911 it gave way to revolution, which finally washed away not only the Qing dynasty but also the ancient imperial system.

With the first signal from Xi'an of a leaning toward reform, Chinese officials and missionaries alike began to submit frequent recommendations. Since the edicts emphasized that most urgent was the securing of men of administrative talent, many were inspired to address the kind of education needed to produce such talent.[81] The Boxer Protocol ending hostilities was signed on September 7, 1901, with the final ratification on November 8 of the foreign indemnities due to be paid by China to the injured parties. The direction was again set for reform but this time by the empress dowager, and it met no opposition.

Richard vigorously renewed his efforts to bring enlightenment to Chinese officials since he was convinced that it was their ignorance that had led to the massacre of more than fifty missionaries and their families in Shanxi Province alone. He no longer had to convince the officials of the need for reform; the critical issues now were the direction and the speed of implementation. This was the role to which Richard now applied himself—using his leading positions at the EAC and the CLS, which formed a new joint committee to draft memorials—to get all arenas of missions expeditiously working in concert for the benefit and enlightenment of the Chinese. He depicted the educational and literary missions as working

---

79. Richard to Baynes, 22 January 1903.

80. Hsü, *The Rise of Modern China*, 410–11, states that this period of reform terminated in 1905. Two of the last three edicts he noted dealt with education: in August 1905, the Civil Service Examination system was abolished; in December 1905, the Ministry of Education was established, but he made no mention of any edict in 1906 other than the prohibition of opium. I place the end date of this reform period at 1906, as this was the year for the establishment of the national system of public education.

81. Correspondent, "Missionary Work and Reform in China," *London Times* (15 November 1901), 6a. The article disclosed that during the year, Richard had telegraphed recommendations for educational reform to the emperor every two or three weeks.

in tandem—literary work providing the "arsenal" of mental and spiritual weapons, and educational work functioning as artillery blasting down the "strongholds of ignorance and superstition."[82]

The "arsenal" in terms of the CLS publications during 1901 may be viewed as monumental, considering that fewer than five missionaries were fully devoted to literary work. Thirty-five "new works and 50,000 copies [had] been printed and published in Chinese, and 22 additional works" were in press. Demand for CLS publications skyrocketed, particularly after the educational edicts of 1901, which ushered in a new era of Court-endorsed Western learning for the Chinese. Meanwhile, in the three years 1899–1902, EAC membership doubled, and sales of its publications (many through CLS book depots) were nearly as great as in the previous twenty-two years.[83]

Soon after the Court returned to Peking in early January 1902, the empress dowager herself began to issue many edicts calling for educational and institutional changes, many of them recapitulations of the edicts promulgated during the 1898 Hundred Days' Reform, with one notable omission—the edict guaranteeing protection of the missionaries. Officials took courage to initiate concrete suggestions. One suggestion was to integrate the schools and traditional examination system; the Court incorporated this idea into an edict issued December 1901.[84]

In January 1902 the Court appointed Zhang Baixi (Chang Pai-hsi) to the position of Chancellor of the Imperial University of Peking, commanding him to present regulations on a new educational system. He proposed

---

82. Richard, "Educational Work is Indispensable," 1901, 91–93, used an easily understood analogy to the different departments of an army to define the different roles in missions work: literary, evangelistic, educational, and medical. All are essential, and each supports the other. According to the *Fourth Triennial Meeting of the EAC*, the new joint committee was a "who's who" of missionary educators—Richard, Allen, Mateer, and Pott included. Exactly what memorial(s) they submitted is not clear, but very likely it was the "Course of Study and Examination Scheme" as arranged by the EAC and the CLS, in the report's Appendix C, v–ix.

83. "Christian Literature for China—The Rev. Timothy Richard, Litt. D., D. D., of Shanghai," *The One Hundred and Tenth Annual Report, Missionary Herald* (May 1902), 220; *Fourth Triennial Meeting*, 5.

84. Richard, *Forty-five Years*, 293; Wang, "Educational Association of China," 88–89, 142–43. Richard had attempted on two different occasions to convince the Chinese government to merge Western curricula with the official examinations. The first time was in 1899 as a representative of the CLS, and the second was early 1900 as the representative of the EAC/CLS Joint Educational Reform Committee. At the time, little interest was demonstrated.

the creation of elementary, primary, and secondary schools under the control and supervision of the Imperial University. Later he was appointed to head the Board of Education, overseeing the embryonic modern system of education.[85]

Commands from the Throne for new changes were being issued even before the previous edicts had been fully implemented. There was no one at the helm experienced in modern education. Since few officials had direct access to information about education in other countries because of the language barrier, they had to rely on a steady diet of translated information, first from Japanese publications and then from CLS publications primarily written by Richard and Allen. In the 1890s and the first several years of the twentieth century, the CLS became the chief interpreter and conveyor of current events.

Nonetheless, Richard and others were highly concerned about the increasing Japanese influence upon Chinese students, both at home and in Japan. Japan had become embroiled in a war with Russia, and with a victory in June 1905, Japan's military and political supremacy was firmly established. This became important in the eyes of some Chinese officials, who noted that Japan, a constitutional monarchy, had defeated the Russian autocracy.[86] The earliest educational edicts in China accorded a place to Western learning, but with considerable reluctance. With Japan once again victorious in war, China now committed itself to learning from Japan how to apply its model—adopting Western learning—to catch up with the West. The proximity to Japan and its use of Chinese characters enabled Chinese officials to overcome their antipathy for Japan and to send students there to study. The *Seventeenth Report of CLS* revealed that approximately "a hundred students from each of the 18 provinces have been sent to Japan to learn how the Japanese have prospered so rapidly." This trickle became a raging torrent in the years 1905–11.[87]

---

85. Bailey, *Reform the People*, 29. For a detailed description of this earliest modern school system, see Kuo, *The Chinese System of Public Education*, 78–85. Richard endorsed the three-tiered system as early as 1888; the concept of the Board of Education was widely published by Richard through a CLS circular in 1894.

86. *Seventeenth Annual Report of CLS* resonated with this concern. See also Reynolds, *China, 1898–1912*, 187.

87. Ibid., 48, noted that in 1896, thirteen students went to Japan to study. By 1906, that number had exploded to at least 8,000 students. With the outbreak of the revolution in 1911, that number dropped immediately by approximately 5,000.

Timothy Richard's Vision

In Shanghai alone there were fifty different book shops that sold a diversity of Japanese-influenced literature. Richard was concerned that China's ignorance of the outside world would make the country susceptible to be led down a disastrous path. It needed time and guidance, and with Christians providing their interpretation of Western learning, Richard believed that China would have access to knowledge that would lead to peace. As was said at the annual meeting by its chair, "Now China is awake, and thirsting for knowledge, and this knowledge it is our task to supply." From another member at this meeting, "the aim of the Society could be summed up in two words—interpreter and inspiration." Richard, in his annual report, clearly envisioned the CLS leading China safely through this stormy time of transition by offering necessary information, with a moral (Christian) foundation, to form the curriculum of Western learning in the new government schools. To burnish the "credentials" of the Christian missionaries, he presented the historical record of missionary efforts to uplift the nations they entered through their Christian philanthropic works in education, medicine, literary endeavors, and social works.[88]

Richard reasserted his grand passion—"We need a model Christian college in every province and at least one model Christian university for all China." Richard also recounted that even a non-Christian member of the gentry had said to him, "that as missionaries were experts in religion, they should be asked to superintend this work in the new government schools." Richard also pointed to the recent establishment of several union colleges of a cross-denominational nature. Such union institutions seemed again to vindicate his earlier advocacy for the reform of higher education in China during his first furlough to England in 1885.[89]

---

88. *Seventeenth Annual Report of CLS*, 11–12, 43, 45. Richard supplied charts in this report, giving the total number of books published in each category by the Roman Catholics, Religious Tract Society, Educational Association of China, and the CLS, and what he designated as "Chinese New Literature." The thirty-six categories included religious as well as different aspects of Western learning, e.g., medicine, universal history, chemistry, statistics, commerce, astronomy, etc. The book totals for organizations pertinent to this study are for the EAC (188), the CLS (387), and Chinese New Literature (1,050). He cited social work by missionaries in China such as establishing orphanages, opium refuges, and campaigns against foot-binding, prostitution, wife-selling, and illiteracy. See Dennis's three-volume study of *Christian Missions and Social Progress*.

89. *Seventeenth Annual Report of CLS*, 13–15, 18. One precedent for a missionary doing government administrative work in education was the Rev. Ernest J. Eitel, who left Shandong, where Richard had known him, and later became government inspector of schools in Hong Kong in 1879. Richard considered Eitel, also a literary man who valued the inclusion of Western learning in the education of the Chinese, one of the

Richard also referred to the efforts of various Chinese officials to promote "modern education." By name, he mentioned the labors of Yuan Shikai, Zhou Fu, Zhang Zhidong, and Duan Fang. All were officials with whom Richard had discussed the need for educational reform. From this seventeenth meeting report, one may infer that Richard was both advocating the establishment of a "system of national education, in which loyalty and patriotism are instilled in order to promote peace and prosperity" by spending "several dollars per inhabitant on it each year," and was proffering the tutelage of the CLS during its implementation.[90]

Statistics for the CLS reveal a continued demand for its publications, just as the 1904 financial report and membership list revealed the stature the Society had attained with Chinese and foreigners alike. Individuals gave donations or subscriptions for the year totaling more than $5,000, with four Chinese listed among the donors. By this time, membership had grown to include more than 200 names—including eight Chinese, nine women, and a preponderance of missionaries—a very different constituency from the CLS Richard came to in 1891.[91]

---

great missionaries to China. See Lodwick, *The Chinese Recorder Index*, Volume One, 136; T. R. (Timothy Richard?), "In Memoriam—Dr. Griffith John," 126. As for the new union schools, Richard mentioned that the Congregationalists, Methodists, and Presbyterians established "a model Christian College in Peking and [Dongzhou]"; the American Presbyterians and English Baptists joined forces in colleges in Shandong and Canton (Guangzhou); "Yale University is attempting to have a Christian College in Hunan, irrespective of denominational differences, simply on the ground that the promoters of the enterprise received their educational training in one University."

90. Ibid., 5, 33. In 1903, there was a total of 25,353,880 pages of new books and reprints published, of which 14,919,280 pages were reprints. For the following year, there were seventy-six titles listed with a total of 30,681,800 pages printed with reprints accounting for 11,425,500 pages. From these lists, however, it cannot be determined how many of these titles were books being written or translated for the Imperial University of Shansi through its Translation Bureau housed within the CLS. Four titles were attributed to Richard. Total sales for the year only amounted to $30,457.51, a precipitous drop of $23,942.12 from the year before. Richard explained this in terms of a shipwreck that destroyed $5,000 worth of books and "cooling ardor." The latter was most probably due to trade competition from Chinese new literature as well as the continuing piracy of the CLS books. The seventeenth annual report also indicated that the Imperial University of Shansi paid rent to the CLS for the use of its facility for the Translation Bureau and that the Boxer indemnity funds for the Imperial University of Shansi in Taiyuan were channeled through the CLS. See chapter 5.

91. Ibid., 15, 23, 26. One Chinese member, Shen Dunhe was the director of the Foreign Affairs Bureau in Shanxi Province, who was involved in the negotiations for the establishment of the Imperial University of Shansi. See chapter 5.

Timothy Richard's Vision

In these early years of the new century, Timothy Richard reached the peak of his missionary career and extent of his influence on historic Chinese reforms. He headed key organizations and publication outlets, was chosen to represent the whole Protestant missionary community in interaction with governments, and could mobilize a vast network that included high-ranking officials both Chinese and Western, as well as reformers in China or in exile. Yet Richard was not immune from personal or professional troubles, as well as the stress of his many new commitments.

During the first half of 1903, Richard traveled to Japan, and after his return he suffered through the final illness from cancer and the death of his beloved wife and partner, Mary. In the same year, he and the CLS board had a major falling out with Young J. Allen, founder and editor of the *Review of the Times*. A dispute over proprietary rights led to legal advice and arbitration, as well as strong language that made the conflict personal. Despite apologies, ill will remained until Allen's death and the closing of the *Review* in 1907.[92]

Early in 1904 Richard was asked to become involved in fund-raising efforts on behalf of the newly formed "International Red Cross committee" in Shanghai, and during that time he served as its secretary for China. During the Russo-Japanese War (1904–5), he was involved in easing the conditions of those involved, primarily thousands of Chinese civilians caught up in the conflict. He also spent time in Shandong for a congress of all religions, and went to Peking for consultations with high government officials. He had little time to devote to thoughtful writing, and he was often absent for internal meetings of the CLS and the EAC, although close associates who shared his views were in charge. (During the EAC triennial meeting of 1905, Richard was on his third furlough in England.)

The years 1905 and 1906 brought far-reaching changes in Chinese education, most notably the demise of the civil service exams based on ancient Confucian literature. In 1905 the emperor issued an edict that affected more than 2 million scholar-officials and brought to an effective end the Confucian examination system that had been in place since the seventh century. This September 2 edict ordered the immediate cessation of the examinations for the *Xiucai* degree (equivalent to a BA); examinations for the *Juren* (MA) and *Jinshi* (PhD) were to be abolished effective the following

---

92. Soothill, *Timothy Richard of China*, 277–85; Whitefield, "The Christian Literature Society for China," Chapter 4, 103–4. In May 1903 Richard traveled to Japan on behalf of the Translation Bureau of the Imperial University of Shansi. He sought appropriate books that could be translated for Chinese students and also examined Japanese educational efforts.

year of 1906. This was in response to a memorial presented to the Court by Yuan Shikai to abolish the examinations "in order to allow the expansion of the modern modes of education." This edict also addressed the need for a standard series of textbooks, careful selection of teachers, and early instruction in modern education by the establishment of primary schools. Subsequently, there was a virtual explosion in the number of primary schools teaching modern subjects, many founded by gentry without government financial support. Richard had discussed these exact issues with missionaries and Chinese officials alike on many occasions since the 1880s, but his first reaction was to warn of the "great danger" that the modern educational system would lie in "inexperienced hands blundering on a gigantic scale."[93]

While these changes echoed missionary advice over the years, at the same time they brought a new measure of influence by Japan that indirectly threatened missionary influence. In 1906, Richard offered a mix of praise and warning. "The immense stride made in education by the Imperial Edicts, changing the ancient mode of education by establishing modern education after the Japanese model in all the provinces, is unexampled in magnitude in the history of the human race." Yet he also put on record his worry that the Chinese were "delaying higher university education" development merely to copy Japanese elementary and secondary education, and were wasting funds sending students to Japan. Most of the students had first to learn spoken Japanese before they could benefit from the lectures, and a majority of them returned to China in one to three years. When they did come back, they had intense feelings against foreign control and influence in China. Richard likely understood this reaction would eventually lead missionaries, and particularly himself and colleagues in the CLS and the EAC, to lose control of the minds of Chinese scholars and officials.[94]

Richard's response was to work toward greater unity within the missionary cohort in order to be more effective in the newly competitive environment. In 1907, he wrote of the "three greatest needs of China" in Christian missions to be a well-supported Christian press, a missionary

---

93. *Eighteenth Annual Report of the CLS*, 7. Perhaps he was expressing some concern over what he perceived as inexperience and politics within the proposed Board of Education. See Bailey, *Reform the People*, 36–37. See the English translation of the edict in the Appendix, *Eighteenth Annual Report of the CLS*, 29–31. Richard was facile with statistics, which he usually presented for the purpose of comparison. In this report, he projected the goal of China's educational development at the end of thirty years based on what Japan had achieved. The conclusion he reached was that China should have over 44 million students in 255,429 primary schools and 2,628 secondary schools and that there should be 486 normal schools training teachers.

94. *Nineteenth Annual Report of the CLS*, 6.

Timothy Richard's Vision

council, and a vision unified through study of a common science of missions.[95] Implicit in all this was a consolidation of missionary efforts and funding for greater efficiency and impact on Chinese society, something Richard had been seeking in vain for more than twenty years. While this cooperative effort had always been needed in his view, now with his thirty-seven years' experience in the country, he sensed it was urgent. If the missionary societies could become a united body operating through a joint council and with a union press, the missionaries still might retain the ear of top government leaders and shape the moral and institutional direction the country was to take. Richard believed that study of a science of missions would result in more full-time literary workers and more educated missionary candidates capable of interacting with Chinese officials.

There certainly were grounds for optimism; there continued to be clear evidence of the high regard some Chinese officials had for the CLS publications and workers. Throughout the first half of the decade, Richard had received a series of honors from the Chinese government as well as Western universities for his central role in educational reform.[96]

With the demise of the ancient examination system in 1905 and the establishment of public education the next year, Richard's "magnificent obsession" had prevailed. While the moral underpinnings of this system were not Christian, as he had worked to make them, and the focus had shifted away from higher education, nevertheless, China had irrevocably changed her system of education. The seed of his original vision for the reform of education in China had, in fact, come to fruition.

END OF AN ERA

By mid-decade in the new century, Richard and the Christian organizations he headed, both the CLS and the EAC, seemed no longer to have a grand passion and purpose. The CLS continued to produce a prodigious amount of literature, both original and translated, and the EAC's 500 members represented "nearly one-ninth of the Protestant missionaries in China and about one-fifth of the missionaries who were really connected with

---

95. Richard, "Some of the Greatest Needs of Christian Missions," 211–12.

96. *Twentieth Annual Report of the CLS*, 8, reported that provincial officials from the Northeast and Northwest frontiers, as well as Canton [Guangzhou], Fujian, Shanxi, and Shandong, had ordered hundreds of copies of one CLS weekly. See concluding chapter 6 regarding Richard's honors.

educational work."⁹⁷ But in reality, most of the EAC standing committees had ceased to function and many of the EAC-produced, CLS-published textbooks were losing out in competition with secular publishing houses like the Commercial Press, which had cooperative arrangements with Japanese publishers.

At the 1909 EAC meeting, Dr. Kuang Fuzhuo (Fong F. Sec), the Chinese head of the Department of English Publications in the Commercial Press, spoke to this issue of competition by making a case for Chinese and missionary cooperation in educational work. A noted Christian himself, Kuang emphasized that since government recognition and registration of all schools was now required, in order to continue work in China, the missionaries had to accept "the government course of study, the prescribed textbooks and the scientific terminology." To this, Richard concurred, "There has been too much independence on the part of the missions. Formerly the government was conservative and independent, [but] now the missions are conservative and apt to act independently of the wishes of the government... A good suggestion of Mr. Fong's is to approach the government through foreign officials, [and] have more respect for our hosts, the Chinese." Richard would repeat this advice in 1912 in a paper examining the future of the EAC in relationship to the newly-established Republic of China.⁹⁸

Clearly, the end of the Protestant mission era was at hand, as many of the pioneers died and as the baton was handed over to the Chinese, both in church circles and in other professional arenas. Li Hongzhang was the earliest key player in the CLS story to pass on in 1901. The indefatigable CLS editor, Young J. Allen, died in 1907 as did the chief CLS donor Thomas Hanbury, following the deaths in 1906 of both Hudson Taylor of the CIM

---

97. Wang, "The Educational Association of China," 170, 173.

98. Fong F. Sec [Kuang Fuzhuo], "The Co-operation of Chinese and Foreign Educationists," 1–6. According to Wang, "The Educational Association of China," 45–46, 49, 69, and 151, the Commercial Press was at that time the largest book company in China. It was established in 1897 in Shanghai as the second book company in China; the founders were Christians who had received at least part of their training in the Presbyterian Mission Press. In 1902 the Commercial Press began cooperating with a Japanese press, establishing a Japanese department headed by a Japanese citizen, which began to edit and publish a series of textbooks for primary and middle schools. By 1906 the Commercial Press was publishing fifty-four different books approved by the Educational Department of the Chinese government. "From 1902 to 1910, more than 300 books were published, some of them exceeding more than 300,000 copies." Richard's response to Fong, in *Sixth Triennial Meeting of the EAC*, 171–74. Richard's comment about the Republic, in "The Future of the Educational Association," 230–38.

and another major CLS writer, the Rev. Joseph Edkins. The emperor and empress dowager both died in 1908, and Zhang Zhidong in 1909. Fittingly, Sir Robert Hart, the Society's president since 1888 and "dean" of the foreign community, would pass on in the year of the 1911 Revolution that brought down the dynastic system. Most of the grand old men of China, foreigners and Chinese alike, were no longer there to steer the course of "New China."

Richard himself was no longer a young man, and he no longer had to struggle to further his personal vision for China once he witnessed the reform of Chinese higher education by the Chinese themselves. When he had first come to the CLS in 1891, it had published only two magazines and had $1,000 in assets. China had no government-supported system of modern education at any level.

> When, twenty-five years later, ill-health compelled him to resign the active office he had six Western colleagues, several associate workers, a staff of eighteen Chinese translators and assistants, and the assets of the Society [CLS] were valued at nearly a quarter of a million dollars. He himself had issued original works or translations numbering over a hundred, and his influence, through literature and personal contact with the most powerful people in the land, had made the name and work of the Society known throughout the Empire.[99]

By 1915 when Richard retired from the CLS, retaining the honorary title of Secretary Emeritus, China had a well-developed system of education on all levels. The Chinese, by their early choice of the Japanese model, nevertheless had redirected their attention to establishing primary schools that were expected "to instill patriotism, loyalty, and concern for the public good," beneficial values certainly, but not those Richard had always sought to inculcate as the Kingdom of God was established in China. Chinese were setting a new direction for their own future that would no longer involve the missionaries, including Richard, as primary adviser and source of information.[100]

---

99. Soothill, *Timothy Richard of China*, 180.

100. Bailey, *Reform the People*, 38, stated that the values inculcated within the Japanese educational system were adopted from the Prussian system. The values Richard had hoped to be instilled from the establishment of the Kingdom of God in China were love, peace, and righteousness. He saw this Kingdom as the dominion of God extended through those who believe in Jesus Christ as the Son of God and Savior of all mankind, not in terms of any geopolitical entity.

5

Fulfilling the Vision

The Imperial University of Shansi, 1901–10

THE HISTORY OF THE Imperial University of Shansi actually dates back to Richard's proposal to Shanxi Governor Zeng Guochuan (Tseng Kuo-ch'üan) to found a college of modern learning in Taiyuan as one of the means of averting future famine. There is no evidence that Zeng made any attempt to implement the suggestion. When his successor, Zhang Zhidong, was looking in the provincial archives for suggestions to enrich the people and avert future famine, he came across Richard's proposals and was intrigued. He sent a special deputation to invite Richard to leave his work as a missionary to become his adviser. Richard declined the government position as he believed his work as a Christian missionary to be even more important.[1] Nevertheless, he indicated he would recommend experts to assist Zhang. Richard himself even did some surveying for Zhang. In 1884 when Zhang was appointed to his next position in Canton, then later in Wuchang, he began reforms very similar to Richard's recommendations, specifically to found colleges that included Western learning and to develop mining and steel smelting.[2]

By 1884 Richard's vision for higher education reform had expanded to include all of China. For more than two decades, Richard continued his efforts make China aware of its need for modern higher education. His perseverance was finally rewarded in 1901 with Chinese government approval

1. Richard, *Forty-five Years*, 172–73.
2. Ayers, *Chang Chih-tung*, 102–6.

Timothy Richard's Vision

of a college for Western learning in Shanxi's provincial capital of Taiyuan and its subsequent founding of a national system of public educational institutions.

Nations that lost citizens and property to violent attacks during the Boxer Uprising of 1900 began to demand indemnities (payments in compensation) from the Chinese government. As early as November 1900, Richard and others had begun to address the issue, with Richard expressing concern not only with justice but with securing the "goodwill instead of the enmity of the people at large."[3] At this point Richard embarked upon one of the most satisfying times of his entire forty-five years in China. In his memoir, he would write, "In 1901, although I had taken a leading part in the Reform Movement, which finally compelled the Government to fly for refuge to Shensi [Shaanxi], I was invited by Prince Ch'ing [Qing] and Li Hung-chang [Hongzhang], who had been appointed Peace Plenipotentiaries, to aid in the settlement of indemnities for the massacres in the Shansi province."[4]

All the missionaries in Shanxi either had been massacred or had fled to other provinces, so no one was left with whom the local officials could negotiate on indemnities. Choosing Richard to confer with seemed to be the reasonable choice. (Other provincial officials were seeking him out for advice as well.) He was well-known by officials and people alike in Shanxi for his humanitarian efforts in famine relief more than twenty years before, and he had served as a missionary there for almost ten years thereafter. Since Prince Qing and Viceroy Li had many contacts with Richard over the years, they also knew him to be a man of integrity who had much experience in China and who exerted much influence within the foreign community. Finally, it was Richard who, as a representative of the Protestant missionaries, had sent memorials on several occasions over the last fifteen years to the Throne pleading for its intervention in the persecution of native and foreign Christians.[5]

The Chinese Peace Plenipotentiaries were eager to settle the Shanxi issues, given that the worst incidents had happened there and foreign troops remained nearby. They had replaced the governor directly responsible for

---

3. All unattributed references to unpublished communications are from BMS MSS. Richard, letter to BMS Home Secretary Alfred Baynes, 19 November 1900, 2.

4. Richard, *Forty-five Years*, 299.

5. Correspondent, "Missionary Work," 6a. "Christian Literature for China," 220, noted that in May 1901 Richard was invited by the governor of Jiangxi province to come there to settle problems resulting from the outbreak of violence against missionaries.

the atrocities and promised the Allied forces that they would "instruct the Governor of Shanxi to protect and provide for the surviving native Christians." Soon thereafter, Richard in Shanghai wired the new governor to ask what had been done and was told that the remains of those killed were buried and famine relief had been distributed among the surviving Christians in Taiyuan and Taigu.[6]

Richard then conferred first with his own Society about filing indemnity claims that were due the end of April. The Baptist Missionary Society (BMS) acknowledged it was going to file claims only for mission property lost or destroyed and missionary personal effects and furniture, but some of the representatives of other Protestant mission societies were considering filing indemnities for the missionaries killed. Richard did not believe this to be appropriate as the indemnity was to be paid to descendants, and the missionary societies could not be considered their descendants. Richard instructed the BMS to notify the heirs and let them decide if they wanted to make a claim for the lives lost.[7]

At this juncture, the newly assigned governor of Shanxi, Cen Chunxuan [Ts'en Ch'un-hsüan], acted on the recommendation of Shen Dunhe, his Foreign Affairs Bureau chief, that he contact Richard. Cen wired the Shanghai *dao dai* [tao tai; hereafter, mayor] on April 23, 1901, to request that Richard come to Shanxi to "settle the missionary and commercial troubles." This new governor of Shanxi was no stranger to reform, having participated in the 1898 Hundred Days' Reform Movement. Shen Dunhe was likely known to Richard, having attended Cambridge University for two years, thus speaking English. They would collaborate several years later in Shanghai, when Shen was a member of the CLS.[8]

---

6. Richard to Baynes, 6 February 1901.

7. Richard to Baynes, 3 April 1901. Soothill, *Timothy Richard of China*, 153, stated that the Roman Catholics "had made large demands, calculated to embitter the feeling of the province against them." For a discussion of the Shanxi indemnity issues pertaining to the Roman Catholics, see Edwards, *Fire and Sword in Shansi*, 165–72. According to Edwards, one item in dispute was the government re-possession of a college (Ling Teh T'ang). The Roman Catholic bishop requested as a condition of the handover that no Protestant ever be allowed to enter it. "This was going beyond his province, and it was a distinct blow at Dr. Richard's proposed Shansi University," and was refused.

8. *Chinese Recorder* 32 (June 1901), 312. "Tsun Chun Hsuan" (sic) to Timothy Richard, English translation of the telegram of 23 April 1901. Lo, *K'ang Yu-wei: A Biography and Symposium* (Tucson: University of Arizona Press, 1967), 77, 111, recorded that Kang, the leader of the Hundred Days' Reform, wrote in his diary that he had discussed with Cen in 1897 some plans "for the organization of a Society of Sagacious Learning

Timothy Richard's Vision

The mayor carried the telegram to Richard, and together they hammered out an initial agreement, with the mayor signing on behalf of the governor. Soon thereafter, the Peace Plenipotentiaries in Peking petitioned the British Consul to pass on to Richard their invitation that he visit Shanxi; however, the Consul did not forward this request as he did not think travel in the interior was safe. Moir Duncan, Richard's former colleague then serving as a British interpreter in Peking (and thus probably privy to the knowledge of this petition), wired Richard to come immediately to Peking.[9]

Richard arrived in Peking on May 14, and by May 25, when he wrote the BMS Home Secretary, he had met with the Chinese and foreign Peace Plenipotentiaries. Meanwhile, he interviewed leading Protestant and Roman Catholic missionaries to see what was being done to settle the missionary problems in north China. Richard also had "wired to the Governor of Shanxi some general principles for the settlement, and [had] now a full scheme for settlement under consideration."[10]

Though these principles were not enumerated in this early correspondence with the BMS Home Secretary, three emerged in the negotiations:

(Sheng-hsüeh hui)." The next year Cen memorialized the government to abolish certain courts. When the Court went into exile during the Boxer Uprising and the subsequent foreign occupation of Peking, Cen met and accompanied it on its travels to Shaanxi. Perhaps this was his attempt to reenter the good graces of the empress dowager to compensate for his earlier reform activity. Regardless, he was rewarded with the governorship of Shanxi. Richard did not indicate in his writings anywhere that he had ever had a personal meeting with Cen prior to 1902. Shen Dunhe not only recommended that the governor invite the missionaries back to Shanxi; during the renegotiations in 1902, he also suggested the names for the two colleges in the amalgamated Imperial University of Shansi. Shen later enlisted Richard's aid when he attempted to start a Chinese girls' school in Shanghai, and also sought Richard's aid in the creation of the "International Red Cross committee" in Shanghai to raise funds for those involved in the Russo-Japanese War being fought in Manchuria. Together they raised from Chinese sources alone more than £55,000 and 10,000 padded suits. See Richard, *Forty-five Years*, 323; Nichols, *Through Hidden Shensi*, 80–82; Woodberry, "Shen Tun-ho," *Through Blood-stained Shansi*, 35–42.

9. Richard to Baynes, 6 May 1901. Richard reported that the agreement included a commitment to send a memorial to the Throne for "approval of a scheme providing for the early establishment of a university at T'ai-yuan-fu ... [where] the students are to have all the privileges of students in the Peking university ..."

10. Richard to Baynes, 25 May 1901, postscript dated 30 May; Edwards, *Fire and Sword in Shansi*, 122–24, 160–65. On May 29 Richard with Dr. Atwood (American Board) presented a "plan of regulations for the settlement of the Mission troubles in Shansi." This plan had seven separate principles, one of which was for the opening of "schools" throughout the province. Though not explicitly stated here, no doubt one of these schools was to be a university of Western learning in the provincial capital.

Fulfilling the Vision

The mission societies would not request or accept money in payment for the loss of lives; the government must provide compensation to provide for the surviving native Christians; and steps must be taken to remove the causes of another such outbreak of violence through the establishment of an institution of Western learning in the provincial capital.[11]

As Richard later wrote, he had presented a proposition "to satisfy the consciences of the foreign nations and to redeem the character of the Chinese themselves from dishonor . . . A university of Western learning where Chinese students should be taught and fitted for positions of usefulness in connection with the government and as professors in other institutions of learning."

> [He] proposed that a fine of half a million Tls. should be imposed upon the province, to be paid in yearly instalments of fifty thousand Tls. and that the money should be devoted to the establishment in Taiyuan fu of a University on Western lines, the aim being to remove the ignorance and superstition that had been the main cause of the massacre of the foreigners . . . [T]hey [the Peace Plenipotentiaries] placed the appointment of the professors, the arranging of the curriculum, and the administration of the funds of the University in my hands for ten years, after which period the control would pass into the hands of the provincial government.[12]

Richard then wrote the BMS a postscript dated May 30 stating that he and two others "saw the Viceroy Li Hung-chang yesterday and presented our regulations for the settlement of mission troubles. The Viceroy said they were good." Richard then was invited by Li "to draw up an outline of the manner in which religious peace was attained in other parts of the world;"

11. "Notes," *The Chinese Recorder* 32 (December 1901?), 625; n.a., "Memorial University," *The Missionary Review of the World* 25 (April 1902), 316. These articles indicated that the refusal of indemnities was at Richard's suggestion. However, n.a., "The Shansi Governor's Proclamation," *The Missionary Review of the World* 25 (June 1902), 460-61, reported it was at the instigation of the China Inland Mission. While it is important who initiated this gesture, the most important aspect is the impact it had on the minds of the Shanxi government leadership. The governor of Shanxi had been sufficiently impressed by the CIM's refusal of indemnities that he issued a proclamation read as a eulogy at the memorial service "held in honor of the Protestant missionaries who died at Taiyuanfu in 1900." See "A Noteworthy Document [Translation of Proclamation]," *The Missionary Review of the World* 25 (April 1902), n.p.; n.a., "A Heathen Panegyric on the Shansi Martyrs," *The Missionary Review of the World* 25 (April 1902), 291-92.

12. "Notes," *The Chinese Recorder* 32 (December? 1901), 625; Richard, *Forty-five Years*, 299; "New University in China," *N. Y. Times*, April 20, 1902, 4-5; "Note," *The Chinese Recorder* 33 (June 1902), 311.

his monograph on "Religious Liberty" was drawn up and circulated among the leading viceroys and governors throughout China.[13] Soon thereafter, Richard indicated that Li and Prince Qing convinced the empress dowager "to sanction the establishment of a University College in Shansi." Her decision may also have reflected the influence of Richard's private communications to the Court in exile.[14]

On September 14, 1901, four months after the plan for Shanxi was first approved, the Court issued a historic edict calling for existing academies in all provincial capitals to be converted to colleges offering both Confucian studies and Western learning.[15] Final ratification by the Chinese government of the overall settlement in Shanxi Province did not come until November 8, perhaps delayed by the illness and death of Viceroy Li. This served as the highest official stamp for the college Richard was creating. With pride, he wrote his home mission secretary that "the native papers were loud in their praise of it as overcoming evil with good."[16] This University—first proposed to and approved by the Shanxi governor by proxy in April 1901, approved by the Peace Plenipotentiaries and empress dowager

---

13. Richard to Baynes, 25 May 1901, postscript of 30 May. "Christian Literature for China" (See note 4) reported the request and distribution of Richard's monograph.

14. Richard, "The China Problem From a Missionary Point of View," 1905, 3. "Missionary Work and Reform in China," *London Times*, November 15, 1901, (6a), disclosed Richard's frequent communications with the Court: "Prompted by the knowledge of the Emperor Kwang Hsu's desire for reform, and supported by the powerful booklet entitled "Learn" ["China's Only Hope," English translation by S. I. Woodbridge] by Viceroy Chang Chih-tung, Mr. Richard telegraphed at regular intervals of a few weeks to officials at Si-ngan-fu [Sian-fu, Xi'an] where the Court stayed for one year, urging the importance of reform in education."

15. Richard, "The New Education in China," 1903, 12, discussed the edict of September: "Each provincial capital was to have a University like the Peking University, whilst the colleges in the prefectures and districts of the various provinces were to be schools and colleges of the second and third class." For a contemporaneous look at Chinese education at the time when Richard first began his higher educational reform efforts, see Martin, *The Chinese*, 1–85.

16. Richard to Baynes, 18 November 1901. Richard to Baynes, 13 November 1901, discussed Li's illness and death on November 7. "Notes," *Chinese Recorder* 32 (December? 1901), 625, stated that though Li and Qing had signed the Boxer Protocol September 7, 1901, when Li died on November 7, the Shanxi agreement was still unsigned. The governor-general of Zhili, Wang Wenshao, replaced him as Peace Plenipotentiary the next day and also signed the Shanxi agreement. "Diary of Events in the Far East," *Chinese Recorder* 33 (January 1902), 48, stated "The Shanxi troubles settled by the establishment of a university, the agreement being settled with Rev. T. Richard, D.O., and stamped by the Shanghai Taot'ai for the Governor of Shanxi."

near the end of May, sanctioned by imperial edict in September, and formally approved in the Shanxi settlement of November 8, 1901—was the primary impetus launching China's new system of public higher education institutions.

Viceroys Zhang Zhidong and Liu Kunyi also made similar calls for educational reform but later in July 1901; both had subscribed to CLS publications and had been well acquainted with Richard's ideas for many years. The next significant edicts to be promulgated on education were on November 16 and 25, 1901, and these officially ordered the provinces to take Yuan Shikai's college in Shandong and its regulations as the model. Yuan too was very familiar with Richard's educational vision through their earlier involvement in reform during 1895–98, and Richard's long-time associate W. M. Hayes worked on Yuan's regulations and became president of the college.[17] No doubt, it was more acceptable to the Throne to acknowledge initiatives for reform from loyal Chinese officials than from a Christian missionary, particularly one who had been closely associated with the radical reform effort of 1898. Official models also were completely under local control, not sharing power with Westerners as in Taiyuan.

More imperial edicts were issued the following year in 1902 to establish the modern system of education for China, particularly higher education, this time based on a memorial by Zhang Zhidong, who had been influenced by Richard as early as the 1880s. By this time, however, Zhang was advocating the Japanese model of education and his focus was on primary and secondary education, not higher education.[18] Nevertheless, Richard's

17. See chapter 4, note 58 on Hayes. Some authors propose it was this Shandong system with W. M. Hayes as president of the new provincial university that was the original impetus as well as model for the reform, while others propose it was the Zhili system with Tenney as president of its new university. Both universities were planned, and the two men appointed, by Yuan Shikai only a few months apart as he was transferred from Shandong to Zhili. "China" column, *London Times*, May 7, 1901, 5d, indicates that Yuan was in the process of establishing two colleges in Shandong, one military and one scientific, around the time Richard was negotiating with the Shanxi governor. The fact remains that Richard had been friends with both missionaries for more than ten years, as well as an acquaintance of Yuan in 1895–98. See arguments for Hayes: Bastid, *Educational Reform*, 35; Hayes, "Foreign Instructors and Intolerance," 234; "Editorial, Watson McMillan Hayes Jubilee 1882–1932," *The China Fundamentalist* 5:1, July–September 1932, 2. See arguments for Tenney: Graybill, *Educational Reform*, 86; Martin, *The Awakening of China*, 213.

18. Anon. [Timothy Richard?], "The Expropriation of Temple Lands in China," 1903, 629–30, discussed a government decision made to carry out the plan to establish lower levels of education by seizing the income from lands associated with the local Buddhist

plan for the college in Taiyuan preceded and influenced the other initiatives by those who had been influenced by him for years or even decades.

Richard had returned to Shanghai in mid-June 1901 to continue with his work at the CLS and on other projects. Before he left Peking, however, he had organized a party of missionaries as a peace commission, which was to return to Shanxi, at the governor's invitation, to negotiate the founding of the college, to reinstate a missionary presence there, and to provide aid and comfort to famine sufferers there and in Shaanxi, the neighboring province to the west. This expedition, which included the first eight missionaries to return to Shanxi since the Boxer uprising, arrived in Taiyuan without incident and was received with great ceremony on July 9, 1901, exactly one year after the missionaries were massacred there in the governor's courtyard. On August 24, Richard wrote BMS Home Secretary Alfred Baynes cryptically that he was in telegraphic and letter correspondence with the group and the governor about education. This was his first mention of the education component of the settlement he had drawn up with the Peace Plenipotentiaries. Finally, on August 26, Richard informed Baynes that he had received a long telegraphic dispatch from the Shanxi governor indicating his "desire to establish a College of Western learning in Taiyuenfu so that when the people know the state of the world that the repetition of last year's massacre will be impossible, etc." Perhaps Richard thought the idea would be more acceptable to the BMS if the request came from the Chinese.[19]

Governor Cen had requested that Richard serve as the school's first president, resident in Taiyuan, or to recommend someone. At this point, Richard solicited financial support from the BMS to pay the salary of one of its missionaries to fill the position. He presented the precedents set by three American mission boards that paid salaries of men who served as presidents of government colleges or universities. Richard wrote Baynes in

---

and Taoist temples, other than those used in State worship, to "be used in the aid of the new prefectural and county schools which it was proposed to establish . . ." The effect of this would be to lessen the control of the people by those who ceased to "represent anything except the ashes of dead superstition." The writer went on to say, "What China needs is Education, but it is not simply the imperfect transfusion of Western Learning into Chinese receptacles, but an enlightenment of the entire intellectual, moral, and spiritual nature of the Chinese race, so as to know not only 'Heaven, Earth, and Man,' but God, who made them all."

19. Richard to Baynes, 24 August and 26 August 1901. Richard to Baynes, 25 May 1901, noted that he returned to Shanghai in part because the Municipal Council told him they would not proceed with the plans for either the Shanghai Chinese Public School or the Shanghai Public Library until his return.

Fulfilling the Vision

late September 1901: "I am strongly pushing the Educational scheme on Shanxi at the expense of the Chinese government under the guidance of a missionary in the hope that it will encourage friendly relations between missionaries and officials. Whether it will succeed or not it is too premature yet to say."[20]

When the final settlement of the Shanxi Boxer indemnity issues took place on November 8, a contract was drawn up and formalized by Richard and the Shanghai mayor on behalf of the Shanxi governor. Then, Richard went ahead with his plans to staff the college. He expected to get the first annual installment of 100,000 Tls. in two months. He himself could not become president because of the pressing nature of his work in Shanghai, so he asked his friend and former colleague from Shandong, A. G. Jones, if he would accept the position for two or three years. When Jones declined the offer, Richard offered the presidency to another long-time colleague, Moir Duncan, who accepted the challenge.[21]

In early spring 1902, Richard traveled to Taiyuan with the first foreign professors to "arrange some fundamental principles in person face to face with the governor" and to open the new university. Richard's aim was "to make the Shansi University a lever for the uplifting of the leaders of the whole province to the level of the kingdom of Heaven as conceived in modern days."[22]

20. Richard to Baynes, 24 August and 26 August, 28 September, 13 November 1901.
Financial precedents included the Methodist Episcopal church supporting a president of a college without requiring him to sever his connection to the mission society, the American Presbyterians supporting Dr. W. M. Hayes "to try a similar experiment" in Shandong, and the "American Board did the same formerly in Japan." He felt that such a resolution would keep the "college from being a merely secular institution." Richard indicated the Shanxi Governor was slow to act. He corresponded with Richard by wire "for some time," and later sent a special commissioner to Shanghai to write out the "definite agreement" about the college.

21. Richard to Baynes, 13 November 1901 and 26 March 1902. See telegrams sent by Richard to A. G. Jones, 26 December 1901 and 4 January 1902.

22. Richard to Baynes, 26 March 1902. Before Richard left Shanghai, he wrote a letter to the editor of the *Chinese Recorder*, which was printed in its March 1902 issue, detailing the need for missionaries to staff the faculties of the newly forming government schools as well as to translate the much needed textbooks.
Soothill, *Timothy Richard of China*, 260, 267, listed the first Western faculty as Timothy Richard, joint chancellor with the Shanxi governor; Moir Duncan, a Scottish missionary with the BMS, whom Richard himself appointed to be principal; and Eric Nystrom, a Swede who was to be professor of chemistry and who remained with the university throughout the period of Richard's chancellorship. These went to Taiyuan in spring 1902 for the opening of the university. Other faculty would follow: Bevan,

Timothy Richard's Vision

When he arrived in Taiyuan, he was dismayed to find that "strong measures were being made to establish a Government University similar to the one I had authority to found. It was to be placed under the control of an anti-foreign official who had done his best to oppose the Western University." He believed this institution violated the original agreement made with Li and Prince Qing, approved by the Court, and validated by the Shanghai mayor for governor Cen. He immediately appealed to the governor, arguing the impracticality of having two rival schools in Taiyuan, but Cen seemed inclined to favor a "healthy rivalry"; serious negotiation ensued, during which Richard proposed a division of labor that might allow the two programs, combined into one institution, to operate more efficiently and frugally. Thinking to garner support, his rival at the other school suggested that students who had already matriculated write an essay on "the advantages and disadvantages of a united university." Quite surprising for him, "out of 108 essays 68 were in favour of union and only 13 definitely against it."[23]

Prolonged renegotiations continued for three and a half months until Cen and Richard reached a compromise. A new contract was drawn up formulating regulations to amalgamate the two institutions into one Imperial University of Shansi. The contract and regulations for the amalgamated institution were signed and sent to Peking where it was then signed and "confirmed by Imperial Seal from Peking, and form[ed] the constitution" of the University. The new institution "should include two departments—a Chinese department, to be controlled by Chinese and to have purely Chinese studies, and a Western department, under [Richard's] control for ten years, to have purely Western subjects."[24]

Williams, Cartwright, Warrington, and Aust.

Nystrom in 1921 established in Shanxi the Sino-Swedish Scientific Research Association, also known as the Nystrom Institute, remaining its director until the early 1930s. See Ludtke and Richter, *Minerva*; Nystrom, *Coal and Mineral Resources*.

23. Richard, *Forty-five Years*, 300; Soothill, *Timothy Richard of China*, 256. A news brief from Shanxi dated 6 June, in "Shansi Advancing in Modern Civilization," *Shanghai Mercury*, June 19, 1902?, prematurely announced the new university.

24. The contract and regulations for the founding of the Imperial University of Shansi were published in the *Peking Gazette*, the official publication of the Chinese government, July 3, 1902. See also Moir Duncan, "Imperial University, Shansi" in "Imperial University," 6–8. Versions were published in several magazines, one of which omitted several lines, thus falsely implying that the Western Department superintended the management and monies of the Chinese Department. See Aisi Li, "Competition and Compromise" for an excellent account of the negotiations that analyses the pragmatic accommodations

Richard's compromise to establish the amalgamated university in Taiyuan in no wise negated the historic impact of his earlier proposal. Creating an authorized institution of Western learning, using money extracted from the provincial government as a fine instead of foreign indemnities, satisfied both the demand by the Western Powers that the Chinese government accept responsibility and be punished for the losses from the Boxer Uprising and the refusal of the various Protestant mission societies to require or accept monetary relief for their missionaries killed. This set a precedent for other similar face-saving solutions, the most well-known being the Boxer Fund for Tsinghua University in Peking.[25]

PIONEERING THE NEW EDUCATION

The founding of the Imperial University of Shansi had a cascading effect upon the other provinces, as it took the lead in several arenas, providing a *de facto* model to the entire empire. First, it was a completely government-supported institution, but with a decidedly Christian bent. While the governor refused to sanction the teaching of the course entitled "Comparative Morals and Religions," the faculty was not expressly forbidden by the agreement to teach either subject. Many of the foreign faculty members in the Western Department were Christians who came to China in missionary service. "Every Sunday, also, the Principal and Faculty held a service in the University premises, and the missionaries were at liberty to work among the students." Furthermore, even though Christian theology was not taught directly, the faculty and Duncan in particular took the opportunity within their lectures, as appropriate, to show "the beneficial results of Christianity."[26]

---

both sides made, in part to deal with criticism from key constituents. She may overemphasize the governor's *de facto* oversight of the Western Department based on his *de jure* power as governor.

25. Ibid., "Shansi Imperial University: A Tribute to Dr. Timothy Richard," *North China Daily News*, December 15, 1910, in BMS MSS. The preparatory program at Tsinghua (Qinghua) University was founded in 1908 with remitted excess American Boxer indemnity funds, which were used to prepare and send its scholars to American universities, usually in the Northeast. See Abe Hiroshi, "Borrowing from Japan: China's First Modern Educational System," in Hayhoe and Bastid, *China's Education*, 73. The Imperial University of Shansi antedated the preparatory program for overseas study by at least six years.

26. Richard, "Of More Value than a Thousand New Missionaries: New China, New Methods," *The Missionary Review of the World* 26 (April 1903), 291. Richard, *Forty-five Years*, 299–309, devoted an entire chapter in his autobiography to the university. He

Timothy Richard's Vision

William E. Soothill, the successor Richard appointed as principal of the Western Department after Moir Duncan's death, took a somewhat different approach. Though a missionary with the United Methodist Free Church Mission from Great Britain, Soothill did not think the University was the "place for religious propaganda." However, he became the first president of the BMS-initiated YMCA club where standing-room only crowds of young men would listen to "lectures on general topics considered from the religious standpoint." Richard also reported that the students gained an even greater interest in the Bible as the "root of Christian civilization" after a chancellor of education in the province exhorted the students to "study the classics of the Western people as well as our own classics."[27]

With foresight from long experience in China, Richard knew that these exciting new changes could become mere paper reforms. So he suggested that the "missionary societies, singly or unitedly, open one or two model universities at once, where the best Chinese will be thoroughly trained to become first-class professors in every branch of knowledge." He also knew that most government universities in Europe and America existed not for the purpose of teaching Christianity but solely for "giving general knowledge." He worked hard to insure that the Imperial University of Shansi would be otherwise. Perhaps prompting his initiatives was the 1903 resignation of W. M. Haynes as president of the Shandong Provincial College over the issue, and the dismissal there of six students who were Christians and refused to bow before the tablets commemorating Confucius.[28]

---

noted in 1903 that "[i]n eleven out of the eighteen provinces we have records of the opening of colleges for the study of Western subjects."

Richard, *Forty-five Years*, 300–301, noted that Governor Cen attempted "to obtain my promise that a regulation be inserted in the Constitution that Christianity never should be taught in the University. Not for a moment could I agree to such a proposal . . ." The morality or ethos underpinning the new educational system was of utmost importance to Richard, and the issue was whether this morality was to be based on Confucianism or on Christianity. Richard knew that outcome depended mainly upon the faculty. For this reason, he issued an urgent appeal to the Christian churches in Europe and the United States to supply the needed manpower, at least until these universities could raise up their own Christian Chinese professors.

27. See "Shansi University. A Tribute to Dr. Timothy Richard," *North China Daily News*, December 15, 1910, in BMS MSS; Soothill, *Timothy Richard of China*, 258; Richard, "What the Bible is Doing in China," 1905, 7.

28. Richard, "The Outlook for Christianity in China," 1902, 341–43; Richard, "Letter to the Editor of the North-China Daily New—The Toleration Question Again," 1903, 431.

Second, the governance of the university was essentially a joint chancellorship held by the governor of Shanxi and Timothy Richard, with the total control of funds, personnel, and curriculum of the Western Department placed in missionary hands. This meant that the Western Department was "an integral part of the Governmental Educational Institution for the province of Shanxi, but the finance, studies, and discipline [were] under the control of foreigners," specifically a Christian missionary. Besides teaching, Principal Duncan had the responsibility for the day-by-day management of personnel and students and proper administration of the resources. He also oversaw the construction of the new facility, which the university moved into by 1906. Perhaps most important, Duncan was responsible for maintaining amicable relations with the Chinese Department.[29]

Third, built into the founding of this university was the planned devolution from missionary to indigenous leadership within the period of ten years. The raising up of indigenous leadership was a persistent theme in all of Richard's efforts in China and entirely consistent with his previous endorsement of self-support and self-direction by the Chinese of their institutions, be it a school or a church. The Imperial University of Shansi was no different. This handover was carried out smoothly in November 1910.[30]

Fourth, during the first three years, students participated in a program of studies that prepared them for the matriculation examination at London University. No other government university in existence at that time in China had a curriculum that prepared its graduates for direct matriculation into a specific university in a Western country. The subjects taught during the earliest years of the university included mathematics, English, chemistry, physics, drawing, zoology, geography, physiology, law, history, and gymnastics. At the end of the three-year preparatory course, students would be awarded certificates entitling them either to employment as teachers in government schools, or entrance to any special course of study to qualify for graduation. The last three years of study offered advanced

---

29. Duncan, "Imperial University, Shansi," 6-8.

30. The initial agreement with Li and Qing was approved in May 1901; however, the renegotiated agreement resulting in the amalgamated university took place by July 1902. Richard announced the devolution on his visit to Taiyuan in November 1910 with the final agreement in June 1911. When the Republican Revolution broke out within four months of the turnover, the university, by necessity, was closed to prevent its destruction. Thanks to the expedient and prudent action of T. L. Kao, a loyal long-term friend of Richard, the university was protected from destruction by renegade troops. The institution was reopened in 1912 completely under Chinese control.

specialized study with degrees offered at the completion in law, sciences, language, medicine, or engineering (mining or civil) after students demonstrated competent knowledge by examination. "The Chinese Government will, by the constitution of the institution, recognize the degrees, and the graduating students will be eligible for public office."[31]

Fifth, the language of instruction was to be solely Chinese, either directly or through interpreters "to ensure a maximum of efficiency in a minimum of time." In the past, mission schools would spend half the day in the study of Western subjects in English and the other half in studying the Chinese classics in Chinese. Richard's plan expedited the process enabling the students to complete their education at the University in six years rather than the usual twelve. This would eliminate the need to study English before proceeding with the University curriculum.[32]

Sixth, the students of the Western Department were all to be Chinese scholars from the province who had passed the Confucian examination level equivalent to either a BA (*Xiucai*) or MA (*Juren*) degree, and who had also passed the Department's entrance examination. Upon completion of their courses, graduates of the Western Department would be qualified to apply for advanced study in the West, and also would be awarded *Juren* status in China if they performed well on a special examination organized by the Ministry of Education. By 1910, all 23 graduates studying in the UK held *Juren* status.[33]

---

31. Duncan, "Imperial University, Shansi," 6-8. According to Soothill, *Timothy Richard of China*, 261–62, "The final examination in these subjects took place in Peking, when those who succeeded were awarded the degree of Doctor (Chin-sze)."

32. "Editorial comment," *Chinese Recorder* 33 (August 1902), 427; Richard, *Forty-five Years*, 302; "Shansi University," *North China Daily News*, December 15, 1910, in BMS MSS. Soothill, *Timothy Richard of China*, 261, indicated that in the beginning no students understood English, nor were any of the professors, other than Duncan, proficient in Chinese. The interpreters they engaged had no knowledge of the subjects and, coming from the coastal areas, could not speak the local dialects. However, they were able to translate the lectures "of the Western professors into Mandarin, which was generally understood, until such time as the professors attained fluency in speaking Chinese or the students ease in understanding English."

33. Richard, *Forty-five Years*, 30; n.a. [Moir Duncan?], "Shansi Imperial University," 461; Duncan, "The Imperial University, Shansi," *East of Asia Magazine* 3 (1904–5), 104; Duncan, "Imperial University, Shansi," 6-8. According to "Historical Summary," *Calendar of the Imperial University of Shansi (Western Department)*, 1908, 4–5, the suspension for several years and then demise of the civil service examinations mandated that another selection process for government officials be devised. "[T]he national adoption of Western methods of education have necessitated some modification in the rules for

Last, the institution had a firm commitment of government financial support. The provincial government was required to include in its budget at least 50,000 Tls. a year for ten years to support this modern higher education. It also was required to provide the necessary facilities until it could complete the construction of appropriate buildings to house the new educational institution.

The governor planned to turn over the "best building" in the city to be used temporarily by the university until its campus could be built. On the very day he was to do this, Cen found out that the head of the Chinese Department, who had opposed Richard's plan from the beginning, was now attempting to undermine Cen's authority with officials in Peking. The governor was so outraged at this official's audacity that "[h]e instantly ordered this official to hand over everything belonging to his Chinese University and to leave T'ai-yuan fu that very day."[34]

In September 1902 the construction plans for the new campus were drawn up and construction began.

> The buildings designed for the Western Department were a reception hall, to contain a reception room for officials and the principal's office, a building containing lecture rooms for law, literature, science, medicine, chemistry, and engineering, with necessary offices for the faculty, laboratories for chemistry and physics, and a room for drawing classes, library, museum, and gymnasium; besides residences for the foreign faculty and bachelor members of the Chinese staff, with all the necessary servants' quarters. It was necessary to have an entrance court that would satisfy Chinese ideas of the style suitable to an Imperial University; this required waiting-rooms for the under officials who accompany the Governor and any other provincial officials on all occasions, and housing for their sedan chairs and runners in bad weather.

Chinese convention was followed in the layout and the actual construction of the buildings; the one exception was the "foreign pattern" of

---

admission, and now candidates are received from Chinese High Schools, subject to their passing the requisite entrance examination." In a sense, the university superimposed a Western education upon a basis of a Chinese education. Moreover, the students were expected to be under thirty years of age and to sign a contract for at least three years attendance. They were charged no fees and were to be given a monthly stipend of 2 to 8 Tls. ($1.50 to $5.00) by the provincial government, not the Western Department. All academic materials, including books and writing materials, were provided at no charge by the respective departments.

34. Richard, *Forty-five Years*, 301.

the doors and windows. Soothill noted "[t]he whole university was lighted by electricity, the apparatus, from boiler to switches, being transported on mule-back from Tianjin, and erected by Mr. N. T. Williams, the mining professor." There was the expectation for a nearby clinic. Construction was completed, and the university was in its new campus by 1906. Enrollment was expected to increase with the advent of the railroad in three or four years, requiring further improvement to the buildings.[35]

At this time in China, there were no suitable textbooks available to meet the needs of the six-year programs. Therefore, Richard anticipated setting aside 10,000 Tls. per year from the university funds for the preparation of textbooks. These textbooks were then provided through a translation department he established for the university housed within the CLS in Shanghai, consisting of "ten Chinese translators and writers and one Japanese translator under the management of a foreign superintendent, the Rev. John Darroch." An attempt was made to standardize terminology by transliterating a list of biographical and geographical names.[36]

LEADING THE WAY

The university's first five years took place in the midst of rapid and extraordinary changes, especially in education, and the university played the important role of a plowshare to break up the fallow ground in this new age for education in China. Within a year of opening for classes with 205 students enrolled, the Imperial University of Shansi had already begun to fulfill one of its purposes—to remove ignorance. This university already

---

35. Peck, "Description of Buildings," in "Imperial University," 9–13; Soothill, *Timothy Richard of China*, 260.

36. Richard, *Forty-five Years*, 303–4. En route to Shanghai after founding the university, Richard visited Yuan Shikai, who was the new viceroy of Zhili. While there, Richard articulated his intention "to devote ten thousand Tls. per annum of the Shansi University funds toward the preparation of textbooks." Yuan thought it a sound idea and agreed to match that amount as well as solicit a similar amount from the new minister of education in Peking. He also expressed confidence that the governors of Shandong and Henan would do likewise. These funds never materialized. Anon. [John Darroch?], "Translation Department," in "Imperial University," 22–23; see ad in *Chinese Recorder* 38 (September 1907). Rent for housing the translation department was paid to the CLS. This translation department served the university for six years, but was eventually closed because of a lack of funds. Nevertheless, during that six years at least eighteen different titles were translated for use at the university. See Appendix 2, p. 169, for a list of known titles of books translated by the department.

had several foreign professors on staff while the other "Western colleges which were being started six months ago in each province have no foreign professors in them. Thus they make it impossible for the students to get a true account of foreigners."[37] By 1904 the Imperial University of Shansi had already developed a good reputation, and by 1906 it clearly achieved some measure of success, for which Richard gave much credit to Moir Duncan. Upon Duncan's premature death that year, he received posthumous honors from the Imperial Court.[38]

37. Duncan, "Imperial University, Shansi," 6-8; Richard to Baynes, 22 January 1903.
Similar articles describing the university were published in the September 1903 issues of [Missionary Herald?] (478–79) and The Chinese Recorder (460–62). "Imperial University," 1–23, included a series of articles on the Imperial University of Shansi. All these articles included lists of officers and staff, with six resident foreign professors. The following combines the corrected information from the articles.

Chancellors: H. E., governor of Shanxi, and Rev. Timothy Richard, D.D. Litt.D.
Directors: Chi King-tao and Ku Ju-yung; Principal: Moir Duncan MA
Professors: law—L. R. O. Bevan, MA (Melbourne), LL.B. (Cambridge), Barrister-at-Law, Gray's Inn, London; science—E. T. Nystrom, C.E., B.Sc. (Stockholm), and R. L. Lyman, BA (Stanford University, USA); language—R. W. Swallow, B.Sc. (Victoria University, Manchester); engineering—M. H. Peck, B.Sc. (California University, US).
Assistant Professors: science—T. H. Li, BA (Tengchow College, Shandong) and T. Y. Yeh, BA (Brest Naval College, France); engineering—J. C. Su (Railway College, Shanghai Kuan); language—Mr. Chou, BA (Queen's College, Hong Kong), and Mr. Sung (Tientsin University); mathematics—O. H. Yu, BA (Anglo-Chinese College, Shanghai); medicine—W. T. Ni, MD (Naval Medical College, T'ientsin).

The names of the language assistant professors, Mr. Chou and Mr. Sung, are not included In the "Imperial University" listing; however, two new names appeared as assistant professors: S. L. Suang, BA (Commercial School, Canton, and T'ientsin University) and C. C. Chang, BA (Naval College, Nanking). Other support staff in the 1904–5 listing: secretary, Mr. He (Nanking); librarian, Mr. Sung (T'ientsin University); cashier, Mr. Kao (Taiyuanfu); usher, Mr. Ma; official attendant, Mr. Li.

38. Bevan, "Imperial University," 1–3, said that the university was referred to as "one of the leading modern universities in China." See "Editorial Comment—Congratulations to Dr. Moir Duncan," Chinese Recorder 37 (May 1906), 281; E. Morgan, "In Memoriam—Rev. M. B. Duncan, M.A, LL.D.," Chinese Recorder 37 (October 1906), 558–61. Richard, Forty-five Years, 306, wrote that the Chinese government "conferred posthumous honours on him by raising his status to the first rank red button [Soothill claims it was second rank]." The year before his death, Duncan had received an honorary LL.D. from Glasgow University in Scotland in recognition of his work in making the Imperial University of Shansi a success. The author visited with Moir Duncan's granddaughter in 1992 and viewed the red button that had been awarded to him. For a unique look at Moir Duncan, see the book published by his late wife and granddaughter for limited circulation: Duncan and Raymer, Lives Lived, 2000.

Timothy Richard's Vision

Not only did the University have its largest enrollment of 339 students in 1906, but it also sent its first graduates abroad for advanced study. Twenty-five students traveled to England for further study in mining and railway engineering, twenty-three with the support of the provincial government; eventually there were more than seventy. "So convinced did the Provincial Government become of the value of modern education that they bore the further expense of sending successful students to England for a further five years' course of study. Thus at one time there were more Shanxi University students in England than from any other educational institution in China." More evidence of the high regard for the university was an extraordinary voluntary grant made by the new Shanxi Governor Bao Fen for the enlargement of the Chemistry Department, which made it the "most efficient and up-to-date institution of its kind in China."[39]

In an editorial comment in the August 1902 *Chinese Recorder*, Richard's funding level in Shanxi was presented as the standard and source of information for the level of provincial funding required by several other universities being established at that time. It noted that "several other provinces are raising Tls. 50,000 per annum (more or less) for the establishment of universities of Western learning in their respective provinces, and that the northern provinces, where the Boxers made the greatest havoc in 1900, are taking the lead."

In another article, Richard listed ten provinces with their funding devoted to opening the new colleges in 1901–1902:

---

39. Richard, *Forty-five Years*, 306; Soothill, *Timothy Richard of China*, 26; Nystrom, *The Coal and Mineral Resources*, 83–85.

Province	Funds Provided
Chekiang (Zhejiang)	50,000 strings of cash/annum
Honan (Henan)	30,000 Tls./annum
Kweichow (Guizhou)	20,000 Tls./annum
Fookien (Fujian)	50,000 Mex. dollars/annum
Kiangsi (Jiangxi)	Over 60,000 Mex. dollars/annum
Kwangtung (Guangdong)	100,000 Tls./annum
Soochow (Suzhou)	Several tens of thousands Tls./annum
Nanking (Nanjing)	———
Shantung (Shandong)	50,000 Tls./annum
Shansi (Shanxi)	50,000 Tls./annum
Chihli (Included Hebei and Peking)	———
Prefectural Colleges in Soochow	10,000 Tls./annum
Prefectural Colleges in Shantung under Roman Catholic Bishop Anzer	2,000 Tls./annum

"This comes to about half a million of Tls. annually for the whole Empire for modern education. Such is the new departure, which dates from 1901–02."[40] While this did not equal the million Tls. for modern education in China that Richard had recommended to Viceroy Li at least a decade earlier, it was a radical departure from the past.

Many other educational changes also began to take place. In August 1901 an edict had been issued, to go into effect the following year, to replace the notorious "eight-legged essay" on the civil service examination with questions about current topics. In September 1901 and October 1902, provincial authorities were ordered by imperial edicts to select students for study abroad. Hanlin and other scholars holding the highest degree were ordered in December 1902 to study in the various departments of the Imperial University of Peking. The July 1905 edict called for opening up civil service exams (in English) to students returning from studying abroad; in later years returned students from the United States often took the highest honors. This breach prepared the way for the *coup de grace*—imperial edicts in August to abolish the ancient civil service examination system and in December 1905 to establish a separate Ministry of Education. These last two edicts clearly marked the demise of the Confucian classics as the core curriculum and the advent of a more modern educational system. This was

---

40. Richard. "The New Education in China," 1903, 13.

Timothy Richard's Vision

confirmed in August 1906 with the establishment of a system of modern public education, to be modeled after the Japanese.[41]

When Richard visited the university in 1908, Bao Fen was by then the governor of Shanxi with whom Richard was serving as joint chancellors. Two of the original foreign professors, Bevan and Nystrom, were still on staff, and new ones had been added. Louis Bevan had served as interim principal 1906–7 after the death of Duncan in 1906. He was now vice-principal under the new principal, William E. Soothill, who would serve in that capacity through the University's devolution to the provincial authorities, a few months prior to the beginning of the 1911 Revolution. He later went to England and became a professor at Oxford University.[42]

In honor of Richard's 1908 visit, the president of the Provincial Assembly convened students from all the provincial schools in a municipal square.

> The President . . . mentioned that some two thousand pupils were gathered there, some from military, some from agricultural, and some from normal schools outside [of] the University, for all the chief teachers in them had at one time or another passed through the University; and not only in T'aiyuan fu, but in all other cities in

---

41. Hsü, *The Rise of Modern China*, 411; Richard, *Forty-five Years*, 305; Abe, "Borrowing from Japan," 57–80. According to Soothill, as many as 30,000 went to Japan for study (263–64). Kuang Fuzhuo (Fong F. Sec), who returned from the US with an MA in education, placed third of 42 candidates who in October 2007 took the first exams in English for returnees designed by the new Board of Education. He was awarded a doctorate of literature and offered placement in the Ministry of Posts and Communications. See Chi Wai Cheung, "Kuang Fuzhuo: From Coolie to Educator and Humanitarian," in Hamrin with Bieler, *Salt and Light*, vol. 2, 66–67.

42. Richard, *Forty-five Years*, 305–6; Soothill, *Timothy Richard of China*, 266–68. Changes in the faculty are revealed by comparing Duncan, "The Imperial University, Shansi," 104 with n.a., "Faculty and Staff," *Calendar of the Imperial University of Shansi* (Western Department), 6th ed., 1908, 2–3. Attrition of the foreign faculty included Lyman, Swallow, and Peck; that of the Chinese faculty included Directors Chi and Ku and Assistant Professors Su, Ni, and Suang. New foreign faculty included E. H. Cartwright (Westminister), language and literature; N. T. Williams (B.Sc., Wales. M.I.M.E., certified colliery manager), mining and engineering; A. W. Warrington (M.Sc., Victoria University), physical science. New members in the Chinese faculty of the Western department included W. S. Feng (Tengchow College, Shandong), C. A. Chen (Pei Yang Telegraph College, T'ientsin), J. Huang (Anglo-Chinese College, Foochow), S. L. Sung (Queen's College, Hong Kong), and C. C. Wu (Chinese graduate). Other new administrative Chinese faculty included Hsieh Yung Lu, Litt.D.; Hanlin as director; Liu Mou Hsiang, MA, as proctor; and C. C. Zhang as the librarian.

Shansi, similar schools were being opened, owing to the stimulus given to education by the University.[43]

Richard all along saw his involvement to be a mentor to the Chinese apprenticed with him in the administration of a modern educational institution. In November 1910, upon Richard's arrival in Peking following his latest trip to England, the Shanxi governor and Provincial Assembly sent an urgent telegram to Richard requesting he come first to Taiyuan before returning to Shanghai. The Provincial Assembly relayed its unprecedented decision to defer its meeting five days awaiting his arrival. Richard was given a rousing reception, and "they spoke in the highest terms of the immense service rendered to the whole province by the University." He realized the time had come to devolve leadership of the university to the Chinese without waiting until the official end of the ten-year period the next year. The plan was announced during this visit, with Richard "convinced that modern education had taken such a deep root in the province that it would never be eradicated." On November 13, 1910, Richard received assurances that the contracts of the foreign professors would be honored and the university enlarged. Two days later he signed the necessary documents devolving the total control of the Imperial University of Shansi to the Chinese, relinquishing "buildings, apparatus and funds of the institution to the Chinese officials and gentry of Shanxi. The officials agreed to carry on the institution perpetually as a university."

By the time of the June 1911 commencement, the foreign professors numbered eight, assisted by fourteen Chinese professors and teachers; and 345 students had been enrolled in the Preparatory Program.

> Of these 252 have already successfully graduated, upon 139 of whom the [MA] degree has been Imperially bestowed. Nearly one hundred of these are now taking a four years' post-graduate course in Law under Professor Bevan, in Advanced Chemistry under Prof. Nystrom, in Mining under Prof. Williams, and in Civil Engineering under Prof. Aust with a view to the [PhD] examination. Two classes of sixty men have just graduated, and there are sixty more in the Preparatory department who graduate next Spring.[44]

43. Richard, *Forty-five Years*, 306–7.

44. Ibid., 307–10. In the almost ten years Richard had been joint chancellor with the governor of Shanxi, he had served with at least five different governors: Cen Chunxuan, Zhao Erxun, En Shou, Ding Baochuan, and Bao Fen. See "Shansi University: A Tribute to Dr. Timothy Richard," *North China Daily News*, December 15, 1910, in BMS MSS; "Dr. Timothy Richard and Shansi University," *The Missionary Review of the World* 24 (July

Timothy Richard's Vision

This handover of the Imperial University of Shansi marked Timothy Richard's final act on the stage of the reform of higher education in China. His vision for change was clearly reflected in the bright lights of the imperial edicts of 1901–6. The university's successful establishment was the zenith of Richard's career in promoting education in China and the cornerstone for China's new system of government-supported higher education. "Whatever the future may bring forth the province has most gracefully acknowledged its past indebtedness to Dr. Richard, and his colleagues."[45]

Since 1910, the University has weathered various wars and political winds and has endured many permutations, but in accordance with the agreement made with Dr. Timothy Richard then, it has continued until today as the premier university in the province. In the Republican era, Shanxi became known as the "Model Province," one of the most progressive parts of China. Its university played a key role in this through its provision of teachers educated in Western learning to schools throughout the province. "Had there been no Timothy Richard such would not have been the case."[46] Yet, in more recent times, Richard's connection with the university has been forgotten or ignored, along with other missionary contributions to China's development. Shanxi University, however, recalled its rich history during

---

1911), 551. Soothill, *Timothy Richard of China*, 267–68, stated that he had expected—contrary to reality—that after the handover the governor would appoint Bevan to head the university and would retain the foreign faculty. However, there were unspecified "opposing forces in Peking" and "jealousy of the university and its success," which had produced "a grudging spirit" in Peking, though not in Shanxi. Soothill listed the foreign teachers as himself, Bevan, Nystrom, Williams, Cartwright, Warrington, and Aust; the eighth professor may have been Richard.

45. "Shansi University: A Tribute to Dr. Timothy Richard," *North China Daily News*, December 15, 1910, in BMS MSS; Davin, "Imperialism and the Diffusion of Liberal Thought," in Hayhoe and Bastid, *China's Education*, 44. Gascoyne-Cecil's *Changing China*, 274–76, provides an interesting appraisal of the university just before its handover. He and his wife had gone to China at the behest of the missionary China Emergency Committee to explore the feasibility of the United Universities Scheme—a British program whereby missionary societies would unite to found universities of Western learning. This was something Richard had requested the BMS to undertake coordinating in 1885!

46. Soothill, cited in Payne, "In Shansi and Shensi." Dr. Paul Monroe, *A Report on Education in Education* (New York: The Institute of International Education, 1922), 34, after a visit to China in 1922, included Shanxi University in a listing of "Chinese Government Institutions of Collegiate Grade Under the Ministry of Education." Five of the institutions had more than 600 students; Shanxi University had 619 students with an annual budget listed as 100,000 (1912 monetary unit not designated). Three others were in Peking; the fifth was Southeastern University in Nanking under the presidency of Guo Bingwen.

Fulfilling the Vision

official celebrations of its centennial on May 8, 2002. This university continues today as one in a vast national network of government-supported schools in provincial capitals that educate young men and women with curricula including modern science along with Chinese and Western cultural and religious studies. Shanxi University is a resounding testimony to the lasting impact of Timothy Richard's vision upon the reform of higher education in late Imperial China.

While the handover of this university was Richard's final act in the reform of higher education institutions in China, it was by no means the end of his career. The fertile mind of this "Renaissance man" continued to explore other ways to cultivate and train the minds of "the four thousand expectant officials." Besides his encouragement of the network of union Christian colleges mentioned above, he also put forth a plan in 1910, in operation through the CLS on a small scale for the next twenty years, for "a systematic home study of the great universal problems."[47]

---

47. Richard, "Turning Point in Human History," 1910, BMS MSS.

6

Giving Honor Where Honor is Due

DURING THE FINAL DECADE of the imperial system in China, 1900–1910, British missionary Timothy Richard had reached the summit of his career as an educator for the social elite and as an adviser to the powerful. The acknowledged representative and spokesman of the Western missionary community, with the resources of several influential organizations and their literary outlets under his supervision, he was an opinion shaper *par excellence*, through both his writings and his personal persuasion. Outside of China, he had become an international statesman who was able to access senior politicians and religious leaders.

Eminent Yale historian Kenneth Latourette in his *History of Christian Missions in China* (1928) described Richard as "one of the greatest missionaries whom any branch of the Church, whether Roman Catholic, Russian Orthodox, or Protestant, has sent to China."[1] At the time of the 1945 centennial of Richard's birth, he was recognized as "the prophet, the writer of books for officials and scholars, the statesmanlike apostle of a social and international Order based on obedience to the laws of God, the 'Nation Builder' of Modern China."[2]

Richard's contributions were recognized by his contemporaries. He was awarded honorary doctorates in 1900 and 1901 by Emory and then Brown University in the United States, and in 1916 by the University of Wales, all in recognition of his efforts on behalf of higher education in

---

1. Latourette, *History of Christian Missions*, 378.
2. Garnier, *A Maker of Modern China*, 7.

Giving Honor Where Honor is Due

China.³ He was given the highest honors awarded to a Westerner by the Chinese Imperial government: In 1902 Richard was appointed by imperial edict as the official adviser to the Chinese emperor for Protestant religious affairs and as joint chancellor of the Imperial University of Shansi. In 1903 he received the highest rank of mandarin (first class, first order, marked by a red button), and several years later his ancestors were ennobled to the same rank three generations back. He was again decorated in 1907 with the Order of the Double Dragon (second class, second order)—a level usually reserved for foreign political dignitaries. For his Manchurian relief efforts for the Chinese victims of the Russo-Japanese War in 1904–5, he was decorated with an International Red Cross medal. All these demonstrate the high esteem in which he was held by Chinese and foreigners alike.⁴

Then, one must ask, how could the name Li T'i-mo-t'ai—Timothy Richard—having been widely known in China in 1906, become anathema in 1951, and finally be virtually unknown in China or the West by the year 2000? The passing of time, of course, is one reason. Another is the shifting winds of politics. Still another is that historians in the West have seemed unable to acknowledge the significant contributions the missionaries made in their host countries, overwhelmingly from altruistic motives. This book is a partial attempt to revive and rectify the record for one man—Timothy Richard.

Who, then, was Timothy Richard? He was a schoolmaster in Wales who came to China in 1870 as a simple Baptist missionary. He began his early educational efforts in China by teaching the brightest famine-orphans

---

3. I ascertained the correct dates for Richard's academic honors through personal communication with the universities. Soothill, *Timothy Richard*, 323–24, included erroneous dates for some awards—1895 for Emory and 1900 for Brown, errors likely taken from Bowser, *Timothy Richard, D.D.*, manuscript in BMS MSS, which also gave a wrong date of 1913 for the honor from the University of Wales.

4. Garnier, *Maker of Modern China*, 85; Forsyth, *Shantung*, 213. "Editorial Notes," *Educational Review* 2 (January 1909), 10, noted that Shanxi Governor Bao Fen had petitioned the emperor to bestow some "reward upon Dr. Timothy Richard for his valuable work in connection with the establishment of Shansi University." The editor congratulated Richard "upon this evidence that his work has been appreciated by the Chinese officials." This most likely refers to the 1907 honor. Richard was joined in this very rare company of foreigners so honored by Sir Robert Hart, the inspector general of the Imperial Maritime Customs Service for nearly four decades. Hart also received the additional honor of a baronetcy in Great Britain. In light of Richard's contributions to improving relations between China and the West at times of crisis and for his enduring pursuit of peace and fraternity among all nations, perhaps posthumous recognition by Great Britain is long overdue.

so that they might later become informed citizens and leaders. He gave scientific demonstrations and lectures for scholars and officials in Shanxi Province about Western learning in science, geography, world history, and current events in order that modern scientific knowledge might replace ignorance and superstition and enable them to improve the welfare of their people.

As early as 1880, he began to articulate a plan to found higher education institutions in provincial capitals to teach scholars this Western learning. Once placed at the helm of the Christian Literature Society (Society for the Diffusion of Christian and General Knowledge among the Chinese) in 1891, Richard wielded his pen as a sword, paring away official resistance to Western learning and at the same time promoting his broader vision for reform by a constant barrage of articles, books, and translations meant to persuade officials of its merits and usefulness. The influential role he played in the 1895–98 Reform Movement was acknowledged then by Chinese and missionaries alike. Identifying himself with the most progressive of the practical missionary educators in the Educational Association of China, Richard sought to unify their vision and mobilize missionary efforts for educational and literary work.

Why was Richard so successful in his efforts in China? He was optimistic and positive, even charming. He had the personality of a pioneer, with unflagging energy and perseverance; he never gave up. He participated in many activities with one stated goal in mind—to bring forth, as best as possible, the Kingdom of Heaven on earth. He was committed to his vision, principles, and goal. He never let anything defeat him; some of his detractors would call this stubbornness in pursuit of his priorities over those of others. To some he was overly tolerant in his tendency to see the best in every person, situation, or belief. He was willing to allow devout non-Christian believers their beliefs. In his own writings and others' accounts of him, he is pictured as slow to speak his opinion, but bold and eloquent in his proclamation of the truth as he knew it. He believed that faith in Jesus as propagated in Christianity was the only way to make good citizens and fully benefit the people of the great nation of China. He constantly whittled away at China's resistance to its essential need for educational reform until it finally gave way. He was realistic about timing; he knew that change would be slow to come to China, taking as many as twenty to thirty years, but in the end change would come. The Chinese officials just needed to be made aware of the need for change, and in his optimistic view, they would proceed expeditiously to make the necessary improvements.

Major change did not come easily for China. At that time, the civil service examination system with the Confucian classics had served as the basis for selecting government officials since the seventh century. There was no systematic approach to schooling, but there was a systematic approach to the examinations for the appointment or promotion of civil officials. Since power and financial reward were ultimately tied to success in these examinations and this success required years of rote learning of Confucian literature, no man who had successfully climbed the tortuous examination ladder wanted to allow another educational system to replace or supplant what he had endured. Fear of the loss of power, prestige, status, money, and position—as well as the problem of many officials being too old to start anew in a very different system requiring different cognitive skills—engendered great resistance to educational reform, which Richard spent many years with much effort to overcome.

The Boxer Uprising, however, was the cataclysmic event that thawed the frozen status quo. And as happened with the abortive Hundred Days' Reform, so it was with the Boxer Uprising; with both there was a counter-reaction, but in opposite directions. With the former, there was a backlash of conservatism; with the latter, there was a tidal wave of reform that would witness the zenith of Timothy Richard's influence.

THE MAKING OF A REMARKABLE MAN

Richard's early life in a Christian home with open discussion of current and religious affairs helped him to develop an openess to the free exchange of new ideas. The last of nine children, he learned early how to negotiate successfully to get what he wanted. He was taught the value of education and witnessed his father on occasions mediating to make peace between members of the community. Richard was imbued with his mother's pleasant and charming nature. Most importantly, he witnessed the genuine nature of his parents' Christian faith, and in his early teens he came to his own faith in Jesus Christ and was baptized. By the time he was sixteen, he had received a "call" from God to foreign missionary service.

Even at a young age while a student, Richard was given responsibility within the classroom. He had the qualities of a born leader that could inspire and encourage others to follow in his steps, and that served him well once he became a schoolmaster himself. His style of leadership was that of a mentor, as he led by example. Working hard to pay for his own education, yet excelling in examinations, he graduated from a theological seminary.

His childhood and earliest education began in a Non-Conformist environment (outside the state Church of England), which contributed to his independent spirit, as did the influence of the history of his homeland of Wales, which had been dominated by the English since the thirteenth century. He directly experienced the prejudice and oppression of the English against the Welsh. He knew what it was to speak one language in the home but be forced to speak another within the educational or work environment. He also saw the modernizing effects of the scientific and industrial revolutions on his homeland, so he quickly learned the importance of practicality in education. It was for this reason that he joined in the reform movement in his seminary to bring about study of the "living" languages and histories of existing civilizations rather than to focus on the dead subjects of the Greek and Roman languages and literatures in the classical curriculum. These experiences would all be reflected in his later work in China.

Richard went to China with the same passion and zeal as did many other young men and women of his time whose hearts were set ablaze "to save the heathen." In 1870 when he arrived in China, however, he was not received warmly, but by rock-throwing and mud-slinging. Most Chinese were not at all interested in what he was there to share. For several years, he was the sole representative of the Baptist Missionary Society in Shandong Province, so he learned quickly to work alone and rely on his own judgment.

A ROAD LESS-TRAVELED

Because of his inquisitive mind, Richard developed a sensitivity and receptivity to the indigenous religions and sought to learn how to use their best doctrines as a way to lead their devotees to belief in Christianity. Within five years, then, he had changed his approach from the traditional evangelistic methods of street chapel preaching to "seeking the worthy," which brought him into more frequent contact with local religious leaders—whether of Buddhism, Taoism, Islam, or local sects—as well as the educated class of scholar-officials seeking advancement through expertise in Confucian literature, which did not promote either creativity or openness to new ideas and methods for solving problems.

Giving Honor Where Honor is Due

This rigid conservatism became especially clear to Richard during North China's great famine of 1876–79, when, in many encounters with officials, his diplomacy and peacemaking skills were supremely tested and honed for the future. During his famine relief efforts, Richard developed and proposed various practical remedies for the prevention of future famines, with mixed results. He began to think that these decision-makers needed an additional sort of education, namely learning based on the Western physical and social sciences and mathematics. As Richard gave lectures to the scholars and officials in Shanxi, he sensed an increasing receptivity to new ideas and ways.

Richard learned early in his work in China that those who were literate were usually devout seekers of truth and as such could be moved intellectually. He sought to use the printed word to try to reach them. For these scholars and officials, the written word was important, almost sacred. Each religious group also had its own body of sacred literature. Richard became intimately familiar with the literature of Taoism, Buddhism, Confucianism, Islam, and secret societies, as well as Jesuit doctrine—out of admiration for the work of Matteo Ricci in China centuries earlier. He began to translate into Chinese material that could impact, or at least appeal to, the ethical nature of the literate Chinese.

Much of this early translation work focused on the impact of Christian faith on the individual life, as he had learned that indirect presentation of devout lives was better received than direct presentation of Christian doctrine. This became a well-defined approach in which both he and his wife Mary were engaged, and for the duration they effectively served as a literary/translation team. Their writings during the first ten years were weighted toward writing or translating biographies.

Richard was an early proponent of training indigenous Christians to the level required to influence the Chinese elite with the West's secular knowledge as well as Christian culture. Even during his earlier famine relief in Shandong, he had included Western learning in a two-track system for the famine-orphan schools: one track for the training in Western learning for those he considered potential leaders; the second for vocational training. Now, he sought to recruit more missionaries to play a critical role in the modernization of China, as the only repositories of Western knowledge available.

As Richard's contacts with elite officials and religious leaders expanded and his priorities and methods changed, this situation caused some concern and tension among his missionary colleagues over the best missions strategy. Most remained focused on reaching the general populace through evangelistic preaching in street chapels and Bible teaching in local schools; some joined him, but many resisted his pressure to change course and adopt scientific education as a primary method of outreach.

When Richard and his family went home on furlough in 1885, he sought to get the BMS to coordinate a united effort among the British mission societies to establish colleges of Western learning in all eighteen Chinese provinces as a means of training native evangelists and future leaders. He encouraged them to begin with a college in Shanxi's capital and to use it as a model for the others. Their leadership in this effort, however, never materialized. In early 1887 Richard returned to Taiyuan deeply disappointed and facing a brewing storm in the missionary community.

Throughout the next few years of active opposition and misunderstanding, Richard never lost his conviction that education could be a practical way of reaching China for Christianity from the top down. But it became clear to him that the educational changes would need to be brought about by the Chinese themselves. His recommended program for study in mission schools, laid out after his first furlough, was intended as a comprehensive curriculum for training native evangelists not only in theology but also in history, science, and culture—both Western and Chinese.

THEOLOGY OF REFORM

Richard never lost sight of the importance of the individual's spiritual salvation, but by 1884 his vision for his work in China had expanded to also include the "salvation" of Chinese society through the agency of modern Western education. In his view, the Kingdom of God was much larger than the saving of individual souls. To him, the gospel as usually preached was only a fraction of the "glad tidings" envisioned by Moses, John the Baptist, and Jesus, who called for prayer for God's will to be done on earth as in Heaven. Christ's kingdom would necessarily contain all that is good in this world and more—a kingdom of peace on earth and good will to men and a kingdom of righteousness for the benefit of the poor and needy. This vision rightly involved the duties of an enlightened government, and this became Richard's primary strategic target. His new mission strategy was the birth of the social gospel as an essentially evangelical impulse.[5]

5. Personal communication on Richard's views of the Kingdom of God, and the link

There was a strong flavor of the philosophy of progressivism in Richard's optimistic conviction that the power of scientific technology and rationalism would naturally and gradually bring about socio-economic progress. A biographer of W. A. P. Martin, a like-minded American ally of Richard's who joined the CLS though based at the Imperial University in Peking, has pointed to a combination of natural theology, millennialism, Enlightenment ideas of progress, and the Great Awakening that created among churches the goal of creating a Christian society where morals and religion would be partners. This perception of a complementary relationship between faith and culture at home led missionaries to project the same goal for their work in other lands. In this sense, the tendency toward cultural imperialism was indirect and unconscious.[6]

Like many of his class in Britain and America, Richard saw education as a primary agent of change. Other missionaries, like CIM's founder James Hudson Taylor, were more inspired by the eschatological urgency also widespread at the turn of the century; in their view this required direct evangelism to save souls before Christ's second coming. Yet one study of their differences concludes that "the two men's attitudes were less conflicting than complementary."[7]

Richard believed that if exposed to Western sciences, the Chinese would observe certain principles in action, which Richard described as the "laws of God" in operation, with God as the first cause or prime mover in these principles. Those Chinese who would come to this rational understanding of God and shed their ignorance and superstition, would then harness the forces of Western science and technology for the improved health and well-being of the masses.

This jump from observation to belief seemed quite rational to Richard, but in his optimism he failed to take into consideration deeper obstacles to a Christian world view, including the materialism that pervaded Chinese philosophy and religion, as well as the gentry's vested interests in the status quo. Most scholar-officials were unable or unwilling to make this "leap of faith."

Meanwhile, his sympathetic but controversial understanding of Mahayana Buddhism as a carrier of Christian-like values, caused many of

---

with the early social gospel, respectively, with Wenzong Wang and Andrew Kaiser, current scholars of Timothy Richard, fall 2012–spring 2013.

6. Covell, *W.A.P. Martin*, 23.
7. Pfister, "Rethinking Missions, 199.

Timothy Richard's Vision

Richard's colleagues to consider his new approach to be unorthodox, even bordering on heresy. BMS Secretary Baynes requested an independent opinion from former missionary James Legge, by then an Oxford University professor. Legge found no evidence of theological error. Later, in 2005, the eminent church historian Samuel Moffett also carefully examined the charge of syncretism and found it unconvincing. He affirmed that Richard never forsook his childhood faith and while differing over strategy, was never far in his theology from that of Hudson Taylor, contrary to many black and white depictions.[8]

In the face of this controversy with his missionary colleagues in Shanxi, to maintain peace and unity Richard finally left missionary work in the province to travel north to Peking and T'ientsin where he endured an agonizing three years of soul-searching. Never content with being idle, however, Richard wrote articles dealing with the benefits of modern education to modernize nations, the multi-faceted benefits of Christianity, and the persecution of Christians in China. He started a small school in his home. He seized every opportunity to cultivate relationships with high government officials.

Through one such relationship during this time of "exile" in North China, Richard was offered the editorship of *The Times* (Shi Bao), a reformist Chinese newspaper in Tianjin. From this new pulpit, he proclaimed loudly and frequently the "good news" of the many positive aspects of the modern West and its learning. Only with this kind of knowledge did Richard believe Chinese leaders could move with equality on the stage of international diplomacy. He compared facts and figures about China with similar information for other nations to illustrate not only China's deficiencies but also its great potential. Richard used charts and diagrams for a visual representation of data, introducing a new form of journalism to the reading public of China, which demonstrated the emerging sciences of sociology and comparative education. With the exception of Young J. Allen, perhaps no other missionary or journalist had so broad a vision or so great an influence as did Richard through such writings.

---

8. Stanley, *The History of the BMS*, 190; Doyle, review of Samuel Hugh Moffett. For an excellent evaluation of Richard's work on Buddhism, see Scott, "Timothy Richard, World Religion," 53–75. Scott explains how Richard fell prey to a faulty approach to comparative religious studies, as well as his own wishful thinking, to mistranslate and misinterpret Buddhist writings, with the result "not only to elevate Mahayana doctrines as expressing religious truth but also to relativize Protestant Christianity," thereby alienating both Buddhists and Christians.

Richard knew, as did some Chinese officials, that the learning in China had little utility other than the selection of members of the Chinese bureaucracy, and while China lived in glorious isolation, this selection was sufficient and necessary. With the encroachment of the West in the mid-nineteenth century, this was no longer a sufficient purpose. By the time China finally promulgated its system of modern higher education as a result of crises in 1898–1901 and then abolished its ancient examination system by mid-decade, neighboring Japan had already had such a modern system for more than thirty years.

CONTENDING FOR HEARTS AND MINDS

The Western Protestant mission era in China ironically helped to open China to influences that turned out to be competitive. Japan's victory against China in 1895 was a rude awakening. Suddenly, China had to face the fact that Japan was not weak but had become an international power with which China would have to contend. A decade later, Japan and Russia engaged in 1904–5 in warfare on Chinese soil with Japan the victor and China the spiritless spectator and helpless victim. Indeed it was time to wake up! China turned east to its former vassal state to learn the secret of its prosperity and progress.

The reasons why late Imperial China turned to Japan are complex but understandable. The first of the reasons was pride. Both China and Japan had imperial systems, and the reform efforts of both sought to reinforce the existing power structure. Moreover, China did not want to submit itself to the direct tutelage of the West. Fragmentation and competitiveness within the missionary community also weakened their efforts to address this new competition. In the arena of education, goals in the various countries were not the same. American education schooled for educated citizenry; British education made gentlemen; German schooling made specialists. Which path and whose advice should be followed?

Expedience argued for accepting Japan's instruction and translations, given the very similar written language, which enabled the Chinese students to have quicker access to translations of Western writings. Proximity also aided Japan, which sent more than 500 teachers to China and received thousands of Chinese students. By 1906 Japan had achieved considerable influence over newspaper and school textbook publication in China. The Japanese came to be viewed as benefactors. Another motivator was cost; it was far less expensive to send students to Japan to be educated, to hire Japanese teachers, and to purchase Japanese translations than to pay Westerners. This was important, given the large indemnities the Qing government had to pay the Western Powers to cover the Boxer damages and deaths. China began to turn from its missionary mentors to accept the Japanese model for the new educational system.

For a time, it appeared the light had dimmed for lobbying by Richard and the EAC to establish Christian underpinnings for the educational process grooming China's future leaders. The Executive Committee continued to promote a national educational scheme with a curriculum based on Christianity and designed a teacher training program that used texts and examinations written by Protestant missionary educators. This was rowing against the current until the Republican revolution of 1911 inspired a renewed focus on Western models of government and education.

In 1912, at the end of his tenure as one of two EAC vice presidents, Timothy Richard prepared a paper that examined the future of the EAC in relation to the newly established Republic of China. He called for united efforts among the denominations and more cooperation with the new government. By that time, Richard had served the EAC and its predecessor for more than three decades, as well as two decades at the helm of the CLS. He had witnessed what few men are privileged to see—the coming to fruition of a vision. But in the new era, the baton was passing to a younger generation of Chinese Christian professionals.

In 1914, after eleven years as a widower, Richard married Dr. Ethel Tribe, a graduate of London University with twenty years of experience as a medical missionary in China. His offer to retire from the CLS was delayed at the Society's request until 1915, when he was given the honorary title of secretary emeritus. He and Ethel took up residence in England in 1916, when Richard published his memoir.[9] He died in 1919 following surgery.

---

9. Walls, *The Cross-cultural Process*, 257; Soothill, *Timothy Richard of China*, 321. According to Walls, 243, Richard had been working on his memoir since at least 1907, when the CLS published an early short version in *Conversion by the Million*. In a 1909 letter, Richard related how fellow missionary Arthur Smith had urged him to give this high priority.

RICHARD'S GLOBAL VISION

While in China, Richard had been thrown into an unplanned role as a senior statesman, as his advice and mediation were sought by imperial and Western antagonists. Through his peace making, he hoped to improve Sino-Western relations so as to reduce widespread Chinese anti-foreignism and open minds to the Christian gospel. Working with missionary educators from all denominations and with Roman Catholic representatives, he developed an ecumenical approach to advising the Court, with an eye to creating greater religious liberty that would allow greater Christian influence. Richard was especially supportive and active in the periodic all-China missionary conferences of 1887, 1890, and 1907 since they resulted in more of the united actions he long had promoted. His career was marked by a rare degree of influence in international church and missionary circles, which he exercised especially during his travels away from the China field. He served as a delegate to the World Baptist Conference in London in 1905 and to the World Missionary Conference in Edinburgh in 1910.

Increasingly, Richard sought audiences beyond Christian circles, in the peace movement and the world of diplomacy. During travel to England for his first furlough in 1896–97, he appealed to mission societies to work together for peace but also published a booklet, "League of Peace for Princes," that he sent to all heirs-apparent in Europe. In 1900, visiting the U.S. to speak at an international mission conference, Richard met U.S. officials in the capital to request political intervention to prevent imminent violence in China, and he also gave speeches in Boston and Paris proposing an international "Parliament of Man" to create and apply international law. Encouraged by enthusiasm within the network of Peace Societies, in 1903 and 1904, both in Tokyo and Peking, he discussed with political leaders his idea for a Federation of the (ten) Powers, with a joint army and navy to keep each other in check and police the world. During the 1904–5 Russo-Japanese War, his mediation and relief efforts as Shanghai's new Red Cross Society's secretary for China enhanced both his authority and experience in peace making.

During his third furlough in 1905, Richard was a delegate to the Lucerne Peace Conference, which he addressed with his proposal to create a federation to ensure universal peace; organizers promised to take it up during the next Hague Conference (although the agenda in 1907 was hijacked by Germany). On the advice of the British and American presidents of the Inter-Parliamentary Union for Peace, Richard returned to China in 1906 via the US with introductions to meet with President Roosevelt, who had just won the Nobel Peace Prize for mediating the Russo-Japanese peace. Richard obtained his tepid agreement to meet with a special envoy from China to discuss disarmament, but new appointees in charge of foreign affairs back in Peking proved both unconvinced and too timid to try. He had greater success with Prince Ito in 1908 and with lectures to various Peace Societies in 1910–11, and he was hopeful that an imminent U.S.-UK treaty of arbitration would kick-start the federation process. But all such hopes were put on hold by the German declaration of war in 1914. Whether Richard may be considered a "foster father" of the post-war League of Nations is worth future exploration.[10]

Another brief look at the philosophical milieu at the turn of the century helps to explain his increasing attention to international relations. The progressive ideology of reform assumed a steady movement toward worldwide economic development and social progress, culminating in a new era of international peace and order. Thus for Richard and other backers of reform, Western education was not just a means of achieving national prosperity and power in China (and elsewhere) for its own sake, but ultimately these outcomes would bring about world peace rooted in Christianity, or even a unified religion.

An assumption of human perfectibility served as the link between some of the more utopian ideas of both Western progressivism and Chinese reformism. When Richard met again in 1913 with 1898 reformers Kang Youwei and Liang Qichao, Kang spoke of his belief in the fatherhood of God and brotherhood of man, and his hope that one day all nations would be united under one government. Liang over the years developed a grand theory of world history in three ages, with the worldwide spread of science, democracy, prosperity, and peace leading to an age of *datong* (great harmony), an ancient Confucian ideal. These ideas may have reflected long contact with Richard, who had drafted a scheme for world federation as far back as 1879, and who had suggested to at least one Chinese official in 1898 that China seek to form a universal arbitration court with the Western Powers to end militarism and war. World War I would shatter such illusions among both Westerners and Chinese.[11]

---

10. Richard, *Forty-five Years*, 367–76; Johnson, "Timothy Richard's Theory," 254, discusses the details of this "Scheme for Federation." See E.I.R., "A Foster Father."

11. Richard, *Forty-Five Years*, 353, 367; Levenson, *Liang Ch'i-Ch'ao*, 38–40.

Giving Honor Where Honor is Due

A RICH BUT LITTLE-KNOWN LEGACY

Historians who have researched the educational reforms of late Qing China have rarely investigated why the Court set up the Imperial University of Shansi, an inland province far from Peking or the coast where the other select modern government institutions were located. As a result, Timothy Richard's Shanxi experience and legacy have been hidden. In similar fashion, few historians have thoroughly rooted out the sources of information about the West obtained by the Chinese reformers. Because China borrowed translations from Japan and there were some Chinese, such as Wang Tao, doing direct translations, it was often assumed that this information came through them. Meanwhile, the writings and publications of Young J. Allen and Timothy Richard remain in the shadows. In particular, Richard's profound influence on the thinking of Kang Yuwei and Liang Qichao is largely unknown.

Not since his birth centennial in 1945 has there been a full appreciation for Richard's work: "In dealing with a man of his calibre there are of course many imponderables which cannot be tabulated or measured, but the seeds sown have since borne good fruit. He builded [sic] better than he knew, and was one of the founders of the new order coming into being in China. His mind gave out flashes of intuition and often lit a flame in other minds."[12]

Notwithstanding all the recognition in China and the West during Richard's own lifetime, there are only a few historians since the mid-twentieth century who recognize the breadth, sincerity, and impact of his work. There are no monuments built in his honor, nor any buildings named for him. This may well change as we learn the results of ongoing current work of a younger generation of scholars, with more objective post-Cold War perspectives on the history of modern China.

A harbinger of renewed respect in China for Timothy Richard appeared in 2002, when he was recognized as a co-founder of Shanxi University in historical displays during its centennial celebration (based on the post-imperial founding date). A replica of the entrance gate of the original university campus is framed by prominent busts of Timothy Richard and Governor Cen Chunxuan. The statues of these two co-founders and joint chancellors of the Imperial University of Shansi keep silent vigil over students passing through this area of the modern campus. Set at an oblique

---

12. Burt, "Timothy Richard," 298.

Timothy Richard's Vision

angle, they both seem to gaze into the future, but appropriately from different perspectives. On May 8, 2002, while attending Shanxi University's celebration, I was among those who remembered the school's earliest beginnings and the world-encompassing vision of the Reverend Dr. Timothy Richard.

Epilogue

IN SEPTEMBER 2011, RUTH Hayhoe was approached by Oxford University's faculty of education and asked if she would travel to Oxford later that year to serve as external examiner for Aisi Li's thesis, by then near completion. She invited me to join her, and I began to do extensive research in order to discover where Timothy Richard was buried. I knew he had died in London in 1919, just three years after his return in 1916 from China and forty-eight years after he had begun his missionary work there in 1870. So I assumed his remains might be in Highgate cemetery, but an extensive search finally ended at Golders Green, London's earliest crematorium, founded in 1902. In the process of this search I also discovered that a great-grandson of Richard, Bjorn Napier Hansen, lived not far from London, and we arranged to meet.

Ruth and I flew from Miami to London on December 17, 2011, arriving in the early morning of December 18 and proceeding to Oxford for the successful doctoral thesis oral examination on Monday morning, December 19. The following day we three returned to London and prepared for a pilgrimage to Golders Green with Bjorn and his wife Sheila.

When we all met at Golders Green on Wednesday morning, the sun was shining on an unusually warm December day. Standing together in the quiet confines of the columbarium, surrounded by niches, each with its plaque of remembrance, we held our own memorial service. Ruth began by reading verses from Matthew 10, which Richard had used to explain the calling that had shaped his work in China—a mandate to reach out to leaders of the people along the lines of Jesus' words: "Whatever town or village you enter, search for some worthy person there and stay at his house until you leave. As you enter the house, give it your greeting. If the house is worthy, let your peace be upon it" (Matt 10:11–13).

I followed this with a prayer of thanksgiving:

Timothy Richard's Vision

> In the name of the Father, the Son and the Holy Spirit: Almighty God and Father of all mankind, Your great love sent Jesus Christ, Your son, to earth to live among us and to shed His blood and die, finally to be raised from the dead. All we who believe that He came to show Your great forgiveness of sin and to welcome us into Your family, became brothers and sisters through Him. I thank You for this and all other gifts and blessings You have given us. Precious Heavenly Father, the three of us stand here, plus Bjorn and Sheila, honoring the man Timothy Richard. In the fullness of time You sent him to live his life and do the good works that You prepared for him to do, even from before the foundations of the earth were created. Thank You for his life, his testimony, and his faith in You, and all his efforts for the uplift of China and peace in China. Thank You for all the wisdom You gave him to negotiate with Governor Cen to settle the Boxer difficulties and to establish the unified Imperial University of Shansi, which continues today more than one hundred years later as Shanxi University. He envisioned that this institution would benefit both the Province and China. We are three generations of scholars who have researched Timothy Richard's contributions to higher education in China. We ask Your blessing for that continued work through Aisi and Ruth. So as we honor this man Timothy Richard, all the glory and praise and thanksgiving belong to You for his life, well lived, but we also thank You for Mary, his helpmate in labors until her death, and also his second wife Ethel who tenderly cared for him a few short years until his death. Thank You for his daughters. Glory to God in the highest, and on earth peace to men on whom His favor rests. Bless us all. Amen.

After the prayer, Aisi placed a vase with four white roses in front of the plaque, which bore the simple words "In Most Happy Memory of Timothy Richard, Li T'i-mo-t'ai. Blessed are the Peacemakers, for they shall be called the children of God." Above Richard's plaque was an empty niche, which the caretaker assured us was likely to remain empty. There I placed a stone and feather from my 2002 visit to the memorial site of Moir Duncan in Shanxi, symbolically bringing these two missionaries together again. This day fulfilled my dream of more than twenty years, to stand at this final resting place and honor the life and contributions of the Welsh Baptist missionary to China (serving 1870–1916), the Rev. Dr. Timothy Richard.

Afterword

IN FRONT OF THE Yilun Hall of the Guozijian (the highest learning center of the old Imperial education system) in Beijing, on the fence underneath the statue of Confucius, I saw hundreds of small red wooden plaques with wishes written on them. The majority of these expressed the same timeless wish: to pass the College Entrance Examination.

I saw this wall of wishes in June 2013, nearly a century after Timothy Richard left China. During this past century, China has changed greatly. It is no longer a country rife with severe famine, widespread poverty, and violent revolts, as it was in Richard's time. Yet certain aspects remain unchanged, as if waves of reforms and revolutions had barely touched them. Among these is the Chinese belief in the value of education.

Young people nowadays who are endeavoring to gain a place in college do not necessarily know how the institution of the university came into being in China. Few can recall who were involved in laying the foundation of China's higher education. Some might perhaps quote a handful of prominent Chinese figures in the late Qing, such as Li Hongzhang and Zhang Zhidong, making the emergence of modern higher education sound almost indigenous. But this is not the whole picture.

After starting my doctoral research on British influence on China's education, focusing on the case of the Imperial University of Shansi, I came to realize that foreign missionaries had significant input into China's transition into an industrial society. Their imprint can be found in many areas: they established clinics and hospitals and subsequently provided medical training to the Chinese; they launched campaigns to abolish foot binding for women; they participated in the founding of charitable organizations; they published newspapers and facilitated the emergence of modern journalism. The list could go on and on. My research focused on the efforts of the missionaries to enlighten the Chinese through systematic education and their contribution to the foundation of contemporary education in China, a story often omitted by mainland Chinese official sources.

My research connected me with Professor Ruth Hayhoe at the New Scholars Workshop, part of the annual conference of the Comparative and International Education Society. She suggested that I visit Dr. Eunice Johnson, who wrote her doctoral thesis on Timothy Richard. After a few emails with Eunice, I postponed my flight back to the UK, and flew to Gainesville, Florida, to meet her.

Upon entering her flat, I was stunned to see the boxes of research materials in the living room. Eunice had already prepared well for my visit, and even sorted the materials for me. For her, my research was far more than a dissertation—it symbolized passing on the quest for the connection between Christian missionaries and China, and thus rediscovering the missionaries' legacy, known these days only to a few.

Going through the materials, including photocopies of primary sources, correspondence with scholars, and pages of research notes, I could almost see Eunice reading in the archives, writing to other researchers, or calling various libraries to find further information. I could also imagine the excitement on her face whenever a new source came to light.

Her research on Timothy Richard and his involvement in Chinese society did not cease with the completion of her thesis. Even while I was there, she was constantly searching for new information on missionary work in China. Such scholarly pursuit makes her an expert on missionary work in China, especially that of Timothy Richard. I remember discussing with her the real identity of an undisclosed Chinese official in Richard's *Forty-five Years in China*. Eunice said that Richard was a gentle person and that it was unlikely he would openly criticize someone; instead, we might find the relevant information in his diaries. She was right.

One drawback of historical research is that historians do not have the luxury of traveling back in time to interview their subjects. However, it sometimes feels like Eunice did just that. I believe that this impression comes from the similarities shared between her and Richard: devotion to their work and concern for education in China, guided by their faith.

As Eunice has shown in this book, Timothy Richard was a dedicated missionary educator. During his time in China, not a single day passed without an expression of his desire to help the country strengthen itself. He turned his vision into action on many kinds of reform through actively engaging with the Chinese. Without a doubt, Richard is one of the most

Afterword

influential missionaries in modern Chinese history, and a pioneer in promoting cross-cultural understanding through international collaboration in higher education. Instead of emphasizing punishment and retaliation, which usually resulted in unresolved or aggravated hostility, Richard's handling of the post-conflict negotiations in 1901 between the Chinese and the missionaries set an example of reaching genuine reconciliation between the two groups, and thereby paved the way for future collaboration. This aspect certainly deserves further research from the perspectives of other fields, such as international relations and post-conflict reconstruction.

It was Richard's belief that the university should not only serve as a training ground for talented young people who would benefit the progress of their country, but it should also act as a platform for bridging different cultures and beliefs. His efforts to collaborate with like-minded Chinese officials eventually led to the creation of what became the Imperial University of Shansi, which housed the moral philosophies of both sides under the same roof. This innovative approach produced young people equipped with both Eastern and Western knowledge who helped transform Shanxi into one of the most advanced provinces in the country at the time.

I hope, one day, when Chinese students think about China's higher education, they will remember that Christian missionaries had an important role in the creation of modern China and its universities. I also hope that the enthusiasm, perseverance, and faith the missionaries had in their work will inspire the Chinese youth to overcome any obstacle and to pursue their dreams.

Aisi Li
January 2014

1. Timothy Richard's birthplace in Ffaldybrenin, Wales, 1845.

2. Richard, recently ordained, departing for China, age 24, November 1869.

3. Timothy and Mary Richard with Eleanor and Mary Celia (below), ca. 1882.

4. Richard, aged 45, just a few months before call to CLS (Christian Literature Society for China), 1890.

廣 學 會

Society for the Diffusion of Christian and General
Knowledge among the Chinese.

1 QUINSAN ROAD,

All Orders for Books and Periodicals to be sent to the Manager Mission Press, Shanghai.

More books published. Memorial ready. More about Mr Walshe

Shanghai, Aug 28th, 1895.

My Beloved Wife

Yours of July 23 which you say will be the last is come to hand. Many thanks for all its sweet contents but I am sorry it is the last. I have also your letter a week previous which arrived since I sent my last.

I write to explain my present movements. Last night I telegraphed to Mr Walshe a C. M. S. man at Shao Hing who wants to go with me to Peking. In a week I intend leaving for Peking and it will be the begining of October I expect before I return. It is to arrange about presenting the memorial.

5. Letter from Richard on SDK letterhead to his wife, telling of imminent travel to Peking to meet with officials and reformers, August 28, 1895.

6. Richard, meeting with elite Hanlin scholar-officials in Peking, September 1895.

7. Mary Richard, ca. 1894.

8. Richard with daughters, L-R Margaret (Maggie), Mary Celia (Mary), Florence (Florrie), Eleanor (Ella), 1908.

9. New office building in Shanghai for Christian Literature Society for China, 1909.

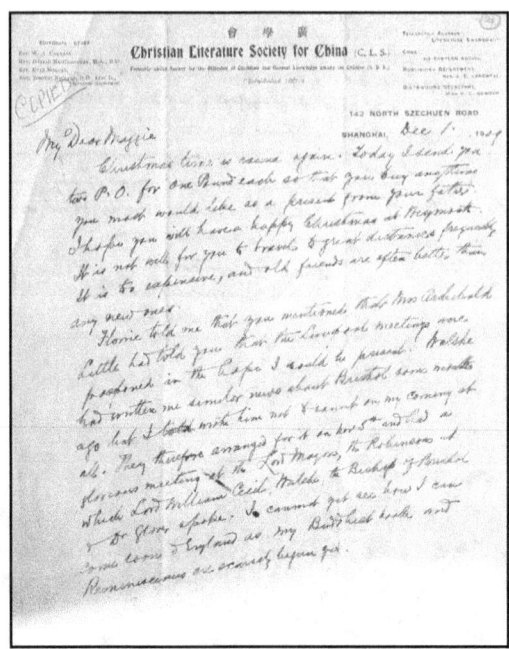

10. Richard's letter to his daughter from the new CLS address, referring to initial work on a Buddhist translation and his memoir, 1909.

11. Richard gave his 8000 volume library to the CLS, 1909.

12. Gov. Cen Chunxuan, co-founder and co-chancellor of the Imperial University of Shansi (IUS).

13. Peace Commission with Chinese officials in Taiyuan, Shanxi, July 1901. L-R seated: A. Orr Ewing, Daodai of Circuit, Dr. E.H. Edwards, Fandai (Treasurer), Daodai Shen Dunhe; standing: unidentified, Maj. Pereira, C.H. Tjader, Dr. Atwood, D.E. Hoste, Dr. Creasy Smith, Rev. Moir B. Duncan (interpreter).

14. IUS co-founder and co-chancellor Richard in Chancellor's robes, n.d.

15–16. The campus of the Imperial University of Shansi: upper, entry gate; lower, library with clock tower, ca. 1906.

17. Administration Building, 1911, in 2002. Stone engraving in the foyer relates the history of the IUS founding and development.

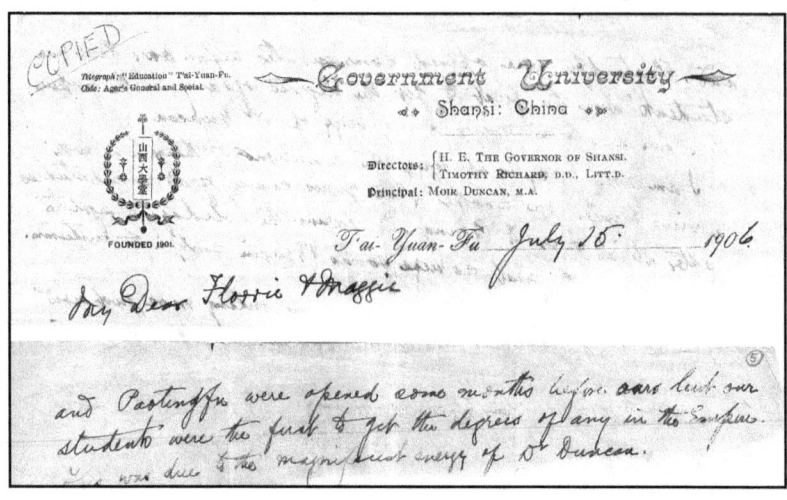

18. Richard wrote a letter to his daughters praising first IUS Principal Moir Duncan, July 25, 1906. (Note "Government University" letterhead listing co-directors Richard and the Shanxi Governor).

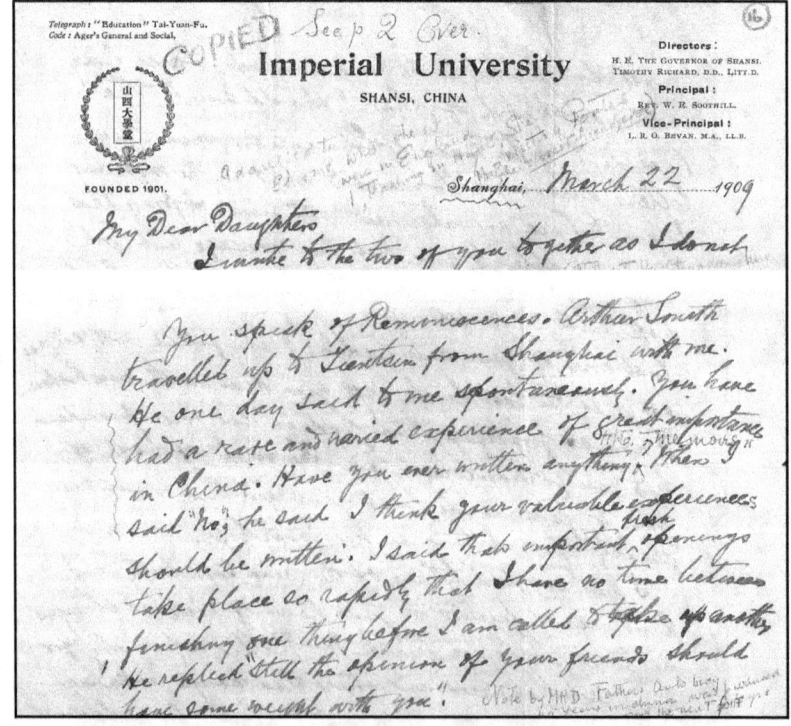

19. Richard wrote a letter to his daughters describing the origin of his memoir, 1909. (Note the change to "Imperial University" letterhead.)

20. University Principal Rev. Moir Duncan.

21. The first IUS graduates leaving for England to study; Richard top center, second Principal William Soothill lower right, summer 1910.

22. The banner reads "commemorating the ceremony for the handover of the Western Department," Richard in the center, L-Shanxi Gov. (Ding Baoquan?), R-Principal Soothill, November 1910.

23–24. Richard with Imperial decoration for the order of the Double Dragon, ca. 1907, and an additional Red Cross medal for humanitarian work in the Russo-Japanese War (1904–5), n.d.

25. Richard in retirement with second wife Ethel Tribe, his daughters and family in New Brunswick, Canada, summer 1916.

26. Richard, age 73, with Ethel, 1918.

27–29. Shanxi U. centennial: Busts of Co-founders Timothy Richard and Cen Chunxuan, in front of a replica of the early campus gate, 2002.

30. Stone inscription sealing the niche containing Timothy Richard's urn, with mementos (above) from Moir Duncan's memorial site in China, Golders Green Crematorium, East Columbarium, London. See Epilogue.

Author's Biographical Sketch and Acknowledgments

MY HEART WAS FIRST opened to Asia during the mid-1950s, when I spent my first two years of junior high school in public schools on Oahu, Hawaii, while my father was stationed at Barber's Point Naval Air Station, but it would be many years before I would actually travel to any Asian country. After graduating from Newberry College in South Carolina and working for two years, I entered graduate school, and in 1970 I received a master of education degree from the University of South Carolina, where I had specialized in testing/psychological services. I then worked for the state as a psychologist, first with the Department of Vocational Rehabilitation, then Fairfield County Follow-Through Program, and finally the South Carolina Commission for the Blind.

These years came to a close in 1979, after I became a born-again, Spirit-baptized Christian and received spiritual confirmation that I was to change professional focus. The next year while I waited, seeking what I should do then, God clearly showed me through his Word and several circumstances that one day I would go to China. This became a reality in 1985 when I taught English in Taiyuan, China, at Shanxi Medical College, followed by stints at Shanxi Finance and Economics College in Taiyuan and later at the Luoyang Institute of Technology in Henan Province. These years were life-changing and enriching, and I wanted to remain in China; but I returned to the US to celebrate my father and mother's fiftieth wedding anniversary. The next year, both my personal situation and the political circumstances in China changed, so I chose to enter a graduate program in Comparative and International Education in the University of Florida's College of Education, where with the relentless encouragement of the program director Dr. Renner, I became a PhD candidate.

I arrived at my research question through what many would call chance, but I believe to be the leading of the Holy Spirit of God. While seeking a paper topic for a course on modern Chinese history, Professor Edward McCord suggested that I research the Shanxi warlord Yan Xishan (Yen Hsi-shan) since I had spent time teaching in Shanxi, and he gave me bibliographical information for a book on Yan. While perusing this book, I learned that the great American educational philosopher John Dewey had lectured at Shanxi University during his two-year sojourn in China (1919–21). I wondered why he would go there; after all, I had visited its campus, and it did not seem special enough to warrant his visit. My interest piqued, I considered doing a dissertation on this period in Dewey's life.

While searching on the computer for materials about China, I came across the entry for *Forty-five Years in China: Reminiscences by Timothy Richard*, printed in 1916. Assuming it would give good context to my Dewey research, I ordered and received the book through interlibrary loan. As I flipped through the pages, my eye caught the chapter title "Famine Relief in Shansi." I said to myself, "That's my province." Further on, the chapter entitled "Shansi University" stunned me. I suddenly realized that I was holding the answer to a question I had asked a companion some five years before in Taiyuan: "Who were the missionaries you say founded Shanxi University?" Now with Richard's autobiography in hand, I had the answer and immediately knew that I would do my dissertation either about this university or its founder, the Welsh Baptist missionary Timothy Richard.

Early in my doctoral program, I elected to take a course in qualitative research from Dr. Robert Sherman; I was tired of thinking of educational research only in terms of statistics. In this class I was inspired, even challenged, to develop a dissertation research question of a qualitative nature that was not only scholarly but also one with which I could passionately wrestle for a number of years. By serendipity, I had already discovered the general subject for my research; now I had "permission" from Dr. Sherman to passionately engage my subject.

As I tried to locate information about Richard, I found that little research had been done on him. Other than a few research papers and a couple of master's theses I located later, the only complete study since 1945 was a doctoral dissertation in 1966 by Sister Virginia Therese (Dr. Rita Johnson), who by this time was retired from St. John's University and living at the Maryknoll Sisters' Motherhouse in New York state. Around the same time, I had a conversation with the Regent Park College Angus Library archivist in Oxford, England, and I discovered that someone had recently requested information about Shanxi University—the granddaughter of the

Author's Biographical Sketch and Acknowledgments

man whom Richard had appointed as the first principal of the Western Department of the Imperial University of Shansi, and she was living in Toronto. In 1992, I was privileged to spend time with both women. First came a couple of wonderful days with a busy, intellectually keen, eighty-something Maryknoll Missioner. On the same train trip, I then spent ten days in Toronto with Doreen Raymer and her husband Ron, pouring over her grandparents' correspondence and doing research at the University of Toronto and at the office of the Overseas Missionary Fellowship (formerly the China Inland Mission). It was on this trip that I met Dr. Ruth Hayhoe, whose research on Chinese higher education had further spurred my curiosity about how an imperial university of modern learning came to be founded in such a remote inland province.

While reading Richard's articles and letters, of which I have since located many inside and outside of archives, it became clear that I could combine the three great passions of my life—Jesus, China, and education—while I engaged in dissertation research on the question, "In what ways did the educational vision Richard disseminated contribute to the reform of higher education in China, l880–1910?" I believe his contributions continue to leave their stamp on higher education and otherwise in China, even in the People's Republic of China in the twenty-first century. It was a personal honor and privilege to present a copy of my dissertation to the officials of Shanxi University on the occasion of the celebration of its centennial on May 8, 2002.

This book publication refines that earlier dissertation to show how Richard's pioneering efforts in education were a central means to achieving an even broader vision—the building of the Kingdom of God among the Chinese. Given the paucity of full-length studies of Richard for nearly seventy years, my offering is a long-overdue attempt to underscore for a new generation of readers Richard's many and varied contributions to China's development and to celebrate his far-reaching vision for change during a most critical time of China's modern history.

Learning about Timothy Richard has been an adventure of discovery—almost like a treasure hunt—and was possible only with the support and assistance of many whom I wish to thank. From the beginning, my steps have been directed by the Holy Spirit of God for the continued revelation and unfolding of his good and perfect will to advance the Kingdom of God on earth as it is in heaven. "Unless the Lord builds the house, they labor in vain who build it" (Ps 127:1a NKJV).

Timothy Richard's Vision

My core dissertation committee remained supportive during the decade of my doctoral program, especially the chairman, Dr. Richard R. Renner, to whom I am deeply grateful for the freedom to combine the great passions in my life. Other University of Florida faculty who served as committee members or advisers included Drs. Arthur Newman, Arthur White, Gene Thursby, Cynthia Chennault, and Michael Ts'in. I am most deeply grateful to Dr. Edward A. McCord who began this journey with me while at the University of Florida and continued with me until its completion, even after joining the faculty at George Washington University in 1994.

I owe many thanks as well to the efforts of many in the following institutions: the College of Education and George Smathers Libraries at the University of Florida; the University of Toronto; Maryknoll Seminary in Ossining, New York; Johns Hopkins University; the University of South Carolina; the University of Wales; Angus Library at Regent's Park College in Oxford (especially Dr. Julian Lock and Ms. Emily Burgoyne); the Overseas Ministries Study Center and the Yale University Divinity School Library (especially Joan Duffy and Martha Smalley) in New Haven, Connecticut; and the Overseas Missionary Fellowship in Toronto. I was also provided access to the archives at the Historical Commission of the Southern Baptist Convention, the National Library of Wales, the Presbyterian Church (USA), and the personal collection of Mrs. Doreen Raymer. I also would thank the late Mrs. Kathrine Gibbs, who provided invaluable assistance in Wales, locating information and photographing significant sites of Richard's life.

I was blessed with scholarships from Kappa Delta Pi International Honor Society in Education (the Gerald H. Read Laureate Doctoral Scholarship in International and Comparative Education); the University of Florida Chapter of Phi Kappa Phi (the Harry H. Sisler Graduate Student Award); the University of Florida Asian Studies Program (the Alice M. Zirger Memorial Scholarship in Asian Studies); and the University of Florida Upsilon Chapter of Kappa Delta Pi (the Robert Curran Memorial Scholarship).

My sisters Claire and Dawn and my brother Loys encouraged and supported me in every sense of the word, and my late father and mother instilled in me the value of education early in my life. Taking steps toward my early vision of going to China was especially pleasant due to the partnership of my dear friend and comrade teacher, Lydia D. Holly, when we taught at Shanxi Medical College in Taiyuan from February 1985 through

Author's Biographical Sketch and Acknowledgments

February 1986. I am grateful for my many Chinese friends and students in China who opened their hearts and lives to me, starting with "Yo-Yo," and am deeply thankful for the continuing faithful prayers and encouragements from the Gainesville Chinese Christian Church since 1988.

I especially wish to acknowledge the personal encouragement, information sharing, and hospitality offered during my visits with Ron and Doreen Raymer of Toronto and Sister Virginia Therese. Friendship, as well as special assistance by correspondence, were offered through the years by Dr. Xu Xiaoguang at Vanderbilt University; Dr. Cyril G. Williams at the University of Wales-Lampeter; Mr. Archie C. Hills, librarian at the Bible College of Wales in Swansea; and Dr. Ruth Hayhoe at the Ontario Institute for Studies in Education. I met Evergreen Family Friendship Service staff at a picnic in Taiyuan during my visit there for the Shanxi University Centennial Celebration in 2002, and this began a mutual relationship of prayer and encouragement for which I continue now to be most humbly grateful.

In 2004 my life took an unexpected turn when I was diagnosed with a rare blood cancer, Waldenstrom's macroglobulinemia. Since then there have been many medical tests, treatments, and health challenges. But in March 2011, I felt strong and well enough to accept Dr. Hayhoe's long-standing invitation to visit her and her husband Walter in south Florida. When Ruth asked specific questions about my dissertation, I had to confess that I had not read it since 2001 and due to cancer treatments did not remember things well, so I really could not discuss it in detail. Instead, we spoke heart to heart about other matters. I had a lovely visit and discovered a sister in the faith. Also during that visit, we daydreamed about going to England together when the Oxford scholar Aisi Li, who had stayed in my home while researching, received her doctorate. See the Epilogue on the fulfillment of that dream in December 2011.

After that trip, I thought my engagement with Richard had ended, but long ago in a recommendation letter she had written for me, Ruth had first suggested this topic was worthy of a book. Now, years later, after Ruth wrote a review of the *Salt and Light* book series edited by Dr. Carol Lee Hamrin, Ruth and Carol have committed their time and resources to make this book publication a reality. Carol has ably and creatively taken the various threads of our efforts to weave together the tapestry of this volume. We thank her colleagues Stacey Bieler, Laura Mason, and Anna Barnes for editorial assistance, and Tom Bieler for technical help on illustrations. Ruth wrote the foreword and did a second read. We invited Oxford scholar Dr. Li to write the afterword, which moved me to tears. Words are insufficient to express my gratitude to all three, but especially to Carol and Ruth who I know are sisters in the faith and have become friends.

We have been granted permission to use previously unpublished photos, letters, and other family information related to Richard, which have been brought to light and graciously shared by Richard's great-grandchildren Phillip Dixon, Bjorn N. Hanson, K. Lewis, and Jennifer Peles. Jennifer has spent many hours finding and digitizing material for us. I am deeply grateful for their efforts on behalf of this book and also the gracious sharing of their lives during this journey into the enduring legacy of their great-grandfather, Timothy Richard of Wales.

TO GOD BE ALL THE GLORY, HONOR, PRAISE, AND THANKSGIVING!

Contributors

DR. CAROL LEE HAMRIN, editor, is senior associate with the Global China Center and a research professor at George Mason University (2000–12), both in Virginia. Hamrin holds a PhD in Chinese and comparative world history from the University of Wisconsin–Madison and served twenty-five years as a research specialist for the US Department of State. Hamrin received the Center for Public Justice Leadership Award for outstanding public service in 2003, has taught in graduate schools in the Washington, DC, area, and has published widely. Her books include three volumes of *Salt and Light: Lives of Faith that Shaped Modern China* (2009, 2010, and 2011), edited with Stacey Bieler; *God and Caesar in China: Policy Implications of Church-State Tensions* (2004), edited with Jason Kindopp; *Decision-Making in Deng's China* (1995), edited with Suisheng Zhao; and *China and the Challenge of the Future* (1990).

DR. RUTH HAYHOE, author of the foreword, is a professor at the Ontario Institute for Studies in Education of the University of Toronto. Her professional affiliations include serving as director of the Hong Kong Institute of Education (1997–2002), head of the Cultural Section of the Canadian Embassy in Beijing (1989–1991), and foreign expert at Fudan University in Shanghai (1980–82). She is the author of *China's Universities and the Open Door* (1989); *China's Universities 1895-1995: A Century of Cultural Conflict* (1996, 2001); and *Portraits of Influential Chinese Educators* (2006); and she is co-author of *Portraits of 21st Century Chinese Universities: In the Move to Mass Higher Education* (2011). Honors include Honorary Fellow (Comparative and International Education Society 2011 and University of London Institute of Education 1998); Silver Bauhinia Star (Hong Kong SAR Government 2002); and Commandeur dans l'ordre des Palmes Académiques (Government of France 2002).

Dr. Aisi Li, author of the Afterword, completed her DPhil in Educational Studies at the University of Oxford. Her thesis, *Competition and Compromise between British Missionaries and Chinese Officials: The Founding of Shanxi University in 1902*, explores the complex process through which a foreign model enters another local context. Her research interests include cross-border partnership in higher education, educational policy transfer, and higher education in transition.

Appendix 1

Chronology of Timothy Richard's Life

1845	Born (October 10) in Ffaldybrenin, Caermarthenshire, Wales.
1859	Baptized in River Caio, Caermarthenshire, Wales.
1860	Received "call" to foreign missionary service.
1865–69	Studied in Haverfordwest Theological College.
1869	Sailed for China (November 17).
1870	Arrived in Shanghai, China (February 12); arrived in Yantai (Chefoo), Shandong (February 27).
1871	Traveled through Manchuria to distribute printed gospels.
1872	Attempted to settle in Ninghai and then Laiyang; returned to Yantai.
1873	Visited Jinan, Shandong, first time.
1875	Settled in Chingzhou, Shandong; developed friendly relations with Muslims, Taoists, other religious leaders, and hermits; baptized first converts outside West Gate of town; prepared catechism and hymn book.
1876–77	Administered famine relief in Shandong.
1877–79	Administered famine relief in Shanxi.
1878	Married Ms. Mary Martin of United Presbyterian Mission, Scotland (October 26); settled in Taiyuan, Shanxi.
1880	Visited Peking to memorialize throne on Russo-China hostilities; met with Li Hongzhang, viceroy of Zhili (north China) in Tianjin.

Appendix 1

1881–84	Offered monthly lectures and scientific demonstrations to officials and scholars in Taiyuan.
1881	Met with Zuo Zongtang, viceroy of Shaanxi and Gansu (northwest China), and Zhang Zhidong, governor of Shanxi; visited sacred Buddhist mountain Wu Tai; returned to Chingzhou to take care of mission during A. G. Jones's furlough; became seriously ill in Jinan.
1884	Visited Peking; met with Sir Harry Parkes regarding protection of missionaries and native Christians; exchanged ideas about the reform of China with Sir Robert Hart; established Evangelical Alliance.
1885–86	Returned to England on first furlough; presented educational scheme for China to Baptist Missionary Society (BMS); made suggestions for improved mission methods; was sorely disappointed in BMS refusal to endorse educational scheme or mission suggestions.
1886	Tried to raise support for educational scheme; visited Europe to investigate education; then to China.
1887	Accused by some Taiyuan colleagues of unorthodoxy; mounted defense against charges of heresy and unorthodox mission methodology; left Shanxi Province, going first to Tianjin and finally staying in Peking.
1888	Developed friendship with Marquis Zeng Jize, son of Zeng Guofan who suppressed the Taiping Rebellion; studied Chinese Mahayana Buddhism and Lamaism; visited Japan to study education and mission methodology; wrote pamphlet *Modern Education*.
1889	Moved to Tianjin; recommended to the BMS the founding of a newspaper for officials and scholars and establishment of a college of Western learning in Jinan, provincial capital of Shandong; considered relocating back to Shandong; made two trips to Shandong, the latter to assist in famine relief and to attend Shandong provincial missionary conference and there contracted "famine fever"; the BMS refused to support establishment of college in Shandong.

Chronology of Timothy Richard's Life

1890	Attended Second General Missionary Conference in Shanghai and read paper "The Relation of Christian Missions to the Chinese Government"; invited by Viceroy Li to become editor of reformist newspaper *Shi Bao* (*The Times*).
1891	Released as editor (June); appointed general secretary of the Society for the Diffusion of Christian and General Knowledge Among the Chinese in October (SDK; hereafter Christian Literature Society for China, name as of 1906); presented educational scheme to Li before leaving Tianjin; relocated to Shanghai; concentrated on literary and translation work; involved with educational work in Shanghai.
1894	Finished translation of Mackenzie's *Nineteenth Century: A History*; invited to three meetings with Zhang Zhidong, now viceroy of Nanjing; met with Zhang Yinhuan, official peace envoy to Japan.
1895	Went to Peking to prepare Mission Memorial for presentation to the Throne; gained interviews with Li, "Prime Minister" Weng Tonghe, Prince Gong, Foreign Office (Zongli Yamen) members, and other officials; presented reform scheme to prime minister, later approved by emperor; met reformer Kang Youwei (October 17) first time; had discussions with various Reform Society members; advised reformers concerning their newspaper and strategies.
1896	Presented Mission Memorial to Foreign Office; had last meeting with Li; Prime Minister Weng Tonghe paid farewell call on Richard, unprecedented for a missionary.
1896–97	Left for second furlough to England; met Viceroy Li aboard ship as Li was going to attend the coronation of the czar of Russia; visited India, Marseilles, Paris, London; appealed to mission societies in interests of peace and federation of nations: published booklet for use of young statesmen.

Appendix 1

1898	Returned to China via Canada and the US; continued efforts to support reform through Reform Society; participated in Hundred Days' Reform movement; assisted reformers to escape after the coup by empress dowager.
1899	Went to Peking to present an educational scheme for China but discussed it privately with several officials instead; met with Sir Robert Hart; was granted interviews with Rong Lu, Kang Yi, and other officials; elected president of the Educational Association of China (EAC).
1900	Spoke in New York at ecumenical conference on missions on "The Need and Value of Literary Work for Missions;" warned of impending upheaval against Christians; appealed to mission, government, and business leaders to protect reformers and Christians in China from persecution; awarded honorary D.D. by Emory College, Oxford, GA; returned to China via Japan; attempted to marshal intervention on behalf of Christians caught in the Boxer Uprising.
1901	Invited by Peace Plenipotentiaries Li and Prince Qing to assist the Chinese government and the governor of Shanxi Province to settle the Boxer indemnity issues with the Protestant missionary societies; presented general principles for settlement to Li and Qing, including one for the establishment of a college of Western learning in the provincial capital of Taiyuan; ratified by Li and Qing with imperial approval by May 30; awarded honorary Litt.D. by Brown University, Providence, RI.
1902	Went in April to Taiyuan for inauguration of the college of Western learning; renegotiated original agreement; with the Shanxi governor co-founded the amalgamated Imperial University of Shansi (IUS) and was appointed joint chancellor with responsibility for the funds, personnel, and curriculum of the Western Department for ten years; approved and recorded in *Peking Gazette* July 3, 1902; appointed by imperial edict to be adviser to the emperor on behalf of Protestant missions.

1900–1902	Involved in developing public education for the Chinese in Shanghai.
1903	Visited Japan to secure textbooks for the IUS; interviewed Baron Kikuchi and Prince Konoye; grieved death of wife, Mary Richard; received highest rank of mandarin with a red button (first rank, first grade).
1904	Became Secretary of the Red Cross Society of China; went to Peking for interviews with Zhou Fu, Rong Lu, Prince Su, and Lu Chuanlin.
1905	Returned to England for third furlough; attended as delegate to World Baptist Conference in London; attended as delegate to Lucerne Peace Conference where he proposed Federation of Nations plan.
1906	Helped to form China Missions Emergency Committee and its delegation to investigate and plan united efforts to address the new situation in China.
1907	Attended Centenary (Third) General Mission Conference at Shanghai; decorated by the Chinese government with the Order of the Double Dragon (second order, second grade).
1908	Visited Korea and Japan; met with Prince Ito Hirobumi.
1909	Elected vice president of the EAC; began writing his memoir.
1910	Attended as delegate the World Missionary Conference in Edinburgh; initiated handover (November 15) of the Imperial University of Shansi to Chinese provincial government authorities.
1911	Completed devolution of the IUS (June); was in Shanghai at the outbreak of the Republican Revolution on October 10.
1912	Re-visited Chingzhou, Shandong, to attend first united conference of the religious leaders of various faiths.
1913	Visited Taoist center at Lao Shan; translated *Mission to Heaven*.

Appendix 1

1914	Visited Changsha, Hunan; married second time—missionary Dr. Ethel Tribe in Yokohama, Japan (August 14); offered to resign as CLS secretary but was persuaded to stay on for a year.
1915	Suffered serious illness; resigned as secretary of the CLS (Autumn) with honorary status as Secretary Emeritus; visited Java.
1916	Returned to England; awarded honorary LL.D. by University of Wales in Aberystwyth for his contributions to higher education in China; published his memoir *Forty-Five Years in China: Reminiscences*.
1918	Received Liang Qichao, who visited on his way to Versailles Peace Conference.
1919	Died April 17 following surgery; cremated and interred in Golders Green Crematorium, Northwest London.

Appendix 2

Compilation of Works in Chinese by Timothy Richard

Sources of the following chronological lists do not use consistent formats for referencing these old and sometimes obscure titles and authors, and the translation back into English from Chinese is inexact, often changing for reprints or new editions. Most are books; some may be tracts or articles. Some publication dates are approximate. Nonetheless, the lists reveal the scale and scope of Richard's literary work.

English Titles of Works in Chinese (Original, Translated, or Edited)	Approximate Date
The Story of the Fall and Redemption, by a Chinese Christian	1874
Philosophy of Plan of Salvation, by J. H. Walker	1875
A Catechism on the Christian Religion	1875
A Collection of Hymns for Use with Catechism	1875
Daniel Quorm, a Cornish Evangelist	1875
Introduction to the Devout Life, by Francis de Sales	1875
Holy Living, by Jeremy Taylor	1875–76
Very Short Tracts, Pasted on Chinese City Walls in Eleven Counties	1876
Adaptation of Standard Chinese Tracts without Idolatry	1876

Appendix 2

How Christianity Fulfills the Highest Aspirations of the Three Religions of China	1876/79
How to Pass the Great Examination (Mrs. Richard's translation of Dr. W. H. D. Rouse's work for India)	1879
The King's Messenger	?
Music of the World, volume one of ten	1880
One Hundred Suggestions for the Improvement of China	1881
Present Needs of China	1882
The World: Its Produce and Merchandise	?
Ten Dialogues on Religion, by Matteo Ricci (Adaptation of Ricci's Tien Chu Shih Yih, with A. G. Jones)	1882
"Stream of Time" (A Chart of the History of the Nations)	1883/94
Modern Education in Seven Nations	1891/99
Benefits of Christianity (Historical Evidence)	1892
Four Great Questions of the Times	1892? 1893?/98
The Earth as a Planet	1892? 1894?
Hope for the People	1893
Relative Strength of Nations	1893
Eight Great European Emperors from Alexander to Napoleon	1893/94
Looking Backward, by Edward Bellamy	1893? 1894?
Productive and Non-Productive Labour	1893? 1894?
Joint Stock Companies	1894?
English Law in China, by Consul G. Jamieson	1894?
Taxation	1894
The Religions of the World	1894
Sketch of the Chinese Endeavor Society	?
Treaties, Regulations, Edicts, etc., in Regard to Mission Work	1894
The Parables, by F. A. Krurnmacher	1894

Compilation of Works in Chinese by Timothy Richard

Salvation of the World	1894
Progress of China's Neighbors	1894/99
Outlines of History of Thirty-one Nations	1894/96
Grace before Meal	1894
Protestant Missionary Pioneers	1894/96
Three Prefaces on the Importance of Western Learning, by Li Hongzhang and Marquis Zeng	?
The Essentials of Recent Western History (a translation of The Nineteenth Century: A History, by Robert Mackenzie, with Cai Ergang/Ts'ai Er-kang)	1894/96
The Warning Bell from the West	1895
Revenue and Expenditure of the Chinese Empire, by Consul G. Jamieson	1895
Tariff and Lekin, by Consul G. Jamieson	?
Essays on Reform, by Seventeen Foreigners, four volumes	1895–96
Memorial on the Aims of Protestant Missions in China, with Statement of Christianity	1895? 1896?
Christian Biographies, ten volumes (with Mary Richard)	1896
The Renaissance of China	1897/99
Scheme of Education	1898
New Collection of Tracts for the Times, Thirty-one Essays	1898/1901
Curse of Opium	?
Right Principles of Universal Progress	1899/1909
Extension of Practical Learning	1900
Childhood of the World, by Edward Clodd	1899
Maps and Bible Pictures, series	1899
Diagram and Statistics of the Chief Religions of the World	1899
A Series of Maps Showing Gradual Discovery of the World	1899

Appendix 2

Social Evolution, by Benjamin Kidd	1899
The Chairman's Hand Book	1899
Elements of Practical Electricity	1899
Agricultural Chemistry	1899
An Essay on Man, by Alexander Pope	1899? 1900?
Reunion of Christendom, by Philip Schaff	1901
Church of the Catacombs, or Fabiola, by Cardinal N. P. Wiseman	1901
Nathan the Wise	1901
World's Hundred Greatest Men, 3 volumes, by F. M. Muller (w/ Cai Ergang and Lin Zhaozhi)	1901
Official Documents on Religious Liberty	1901/3
Old Testament Stories	1901
Everybody's Pocket Cyclopedia	1901
A Brief History of the Indian Peoples	1901
The Indian Empire, six volumes	1902
Permanent Peace and Prosperity for China	1902? 1903?
Relations of Advanced and Backward Nations	1903
The Christian Church, by Dean R. W. Church	1903? 1904?
The World's History, by Sir Roper Lethbridge (with Ding Xiong, Fei Xilin, Lu Fengsan)	1903
Outline of World History	1904
Outline of Timothy Richard's Work for China	1904
Anthropology of Universal Civilization, by Sir E. B. Tylor (edited with W. G. Walshe)	1904
England in Egypt, by Alfred Milner	1907
Industrial History of England	1907
Christian Theology (Catechism), by Sir Oliver Lodge (with A. G. Jones)	1907
History of the Indian Empire, by W. W. Hunter	1907
Twelve Years' Programme	1907
Peace for the World	1908

Compilation of Works in Chinese by Timothy Richard

Select Masterpieces of Biblical Literature, by R. G. Moulton (edited)	1908
The Substance of Faith Applied to Science, by Sir Oliver Lodge	1908
Essence of Christianity (with Cai Ergang and Dai Shiduo)	1908/9
A Primer of the Peace Movement	1909
Biographies of Eminent Christian Statesmen, Series	1912
Tracts for the Times	1912

TEXTS TRANSLATED INTO CHINESE FOR IMPERIAL UNIVERSITY OF SHANSI 1901-10

Atlas of Physical Geography, by Alexander K. Johnston

Atlas of Popular Astronomy, by Alexander K. Johnston

General History for School and Colleges, by F. V. N. Myers

History of Commerce in Europe, by H. de B. Gibbins

One Thousand Biographies, selected from Biographical Dictionary, by Chamber

The Wonderful Century, by Alfred Russel Wallace

Chronological Tables of the Chinese Dynasties, from the Chou to the Ch'ing

History of Russia, by Alfred Rambaud

Algebra, two volumes

Arithmetic, two volumes

Botany

Evolution, by Edward Clodd

Mineralogy

Pedagogy

Physics

Physiography

Physiology

Zoology

Appendix 2

SOURCES FOR LISTS ABOVE

Most of the Circulars Sent Out in Behalf of the Diffusion Society and the Christian Literature Society Between 1891–1901 by Timothy Richard (Shanghai: Christian Literature Society, 1907).

Semi-Jubilee Report of the CLS (1912), 31, summed up Richard's chief publications as:

1. 50 Books on the Works of God in order to improve the material condition of China

2. 37 Books on the Laws of God to improve the social, national, and international relationships

3. 33 Books on the Providence of God to improve education

4. 48 Books on the Grace of God to improve religion and character

Bowser, Hilda. *Timothy Richard, D.D., Litt.D., LL.D., An Outline of His Life and Work in China* (Shanghai: Christian Literature Society, 1914), 5–7. This source should be used with caution as it contains significant errors.

Clayton, G. A. *A Classified Index to the Chinese Literature of the Protestant Churches in China* (Shanghai: China Christian Publishers' Association, April 1918).

Lodwick, Kathleen. *The Chinese Recorder Index: A Guide to Christian Missions in Asia, 1867–1941*, Volume One (Wilmington, DE: Scholarly Resources, Inc., 1986), 405–6, lists articles in the *Chinese Recorder* by or about Timothy Richard.

MacGillivray, D. *Descriptive and Classified Missionary Centenary Catalogue of Current Christian Literature* (Shanghai: Christian Literature Society, 1907).

Mcintyre, W. E. *Baptist Authors: A Bibliography* (np, 1914).

Starr, Edward Caryl. *A Baptist Bibliography*, vol. 19 (Philadelphia: Judson Press, Samuel Colgate Baptist Historical Collection, Colgate University, 1947–76).

Whitefield, Douglas Brent. Appendix: CLS Chinese-language Books 1887–1911, "The Christian Literature Society for China: The Role of its Publications, Personalities, and Theology in Late-Qing Reform Movements" (PhD diss., University of Cambridge, 2001), 187–194.

Sources of Illustrations*

Cover Image, Richard, *Forty-five Years*, op 332.

1. Courtesy Fiona Dunlop.
2. Timothy Richard, *Forty-Five Years*, op 34.
3. Alfred Jones Papers, Special Collections, Yale Divinity School Library.
4. Courtesy Phillip Dixon.
5. Courtesy Jennifer Peles.
6. Reeve, *Timothy Richard*, 95, also in Richard, *Forty-five Years*, op 256.
7. Reeve, *Timothy Richard*, 125.
8. Courtesy Bjorn N. Hansen.
9. Richard, *Forty-five Years*, op 354.
10. Courtesy Jennifer Peles.
11. Soothill, *Timothy Richard of China*, op 280, also in Reeve, *Timothy Richard*, 139.
12. Richard, *Forty-five Years*, op 300.
13. Photo from Reeve, *Timothy Richard*, 113; list of names from Edwards, *Fire and Sword*, 140.
14. Courtesy Jennifer Peles.
15. Soothill, *Timothy Richard of China*, op 256.

* Photoshop was used to improve visual quality of scanned digital images by adjusting contrast and grayscale curves, some cropping, and minor touchups. All photographs from the early biographies of Timothy Richard, and from his memoir, are in the public domain. Some of the originals can be found in the Baptist Missionary Society Archives, the Angus Library and Archive, Regent's Park College.

Sources of Illustrations

16. Soothill, *Timothy Richard of China*, op 256.
17. Author's collection.
18. Courtesy Jennifer Peles.
19. Courtesy Jennifer Peles.
20. Richard, *Forty-five Years*, op 305.
21. Reeve, *Timothy Richard*, 135.
22. Reeve, *Timothy Richard*, 147.
23. Courtesy Jennifer Peles.
24. Richard, *Forty-five Years*, op 332.
25. Courtesy K. Lewis.
26. Courtesy Phillip Dixon.
27. Author's collection.
28. Author's collection.
29. Author's collection.
30. Courtesy Bjorn N. Hansen.

Bibliography

ARCHIVAL MATERIAL

Timothy Richard Papers, (English) Baptist Missionary Society (BMS) Archives (1880–1914), The Angus Library and Archives, Regent's Park College, (cited as BMS MSS), is the most extensive collection of Richard's personal papers. The author used the 200 Mss. available on microfilm from the Historical Commission, Southern Baptist Convention, Nashville, Tennessee, and which is also now at the Yale University Divinity School Library Special Collections (Microfilm: Film Ms56). All unpublished communications cited in this volume are from this collection, unless otherwise noted. Contextual clues indicate that many of Richard's papers have not been found, and may have been lost or destroyed during political crises in China or the bombing of London during World War II.

Timothy Richard Papers, Wyre Lewis Collection, National Library of Wales at Aberystwyth. (Cited as NLW.)

Moir and Jessie Duncan Papers, Personal Collection of Doreen Raymer, Toronto, Canada.

Eunice Johnson Collection on Timothy Richard 1867–2002 (Record Group 232), Yale University Divinity School Library Special Collections, China Records Project. This material—including the BMS MSS microfilm and sources listed below—is the most extensive collection of Timothy Richard material, primarily in English, in one location.

PUBLISHED WORKS BY TIMOTHY RICHARD IN ENGLISH (CHRONOLOGICAL ORDER)

1880–1889

"Some Thoughts About Christian Missions—Examinations." *Chinese Recorder* 11 (July–August 1880) 293–95.

"Thoughts on Christian Missions; Difficulties and Tactics." *Chinese Recorder* 11 (November–December 1880) 430–41.

"Christian Persecutions in China—Their Nature, Causes, Remedies." *Chinese Recorder* 15 (July–August 1884) 237–48.

Bibliography

"Outline—How to Get a Higher Class of Missionaries for China." 1885. Handwritten mss. BMS MSS.

"The Political Status of Missionaries and Native Christians in China." Extracted from *Chinese Recorder* March 1885. Reprinted in *Memorandum on the Persecution of Christians in China*. Shanghai: American Presbyterian Press, 1885.

Wanted: Good Samaritans for China. London: BMS, 1885. BMS MSS.

A Scheme for Mission Work in China. London: BMS, [1885?]. BMS MSS.

Fifteen Years' Missionary Work in China. An Address at the Annual Meeting of the BMS, Exeter Hall, April 30, 1885. BMS MSS.

"Translation of Order of Study in Our Religion." 1887. Handwritten mss. BMS MSS.

With Arthur Sowerby and J. I. Turner. "Statement of Facts being the Report of the Subcommittee on the Province of Shansi." February 1887. Handwritten mss. BMS MSS.

"How One Man Can Preach to a Million." *Chinese Recorder* 20 (November 1889) 487–98.

1890–1899

"Relation of Christian Missions to the Chinese Government." *Records of the General Conference of the Protestant Missionaries of China*. Shanghai. May 2–20, 1890. Shanghai: American Presbyterian Press, 1890, 401–15.

"Historical Evidences for Christianity—The Material Benefits." *Chinese Recorder* 21 (April 1890) 145–50.

"The Intellectual Benefits." *Chinese Recorder* 21 (May 1890) 228–32.

"Political Benefits of Christianity." *Chinese Recorder* 21 (October 1890) 435–48.

"The Social Benefits of Christianity." *Chinese Recorder* 21 (November 1890) 500–9.

"The Moral Benefits of Christianity." *Chinese Recorder* 22 (January 1891) 25–32.

"The Spiritual Benefits of Christianity." *Chinese Recorder* 22 (April 1891) 172–77.

"The Spiritual Benefits of Christianity, concluded." *Chinese Recorder* 22 (May 1891) 197–203.

"The Historical Evidences of Christianity—Present Benefits." *Chinese Recorder* 22 (October 1891) 443–51.

"The Historical Evidences of Christianity—Present Benefits, concluded." *Chinese Recorder* 22 (November 1891) 491–98.

[History of?] *The Anti-Foreign Riots in China*. Shanghai: North China Herald Office, 1892.

"Scheme for the General Enlightenment of China." *Chinese Recorder* 23 (March 1892) 131–32.

"Letter to the Editor of the *Chinese Recorder*—SDK." *Chinese Recorder* 23 (May 1892) 237–38.

"Address of Welcome." *Records of the Triennial Meeting of the Educational Association of China (EAC), May 2–4, 1893*. Shanghai, 1893.

How to Multiply Trade in China. Shanghai: SDK, March 1894. BMS MSS.

How to Multiply Trade in China (condensed). Shanghai: SDK, March 1, 1894. BMS MSS.

"A Practical Plan for Education." *Chinese Recorder* 25 (June 1894) 255.

"God's Various Methods of Blessing Mankind." *Chinese Recorder* 25 (June 1894) 272–82.

"Murray's New Phonetic System of Writing Chinese Characters." *Chinese Recorder* 25 (August 1894) 389–90.

"China's Appalling Need of Reform." *Chinese Recorder* 25 (November 1894) 515–21.

The China Mission Handbook. First Issue. Shanghai: American Presbyterian Press, 1896.
"Memorial to the Chinese Emperor on Christian Mission." *The Peking and Tientsin Times,* March 7, 1896. BMS MSS.
"Memorial to the Chinese Emperor on Christian Missions (Translation)." *Chinese Recorder* 27 (April 1896) 177–83.
Prospectus of a Society for Aiding China to fall in with Right Principle of Universal Progress. London: BMS, July 1897. BMS MSS.
"The Crisis in China, and How to Meet It." *Chinese Recorder* 29 (February 1898) 78–87. This was first printed as a pamphlet under the same title in March 1897 by the BMS in London.
"New China and Its Leaders." *Chinese Recorder* 29 (September 1898) 415–17.
"Non-Phonetic and Phonetic Systems of Writing." *Chinese Recorder* 29 (September 1898) 540–45.
"Educational Problems in China." In *Records of the Third Triennial Meeting of the EAC, May 17–20, 1899.* Shanghai: American Presbyterian Mission Press, 44–48.

1900–1904

"Reinforcements for the Christian Literature Society for China." *Chinese Recorder* 31 (March 1900), 159–60.
Philosinensis [Timothy Richard pseudonym?]. "China Old and New." *North China Herald,* August 22, 1900, 409–10; August 29, 1900, 463.
"Christian Literature." *Chinese Recorder* 31 (December 1900) 597–603.
Christian Literature: Its Extent and Its Value. Shanghai: SDK, [1900?]. BMS MSS.
"Literature as an Evangelistic Agency." In *Ecumenical Missionary Conference,* vol. 2. New York: American Tract Society, 1900, 74–76.
"In Memoriam of Rev Alexander Williamson." *Chinese Recorder* 32 (February 1901) 55–60.
"Educational Work Is Indispensable." *Chinese Recorder* 32 (February 1901) 91–93.
"One Great Missionary Secret." *Chinese Recorder* 32 (March 1901) 124–25.
"An Appeal to Missionaries for Books Suitable for Mandarins." Circular No. 114. Shanghai: SDK, April 19, 1901. BMS MSS.
"Some New Conditions of Missionary Work in Pacified China." Circular No. 115. Shanghai: SDK, April 30, 1901. BMS MSS.
"How a Few Men May Make a Million Converts." *Chinese Recorder* 32 (June 1901) 267–80.
"The Regeneration of China." *Chinese Recorder* 32 (December 1901) 614.
"The Outlook for Christianity in China." *The Missionary Review of the World* (May 1902) 341–43.
"Of More Value Than a Thousand [Ten Thousand?] Missionaries; New China New Methods." *Chinese Recorder* 34 (January 1903) 1–9. This paper appeared under the same title in a condensed form in *The Missionary Review of the World* (April 1903) 291–95.
"The New Education in China." *Contemporary Review* 83 (January 1903) 11–16.
"Letter to the Editor: The Toleration Question Again." *North China Herald,* March 5, 1903, 431.

Bibliography

[Timothy Richard?]. "The Expropriation of Temple Lands in China." *North China Herald*, April 2, 1903, 629-30.

"The Shansi University from Within." *Missionary Herald* (April 1903) 193-95.

"Christian Literature in India." *Chinese Recorder* 34 (June 1903) 265-70.

"Shansi Imperial University." *Chinese Recorder* 34 (September 1903) 460-63.

"Timothy Richard's Relations with the Chinese Government and the Christian Church." *Chinese Recorder* 34 (December 1903) 617-18.

"The Forces Which Are Molding the Future of China." *The Missionary Review of the World* NS 27 (February 1904) 86-89.

1905-1909

"The China Problem: From a Missionary Point of View." *China: a Quarterly Record of the Christian Literature Society for China* (January 1905) 289-97. Richard printed this same article and presented it to the Missions Committee of the BMS in London in May 1905 while on furlough.

Some Hints for Rising Statesmen. Shanghai: SDK, 1905. BMS MSS. Circulated privately in 1899 as *A League of Princes*.

"Thirty-five Years in China: A Talk With Rev. Timothy Richard." *Christian World* (February 2, 1905). BMS MSS.

"Speech." Christian Literature Society for China. March 17, 1905. BMS MSS.

What the Bible Is Doing in China. London: British and Foreign Bible Society, May 3, 1905. BMS MSS.

"What the Bible is Doing in China: A speech at the Bible Society's Anniversary in Exeter Hall." Annual Meeting of the British and Foreign Bible Society. *The Record*. May 5, 1905. BMS MSS.

Calendar of the Gods. Shanghai: Methodist Publishing House, 1906.

"Appeal to the Arthington Committee." March 13, 1906. Typewritten mss. BMS MSS.

"China and the West." *Living Age* 30 (March 1906) 636-38.

"The Awakening of China." *Living Age* 31 (April 21, 1906) 131-45.

Conversion by the Million. 2 vols. Shanghai: Christian Literature Society (CLS), 1907.

Most of the Circulars Sent Out In Behalf of the Diffusion Society and the Christian Literature Society Between 1891-1901 by Timothy Richard. Shanghai: CLS, 1907. BMS MSS. (Circulars are available on microfilm from Claremont College, Claremont, CA.)

"Some of the Greatest Needs of Christian Missions." *Chinese Recorder* 38 (April 1907) 211-12.

Guide to Buddhahood: Being a Standard Manual of Chinese Buddhism. Shanghai: CLS, 1907.

The Awakening of Faith in New Buddhism. n.p., 1907.

"Conversion by the Million." *Chinese Recorder* 38 (October 1907) 540-42.

"Present National Movements." *North China Daily News*, January 14, 1909. BMS MSS.

"Kang Yu-wei." *Shanghai Mercury*, January 25, 1909. BMS MSS.

"Civilizations Tested." *North China Daily News*, September 30, 1909. BMS MSS.

"The Late Prince Ito." *The National Review*, October 30, 1909. This same article appeared in the *Chinese Recorder* 40 (November 1909).

"Letter to the Editor." *North China Daily News*, [1909?]. BMS MSS.

Bibliography

1910–1919

"The China Giant Awakes." *British Weekly*, October 13, 1910. BMS MSS.

The New Testament of Higher Buddhism. Edinburgh: T. & T. Clark, 1910.

Historical Evidences for Christianity. 2nd ed. Shanghai: Commercial Press, 1911. First edition published in 1885.

"Turning Point in Human History." *Baptist Times & Freeman*, October 14, 1910. Reprinted in "Letters to the Outlook." *Outlook*, January 7, 1911, 45–46, and in *The Advocate of Peace* 73 (March 1911) 66.

"The Future of the Educational Association." *Chinese Recorder* 43 (April 1912) 230–38.

[Timothy Richard?]. "In Memoriam—Dr. Griffith John." *Journal of the North-China Branch of the Royal Asiatic Society* 43 (1912) 126.

With Donald MacGillivray. *A Dictionary of Philosophical Terms Chiefly from the Japanese*. Shanghai: CLS, 1913.

With Ch'ang Ch'un Ch'iu. *A Mission to Heaven: A Great Chinese Epic and Allegory*. Shanghai: CLS, 1913.

Epistle to All Buddhists Throughout the World. Shanghai, CLS, 1913 and 1916.

Contemporary Inspiration Through the Ages. Shanghai: [CLS?], 1914.

Forty-five Years in China: Reminiscences by Timothy Richard. London: T. Fisher Unwin, and Frederick A. Stokes, 1916.

"Some Forces in Modern China." *Contemporary Review* (December 1916) 749–54.

The Awakening of Faith in Mahayana Doctrine. 2nd ed. Edinburgh: T. & T. Clark, 1918.

"Notes on His Visit—Liang Chi Chao." [1919?]. Handwritten mss. NLW.

PUBLISHED WORKS ABOUT TIMOTHY RICHARD IN ENGLISH*

Short biographies include:

Biographical Dictionary of Chinese Christianity at http://www.bdcconline.net/en/stories/r/richard-timothy.php, accessed 15 February 2014.

Bohr, Paul Richard. "The Legacy of Timothy Richard." *International Bulletin of Missionary Research* 24/2 (April 2000) 75–79.

The studies below rely heavily on Richard's autobiography. Writers of the earliest books (before 1930) had a personal relationship with Richard and thus include occasional nuggets of information not found in Richard's autobiography. Some of these are now available in reprint. Those dated 1945 were written in honor of the centenary of Richard's birth.

Barr, Pat. *To China with Love: The Life and Times of Protestant Missionaries in China, 1860–1900*. London: Secker & Warburg, 1972.

Bohr, Paul Richard. *Famine in China and the Missionary: Timothy Richard as Relief Administrator and Advocate of National Reform, 1876–1884*. Cambridge: East Asia Research Center, Harvard University, 1972.

* Note: The bibliography reflects the author's dissertation research through 2001; asterisks mark a few more recent studies used in editing this volume.

Bibliography

Bowser, Hilda. *Timothy Richard, D.D., Litt.D., LL.D.: An Outline of His Life and Work in China.* Shanghai: CLS, 1914.
Burt, E.W. "Timothy Richard: His Contribution to Modern China." *International Review of Missions* 34 (July 1945) 293–300.
———. "The Centenary of Timothy Richard." *The Baptist Quarterly* (January–April 1945) 343–48.
Cowell, H. J. "Timothy Richard, Missionary and Mandarin: A Centenary Tribute." *The Asiatic Review* 41 (1945) 397–403.
Evans, E. W. Price. *Timothy Richard: A Narrative of Christian Enterprise and Statesmanship in China.* London: Carey Press, 1945.
Garnier, A. J. *A Maker of Modern China.* London: Carey Press, 1945.
Johnson, Rita T. "Timothy Richard's Theory of Missions to the Non-Christian World." Ph.D diss., St. John's University, 1966.
Kikuchi, Ben Hideo. "Timothy Richard's Influence on the Missionary Movement and Chinese Reform in Late Ch'ing China." MA thesis, University of Oregon, 1969.
Latourette, Kenneth Scott. "Timothy Richard: He Sought All of China." *These Sought a Country.* New York: Harper & Brothers, 1950, 88–110.
MacGillivray, D. *Timothy Richard of China: A Prince in Israel.* Shanghai: CLS, 1920.
Reeve, Rev. B. *Timothy Richard, D.D.: China Missionary, Statesman, and Reformer.* London: S. W. Partridge, [1911?].
Soothill, William E. *Timothy Richard of China: Seer, Statesman, Missionary & the Most Disinterested Adviser the Chinese Ever Had.* London: Seeley, Service, 1924.

ADDITIONAL PRIMARY AND SECONDARY REFERENCES

Abe, Hiroshi. "Borrowing From Japan: China's First Modern Educational System." In *China's Education and the Industrialized World: Studies in Cultural Transfer.* Edited by Ruth Hayhoe and Marianne Bastid. Armonk, NY: Sharpe, 1987.
Altbach, Phillip, and Viswananathan Selvaratnam, eds. *From Dependence to Autonomy: The Development of Asian Universities.* Dordrecht: Kluwer Academic, 1989.
Annual Report of the Society for the Diffusion of Christian and General Knowledge Among the Chinese (SDK). Shanghai: SDK, *the Sixth*, 1893; *the Tenth*, 1897; and *the Seventeenth*, 1904.
Annual Report of the Christian Literature Society for China (CLS, formerly the SDK). Shanghai: SDK, *the Eighteenth*, 1905; *the Nineteenth*, 1906; *the Twentieth*, 1907; *the Twenty-first*, 1908; *the Twenty-second*, 1909; *the Twenty-third*, 1910; *the Twenty-fourth*, 1911; *the Semi-Jubilee or Twenty-fifth*, 1912; *the Twenty-sixth*, 1913; *the Twenty-seventh*, 1914; *the Twenty-eighth*, 1915; *the Twenty-ninth*, 1916; *the Thirtieth*, 1917; *the Thirty-first*, 1918; *the Thirty-second*, 1919; *the Thirty-third*, 1920; *the Thirty-fourth*, 1921; and *the Thirty-fifth*, 1922.
Armstrong, Alex. "English Baptist Mission." *Shantung.* Shanghai: Shanghai Mercury Office, 1891.
Ayers, William. *Chang Chih-tung and Educational Reform in China.* Harvard East Asia Series 54. Cambridge: Harvard University Press, 1971.
Bailey, Paul J. *Reform the People: Changing Attitudes Towards Popular Education in Early Twentieth Century China.* Edinburgh: Edinburgh University Press, 1990.

Bibliography

"The Baptist Missionary Society: Annual Public Meeting." *Baptist Times* (May 3, 1905). BMS MSS.
Bastid, Marianne. *Educational Reform in Early 20th-Century China*. Translated by Paul J. Bailey. Ann Arbor: Center for Chinese Studies, University of Michigan, 1988.
Bays, Daniel, ed. *Christianity in China: From the Eighteenth Century to the Present*. Stanford: Stanford University Press, 1996.
*———, and Ellen Widmer, eds. *China's Christian Colleges: Cross-Cultural Connections, 1900–1950*. Stanford, CA: Stanford University Press, 2009.
Beach, Harlan. *A Geography and Atlas of Protestant Missions*. Vol. 1: *Geography*. New York: Student Volunteer Movement for Foreign Missions, 1902.
Bennett, Adrian A. *Missionary Journalist in China: Young J. Allen and His Magazines, 1860–1883*. Athens: University of Georgia Press, 1983.
Bevan, L. R. O. "Taiyuenfu: Historical and Mythological." *East of Asia Magazine* 3 (1904–5) 97–100. See "Imperial University": 1–3.
Biggerstaff, Knight. *The Earliest Modern Government Schools in China*. Ithaca, NY: Cornell University Press, 1961.
"Book Review—History of the War Between China and Japan." *North China Herald* (May 15, 1896) 654–55.
Borthwick, Sally. *Education and Social Change in China: The Beginnings of the Modern Era*. Stanford: Hoover Institution Press, Stanford University, 1983.
Boulger, Demetrius Charles. *China*. New York: Peter Fenelon Collier & Son, 1900.
Boxer Rising: A History of the Boxer Trouble in China Reprinted from the Shanghai Mercury. New York: Paragon Book Reprint Corp., 1967.
Britton, Nelson. "Li-ti-mo-tai of China: The Story of a Great Life." *The Chronicle* (May 1907) 79–80. BMS MSS.
Britton, Roswell. *The Chinese Periodical Press, 1800–1912*. Shanghai: Kelly & Walsh, 1933.
Broomhall, A. J. *Assault on the Nine. Book Six: 1875–1887*. London: 1988. In *Hudson Taylor & China's Open Century. Books One-Seven*. London: Hodder & Stoughton and the Overseas Missionary Fellowship, 1981–89.
Brown, J. Cumming. *The Awakening of China*. Edinburgh: Elliott, 1897.
Buck, D. "Educational Modernization in Tsinan 1899–1937." In *The Chinese City between Two Worlds*, edited by M. Elvin and W. Skinner, 171–212. Stanford: Stanford University Press, 1974.
Cameron, Meribeth E. *The Reform Movement in China, 1898–1912*. Stanford: Stanford University Press, 1931.
Carlyle, G., ed. *The Collected Writings of Edward Irving*. London: Strahan, 1864–1865.
Cary-Elwes, Columba. *China and the Cross: A Survey of Missionary History*. New York: Kenedy & Sons, 1957.
Chang Chih-tung. *China's Only Hope: An Appeal*. Translated by Samuel I. Woodbridge. Edinburgh: Oliphant, Anderson & Ferrier, 1901.
"Chat with Dr. Timothy Richard." *The Baptist*, February 23, 1905. BMS MSS.
Chen Chi-yun. "Liang Ch'i Ch'ao's 'Missionary Education': A Case Study of Missionary Influence on the Reform." Papers on China no. 16. Cambridge: Harvard University Press, 1962.
Chen Wei Cheng. "The Educational Work of Missionaries in China." Ph.D. diss., University of Michigan, 1910.

Bibliography

Chesneaux, Jean, Marianne Bastid, and Marie-Claire Bergère. *China: From the Opium Wars to the 1911 Revolution.* Translated by Anne Destenay. New York: Pantheon, 1976.

"China." *London Times*, May 7, 1901, 5d.

"China and Timothy Richard: Outline Studies for Group Discussion." London: Carey, n.d. [1945?].

Christian Literature and the Reform Movement. Edinburgh: CLS, 1911. BMS MSS.

"Christian Literature for China—The Rev. Timothy Richard, Litt.D., D.D., of Shanghai." The One Hundred and Tenth Annual Report. *Missionary Herald* (May 1902) 220.

Clayton, G. A. *A Classified Index to the Chinese Literature of the Protestant Churches in China.* Shanghai: China Continuation Committee, 1913.

Cleverley, John. *The Schooling of China: Tradition and Modernity in Chinese Education.* Sydney: Allen & Unwin, 1985.

Cliff, Norman H. "Building the Protestant Church in Shandong, China." *International Bulletin of Missionary Research* 22:2 (April 1998) 62–68.

Cloyd, David E. *Modern Education in Europe and the Orient.* New York: Macmillan, 1917.

Coates, Olive Mary. "Mrs. Moir Duncan—One of the Pioneers." *Scottish Baptist Magazine* (January 1967) 3–4.

Cohen, Paul. *History in Three Keys: The Boxers as Event, Experience, and Myth.* New York: Columbia University Press, 1998.

———. *Missionary Approaches: Hudson Taylor and Timothy Richard.* Cambridge: Harvard University, China Papers 11, 1957.

Correspondent. "Missionary Work and Reform in China." *London Times*, 15 November 1901. 6a.

Covell, Ralph. *W. A. P. Martin: Pioneer of Progress in China.* Washington, DC: Christian University Press, 1978.

———. *Confucius, the Buddha, and Christ: A History of the Gospel in Chinese.* Maryknoll, NY: Orbis, 1986: 125–28.

[Darroch, John?]. "Translation Department." *East of Asia Magazine* 3 (1904–5) 118–19. See "Imperial University": 22–23.

Davin, Delia. "Imperialism and the Diffusion of Liberal Thought: British Influence on Chinese Education." In *China's Education and the Industrialized World: Studies in Cultural Transfer*, edited by Ruth Hayhoe and Marianne Bastid. Armonk, NY: Sharpe, 1987, 33–56.

"The Death of Mrs. Timothy Richard." *North China Herald*, 17 July 1903, 103.

Dennis, Rev. James S., *Christian Missions and Social Progress.* 3 vols. New York: Fleming H. Revell, 1897, 1898, 1906.

"Diary of Events in the Far East." *Chinese Recorder* 33 (January 1902) 48.

*Doyle, G. Wright. Review of Samuel Hugh Moffett, *A History of Christianity in Asia: Volume 2, 1500-1900* (Maryknoll, NY: Orbis, 2005). http://www.globalchinacenter.org/analysis/christianity-in-china/a-history-of-christianity-in-asia-volume-2.php, accessed 11 November 2013.

"Dr. Timothy Richard and Shansi University." *The Missionary Review of the World* 24 (July 1911) 551.

Duncan, Jessie and Doreen Raymer. *Lives Lived of Moir and Jessie Duncan.* Toronto: WindyRidge, 2000.

Duncan, Moir. "Shansi Imperial University." *Chinese Recorder* 34 (September 1903) 460–63.

Bibliography

[———?]. "Shansi Imperial University." [*Missionary Herald?*] (September 1903) 478–79.

"The Imperial University, Shansi." *East of Asia Magazine* 3 (1904–5) 102–5. See "Imperial University": 6–8.

Eddy, Sherwood. *I Have Seen God Work in China*. New York: Association Press, 1944.

"Editorial Comment." *Chinese Recorder* 33 (August 1902) 427.

"Editorial Comment—Congratulations to Dr. Moir Duncan." *Chinese Recorder* 35 (May 1906) 281.

"Editorial Notes." *Educational Review* 2 (January 1909) 10.

Edmunds, Charles K. *Modern Education in China*. Bulletin 1919, No. 44. Department of the Interior, Bureau of Education. Washington, DC: Government Printing Office, 1919.

"Educational Resolutions Adopted by the Centenary Missionary Conference." *Chinese Recorder* 38 (June 1907) 328–31.

Edwards, E. H. *Fire and Sword in Shansi*. New York: Fleming H. Revell, 1903. Reprinted, New York: Arno, 1970.

Elliott, Jane. *Who Died for Civilization? Who Died for His Country? A Revised View of the Boxer War*. Ann Arbor: University of Michigan Press, 2001.

Elman, Benjamin A., and Alexander Woodside, eds. *Education and Society in Late Imperial China, 1600–1900*. Berkeley: University of California Press, 1994.

Esherick, Joseph W. *The Origins of the Boxer Uprising*. Berkeley: University of California, 1987.

"Examination Scheme." *Chinese Recorder* 29 (August 1900) 420–23.

"Faculty and Staff." Calendar of the Imperial University of Shansi (Western Department), 6th ed. (1908) 2–3. BMS MSS.

Fairbank, John K., Edwin Reischauer, and Albert M. Craig. *East Asia: Tradition & Transformation*. New Impression. Boston: Houghton Mifflin, 1978.

Fenn, William Purviance. *Christian Higher Education in Changing China, 1880–1950*. Grand Rapids: Eerdmans, 1976.

Feuerwerker, Albert. *China's Early Industrialization: Sheng Hsuan-huai (1844–1916) and Mandarin Enterprise*. New York: Atheneum, 1970.

Fisher, Daniel. *Calvin Wilson Mateer: Forty-five Years a Missionary in Shantung*. Philadelphia: Westminster, 1911.

Fong F. Sec (Kuang Fuzhuo). "The Co-operation of Chinese and Foreign Educationists in the Work of the Association." *Educational Review* 2 (July 1909) 1–6.

Forsyth, Robert Coventry. *Shantung: The Sacred Province of China*. Shanghai: CLS, 1912.

———. *The China Martyrs of 1900*. New York: Revell, n.d. [1904?].

Franke, Wolfgang. *China and the West*. Translated by R. A. Wilson. Columbia: University of South Carolina Press, 1968.

Fu Lan. "The Chi-nan-fu College." *Chinese Recorder* 33 (May 1902) 247–49.

Gascoyne-Cecil, Lord William. *Changing China*. London: Nisbet, 1910.

Gasster, Michael. *China's Struggle to Modernize*. New York: Knopf, 1972.

Gill, Frederick C. "April 12—Timothy Richard." *The Glorious Company*, vol. 1. London: Epworth, 1958.

"Government Universities." *Chinese Recorder* 33 (September 1902) 463–64.

Gracey, J. T. "The Protestant Literary Movement in China." *The Missionary Review of the World* 27 (January 1904) 25–29.

Graham, Gael. *Gender, Culture, and Christianity: American Protestant Mission Schools in China, 1880–1930*. New York: Lang, 1995.

Bibliography

Graybill, Henry Blair. *The Educational Reform in China*. Hong Kong: Kelly & Walsh, 1911.

H., M. A. "Editorial. Watson McMillan Hayes Jubilee 1882–1932." *The Chinese Fundamentalist*. (July–September 1932) 2. (Available from the Archives of the American Presbyterian Church, Philadelphia, PA.)

*Hamrin, Carol Lee, with Stacey Bieler, eds. *Salt and Light: Lives of Faith that Shaped Modern China*. Studies in Chinese Christianity. Eugene, OR: Pickwick Publications, 2009.

*———. *Salt and Light, Volume 2: More Lives of Faith that Shaped Modern China*. Studies in Chinese Christianity. Eugene, OR: Pickwick Publications, 2010.

Harrell, Paula. *Sowing the Seeds of Change: Chinese Students, Japanese Teachers, 1895–1905*. Stanford, CA: Stanford University Press, 1992.

Hart, Robert. "These From the Land of Sinim: Essays on the Chinese Question." London: Chapman & Hall, 1901.

Hayes, W. M. "Foreign Instructors and Intolerance." *Chinese Recorder* 33 (May 1903) 234.

Hayhoe, Ruth. *China's Universities, 1895–1995: A Century of Conflict*. New York: Garland, 1996.

———, ed. *Education and Modernization: The Chinese Experience*. Oxford: Pergamon, 1992.

———, and Marianne Bastid, eds. *China's Education and the Industrialized World: Studies in Cultural Transfer*. Armonk, NY: Sharpe, 1987.

———, and Lu Yongling, eds. *Ma Xiangbo and the Mind of Modern China, 1840–1939*. Armonk, NY: Sharpe, 1996.

Headland, Isaac Taylor. *China's New Day*. West Medford, MA: The Central Committee on the United Study of Missions, 1912.

———. "Missionary Influence in Chinese Reform." *The Missionary Review of the World* 22 (January 1909) 26–27.

"A Heathen Panegyric on the Shansi Martyrs." *The Missionary Review of the World* 25 (April 1902) 291–92.

Hemmens, Harry L. "Timothy Richard." *Our Standard Bearers*. London: BMS, n.d. BMS MSS.

"Historical Summary." Calendar of the Imperial University of Shansi (Western Department), 6th ed.: 1908. BMS MSS.

Ho Ping-ti. *The Ladder of Success in Imperial China*. New York: John Wiley & Sons, 1964.

Holloway, Brenda. *Timothy Richard of China: A Pageant*. London: Carey, 1945.

Hsü, Immanuel. *The Rise of Modern China*. 41st ed. New York: Oxford University Press, 1990.

Hurt, John. *Education in Evolution: Church, State, Society and Popular Education, 1800–1870*. London: Hart-Davis, 1971.

Hyatt, Irwin T., Jr. *Our Ordered Lives Confess: Three Nineteenth-Century American Missionaries in East Shantung*. Cambridge: Harvard University Press, 1976.

"Imperial University at Taiyuenfu, Shansi." *The East of Asia Magazine Special Educational Number*. Shanghai: North China Herald, June 1904, 1–23.

"Is There a Yellow Peril?" *The Western Daily Press*. Bristol, [England], May 15, 1905. BMS MSS.

Johnston, James. "Dr. Timothy Richard: A Missionary Statesman in China." *The Congregationalist & Christian World*. May 19, 1906. BMS MSS.

Judge, Joan. *Print and Politics: Shibao and the Culture of Reform in Late Qing China*. Stanford, CA: Stanford University Press, 1996.

Bibliography

Keenan, Barry C. *Imperial China's Last Classical Academies: Social Change in the Lower Yangzi, 1864–1911*. China Research Monograph 42. Berkeley: Institute of East Asian Studies, University of California-Berkeley, 1994.

———. "Lung-men Academy in Shanghai and the Expansion of Kiangsu's Educated Elite, 1865–1911." *Education and Society in Late Imperial China, 1600–1900*. Edited by Benjamin A. Elman and Alexander Woodside, 493–524. Berkeley: University of California Press, 1994.

Kemp, E. G. *Chinese Mettle*. London: Hodder & Stoughton, 1921.

Kranz, Paul. "List of Educational Articles from the 'Recorder,' 1869–1894." *Chinese Recorder* 26 (May 1895) 228–32.

Kuo Ping Wen. *The Chinese System of Public Education*. New York City: Teachers College series, Columbia University, 1915.

Kwong, Luke S. K. *A Mosaic of the Hundred Days: Personalities, Politics, and Ideas of 1898*. Cambridge: Council on East Asian Studies, Harvard University Press, 1984.

Latourette, Kenneth Scott, *History of Christian Missions in China*. London: SPCK, 1928.

———. *The Chinese: Their History and Culture*. 3rd ed. Revised. New York: Macmillan, 1947.

Levenson, Joseph R. *Liang Ch'i-Ch'ao and the Mind of Modern China*. Berkeley: University of California Press, 1967.

*Li, Aisi. "Competition and Compromise between British Missionaries and Chinese Officials: the Founding of Shanxi University in 1902." Ph.D. diss., Oxford University, 2012.

Li, Anthony C. *The History of Privately Controlled Higher Education in the Republic of China*. Westport, CT: Greenwood, 1954.

Lo, Lung-pang, ed. and trans. *K'ang Yu-wei: A Biography and Symposium*. Tucson: University of Arizona Press, 1967.

Lodwick, Kathleen, compiler. *The Chinese Recorder Index: A Guide to Christian Missions in Asia, 1867–1941*, Volume I. Wilmington, DE: Scholarly Resources, 1986.

Ludtke, Gerhard, and Fredrich Richter. *Minerva: Jahrbuch der Gelehrten Welt*. Berlin: de Gruyter, 1933.

Lund, Renville Clifton. "The Imperial University of Peking." Ph.D. diss., University of Washington, 1956.

Lyman, E. R. "Psychological." *East of Asia Magazine* 3 (1904–5) 110–14. See "Imperial University": 14–17.

———, ed. *A Century of Protestant Missions in China (1807–1907)*. Shanghai: American Presbyterian Mission Press, 1907.

———, ed. *Descriptive and Classified Missionary Centenary Catalogue of Current Christian Literature*. Shanghai: CLS, 1907.

Mackenzie, Robert. *The Nineteenth Century: A History*. 15th ed. London: Nelson, 1909. (A 72-page edition was first published in 1880 by G. Munro of New York. Richard read and translated the 472-page edition published by Thomas Nelson of New York and London in 1889.)

The Man Who Could Not Be Denied. London: Carey, 1945.

Martin, W. A. P. *The Awakening of China*. New York: Doubleday, Page, 1907.

———. *The Chinese: Their Education, Philosophy, and Letters*. London: Trübner, 1881.

Miyazaki, Ichisada. *China's Examination Hell: The Civil Service Examinations of Imperial China*. Translated by Conrad Schirokauer. New Haven: Yale University Press, 1981.

Bibliography

Morgan, E. "In Memoriam—Rev. M. B. Duncan, M.A., LL.D." *Chinese Recorder* 37 (October 1906) 558–61.

Nevius, John L. *China and the Chinese*. Revised edition. Philadelphia: Presbyterian Board of Publication, 1882.

"New China and Its Leaders." *Chinese Recorder* 29 (September 1898) 418–19.

Nichols, Francis H. *Through Hidden Shensi*. New York: Scribner, 1905.

"Notes." *Chinese Recorder* 32 (1901).

"Notes." *Chinese Recorder* 33 (June 1902) 302, 311.

"Notes." *Tyndale Messenger*. July 1905.

"A Noteworthy Document." *The Missionary Review of the World* 25 (April 1902) n.p.

Nystrom, Erik Torsten. *The Coal and Mineral Resources of Shansi Province, China*. Stockholm: Norstedt, 1912.

"Obituary: Timothy Richard." *Journal of the North-China Branch of the Royal Asiatic Society* 50 (1919) 247–48.

"Obituary: Timothy Richard, D.D., LL.D., Litt.D." *The China Mission Year Book 1919* (Tenth Annual Issue). Edited by E. C. Lobenstine and A. L. Warnshuis. Shanghai: Kwang Hsueh, 1920.

"Obituary: Timothy Richard and the Christian Literature Society." [1921?] Typewritten mss. NLW.

"Officers and Committees." *Chinese Recorder* 33 (June 1902) 302.

Payne, Ernest. "Timothy Richard of China, 1845–1919." In *The Great Succession: Leaders of the Baptist Missionary Society During the 19th Century*, 102–14. London: Carey, 1938.

———. "In Shansi and Shensi." *Northern Messenger Sunday School Paper*. Montreal, [1933?].

Peake, Cyrus H. *Nationalism and Education in Modern China*. New York: Columbia University, 1932.

Peck, Myron H. "Description of Buildings." *East of Asia Magazine* 3 (1904–5) 105–10. See "Imperial University": 9–13.

Pepper, Suzanne. *Radicalism and Education Reform in 20th-Century China*. Cambridge: Cambridge University Press, 1996.

Peterson, Glen, Ruth Hayhoe, and Yongling Lu, eds. *Education, Culture and Identity in Twentieth-Century China*. Ann Arbor: University of Michigan Press, 2001.

*Pfister, Lauren. "Rethinking Missions in China: James Hudson Taylor and Timothy Richard." In Andrew Porter, *The Imperial Horizons of British Protestant Missions, 1880–1914*. Studies in the history of Christian Missions. Grand Rapids: Eerdmans, 2003. Originally a Position Paper from a consultation on "Imperial Horizon of Protestant Mission. 1880–1914," Cambridge, April 7–9, 1998. University of Cambridge, North Atlantic Missiology Project, No. 68.

Pomerantz-Zhang, Linda. *Wu Tingfang (1842–1922) Reform and Modernization in Modern Chinese History*. Hong Kong: Hong Kong University Press, 1992.

Potts, F. L. Hawks. *The Emergency in China*. New York: Missionary Education Movement of the United States and Canada, 1913.

Price, Fred. *History of Caio, Caermarthenshire, Swansea, Wales*: The Author. Printed by B. Trerise, 1904.

"Programme of Triennial Meeting." *Chinese Recorder* 33 (April 1902) 199–200.

"Provincial Education in Shansi." *North China Herald* (December 18, 1903) 1296.

Purcell, Victor C. *The Boxer Uprising*. Cambridge: Harvard University Press, 1963.

Reardon-Anderson, James. *The Study of Change: Chemistry in China, 1840–1949*. Cambridge: Cambridge University Press, 1991.
Records of the General Conference of Protestant Missionaries of China. Shanghai, May 10–24, 1877; Shanghai, 1878. May 7–20, 1890; Shanghai, 1890.
Records of the Triennial Meeting of the EAC. Shanghai, May 2–4, 1893. Shanghai, 1893.
Records of the Second Triennial Meeting of the EAC. Shanghai, May 6–9, 1896. Shanghai, 1896.
Records of the Third Triennial Meeting of the EAC. Shanghai, May 17–20, 1899. Shanghai, 1900.
Records of the Fourth Triennial Meeting of the EAC. Shanghai, May 21–24, 1902. Shanghai, 1902.
Records of the Fifth Triennial Meeting of the EAC. Shanghai, May 17–20, 1905. Shanghai, 1905.
Records of the Sixth Triennial Meeting of the EAC. Shanghai, May 19–22, 1909. Shanghai, 1910.
"Reinforcements for the Christian Literature Society for China." *Chinese Recorder* 31 (March 1900) 159–60.
Reports of the Mission Among the Higher Classes in China (The International Institute of China), 27th and 28th. Shanghai, 1911; 56th and 57th. Shanghai and Peking, 1926.
Reynolds, Douglas R. *China. 1898–1912: The Xinzheng Revolution and Japan*. Cambridge: Council on East Asian Studies, Harvard University, 1993.
R., E. I. [Eleanor Richard?]. "A Foster Father of the League of Nations." *Peking & Tientsin Times*, March 1919. Typewritten mss. NLW.
Richard, M[ary?]. "The Martyrs of 'Young China.'" *Sunday at Home* 46 (1899) 285–88.
———. "The Christian and the Chinese Idea of Womanhood and How Our Mission Schools May Help to Develop the Former Idea." *Chinese Recorder* 31 (January 1900) 10–16; (February 1900) 55–62.
Richardson, Don. *Eternity in Their Hearts*. Ventura, CA: Regal, 1981.
Schurmann, Franz, and Orville Schell. *Imperial China: The Decline of the Last Dynasty and the Origins of Modern China, the 18th and 19th Centuries*. New York: Vintage, 1967.
Schwartz, Benjamin. In *Search of Wealth and Power: Yen Fu and the West*. Cambridge: Harvard University Press, 1964.
*Scott, Gregory Adam. "Timothy, Richard, World Religion, and Reading Christianity in Buddhist Garb." *Social Sciences and Missions* 25 (2012) 53–75.
"Shanghai Mercury." *The Boxer Rising: A History of the Boxer Trouble in China*. 1900. Reprinted, New York: Paragon, 1967.
"Shansi Advancing in Modern Civilization." *Shanghai Mercury*. June 19, [1902?]. n.p. BMS MSS.
"Shansi University: A Tribute to Dr. Timothy Richard." *North China Daily News*. December 15, 1910. BMS MSS.
Sites, Lacey. "The Educational Edicts of 1901 in China." *Educational Review* 25 (January 1903) 67–75.
"The Educational Conquest of China." *Contemporary Review* 98 (October 1910) 403–8.
"Special Commissioner." "The Fate of China: A Chat With Rev. Dr. Timothy Richard." *The Christian Commonwealth*. March 23, 1905. BMS MSS.
Spence, Jonathan D. *The Gate of Heavenly Peace: The Chinese and Their Revolution, 1895–1980*. New York: Penguin Books, 1981.

Bibliography

———. *To Change China: Western Advisers in China, 1620–1960*. New York: Penguin, 1980.

Stanley, Brian. *History of the Baptist Missionary Society, 1792–1992*. London: Continuum, 1992.

Stauffer, Milton, ed. *The Christian Occupation of China*. Shanghai: China Continuation Committee, 1922.

Stephens, Margaret Anne. "The Impact of the West: Timothy Richard and Reform in China." MA thesis, George Washington University, 1979.

Swallow, R.W. "Education and Reform in China." *The Imperial and Asiatic Quarterly Review and Oriental and Colonial Record* 20/1 (July 1905) 138–47.

Tan, Chester. *The Boxer Catastrophe*. New York: Octagon, 1955.

Tang Xiaobing. *Global Space and the Nationalist Discourse of Modernity: The Historical Thinking of Liang Qichao*. Stanford: Stanford University Press, 1996.

"Taught by War—an Interview with the Rev. T. Richard." *The Daily News*. August 30, 1897. BMS MSS.

Teng Ssu-yü and John K. Fairbank. *China's Response to the West: A Documentary Survey, 1839–1923*. Cambridge: Harvard University Press, 1961.

Tucker, L. *Notes on the Life and Work of Dr. Timothy Richard of China*. London: Shaw, [1908?]. BMS MSS.

*Uhalley, Stephen Jr., and Xiaoxin Wu, eds. *China and Christianity: Burdened Past, Hopeful Future*. Armonk, NY: Sharpe, 2001.

U.S. Senate Committee on Foreign Relations. *Chinese Indemnity Fund*. 48th Cong., 2d sess., 1885. S. Rept. 1190.

Varg, Paul A. *Missionaries. Chinese and Diplomats: The American Protestant Missionary Movement in China, 1890–1952*. New York: Octagon, 1977.

*Walls, Andrew F. *The Cross-cultural Process in Christian History*. Maryknoll, NY: Orbis, 2002.

Wang Shu-hwai. "The Educational Association of China, 1890–1912: Its History and Meaning in the Missionary Education in China." MA thesis, University of Hawaii, 1963.

Warr, Winifred. *Far Into China: The Story of Timothy Richard, Pioneer*. London: Carey, n.d. [1945?].

Wei, Betty Peh-T'i. *Shanghai: Crucible of Modern China*. Hong Kong: Oxford University Press, 1987.

*Whitefield, Douglas Brent. "The Christian Literature Society for China: The Role of its Publications, Personalities, and Theology in Late-Qing Reform Movements." Ph.D. diss., Cambridge University, August 28, 2001.

Whyte, Bob. *Unfinished Encounter: China and Christianity*. London: Fount Paperbacks, 1988.

Williamson, H. R. *British Baptists in China, 1845–1952*. London: Carey Kingsgate, 1957.

———. "Timothy Richard, 1845–1919." *Baptists Who Made History: A Book about Great Baptists Written by Baptists*. London: Carey Kingsgate, 1955, 96–107.

Wilson, C. E. "Timothy Richard, 1845–1919." London: BMS, [1919?] Typewritten mss. BMS MSS.

Wong, Timothy Man-kong. "Timothy Richard and the Chinese Reform Movement." *Fides et Historia* 31/1 (summer–fall 1999) 47–59.

Woodberry, K. C., Mrs. *Through Blood-Stained Shansi*. New York: Alliance, 1903.

*Woodberry, Robert D. "The Missionary Roots of Liberal Democracy." *American Political Science Review* 106:2 (May 2012), 244–74.

Wright. Daniel B. "J. Hudson Taylor, 1832–1905, and Timothy Richard, 1845–1919: Two Unique Tools for God's Task in China." Unpublished student paper, Fuller Theological Seminary, winter 1987.

Wright, Mary C. *The Last Stand of Chinese Conservatism: The T'ung-Chih Restoration. 1862–1874*. New York: Atheneum, 1967.

Wu Yung. *The Flight of an Empress*. New Haven: Yale University Press, 1936.

Xu Xiaoguang. "A Southern Methodist Mission to China: Soochow University, 1901–1939." Ph.D. diss., Middle Tennessee State University, 1993.

Yam Tong Hoh. "The Boxer Indemnity Remissions and Education in China." Ph.D. diss., Columbia University, 1933.

Young, J. H. "The Rev. Timothy Richard, D.D., Litt.D. of China." *Missionary Herald* (January 1902) 16–19.

Index

Addis, Sir Charles S., 66
Allen, Young J., 20n36, 51, 55, 65–68, 74n64, 80n82, 81, 84, 87, 120, 125
Arsenal, 37, 38n16, 51n4

Baptist Missionary Society, English (BMS), xiii, 4, 5, 10–13, 17, 20, 22, 25–27, 31–39, 50, 51, 53n6, 60, 64, 65, 74, 90–93, 96, 97, 99, 100, 102, 109–111, 113, 116, 118, 120, 160
Baynes, Alfred, 13n15, 17n28, 20n34–35, 26n48, 27n50, 29n53, 33, 36, 37n13, 39, 40n23, 42n26–27, 42n29, 43n30–31, 44, 45n36, 46n38, 74n63, 78n74, 79n79, 90n3, 91n6–7, 92n9–10, 94n13, 94n16, 96, 97n20–22, 105n37, 120
Bevan, L.R.O. (Louis), 97n22, 105n37–38, 108–110n44
Boxer Uprising, 3, 63n29, 76–79, 90, 92, 96, 99, 106, 115, 122, 128, 162; Protocol 79, 94
Buddhism, 13, 15, 37, 39, 95n18, 116, 117, 119, 120n8, 160

Caermarthenshire, 8, 159
Cai Ergang (Ts'ai Er-kang), 68, 167–69
Cen Chunxuan (Ts'en Ch'un-hsüan), x, 78n76, 91, 92, 96, 98, 100, 103, 109n44, 125, 128
Chancellor, 80, 97n22, 100, 101, 105n37, 108, 109n44, 113, 125, 162
Chang Chih-tung. *See* Zhang Zhidong
Chang Pai-hsi. *See* Zhang Baixi
Chang Yin-huan. *See* Zhang Yinhuan
China Inland Mission (CIM; Overseas Missionary Fellowship), xiii, 10, 13n16, 14n19, 18n31, 20n34, 28, 35, 36n11, 37n13, 87, 93n11, 119, 153, 154
Chinese Book and Tract Society, 50
Chinese Department, 98, 101, 103
Chinese Imperial Maritime Customs (Imperial Chinese Customs), 27, 47, 54, 57
Chinese Progress, The, 66, 69n45
Chinese Telegraph Administration, 66
Ch'ing, Prince. *See* Qing, Prince
Ch'ing-chow. *See* Weifang
Christian Literature Society (CLS), xiii, 4, 5, 29, 46, 47, 50, 51–60, 63–69, 72, 74–76, 79–88, 91, 95, 96, 104, 111, 114, 119, 122, 161, 164. *See also* Society for the Diffusion of Christian and General Knowledge among the Chinese (SDK)
Ci Xi. *See* Empress Dowager
Commercial Press, 87
Cornaby, W. A., 76

Darroch, John, 104
donations from Christians, 15, 55n11, 83
Duan Fang, 83
Duncan, Moir, x, xi, 33, 92, 97, 98n24, 99–102n31–33, 105, 108, 128

Edkins, Joseph, 36, 55, 88
Educational Association of China (EAC), xiii, 4, 5, 48, 56, 71–76, 79, 80, 82n88, 84–87, 114, 122, 162–63
Empress Dowager (Ci Xi), 53n7, 64, 70, 75n67, 76, 78–80, 88, 92n8, 94, 162

191

Index

Evangelical Alliance, 27, 160
examination, civil service, 3, 5, 26n49, 53, 59, 67, 70n47, 79n80, 102n33, 107, 115
famine relief, 2, 15, 16n22, 17–20, 30, 43, 52, 90–91, 117, 152, 159–60
Famine Relief Committee, 18
feng shui, 14n18, 16–17, 19
Ferguson, J. C., 66n38, 73, 74n64
Fong F. Sec. *See* Kuang Fuzhuo
Foreign Affairs Office, 56, 61, 161
furlough, 4, 12n14, 24, 29, 31, 33, 34, 35, 55, 62–65, 73, 82, 84, 118, 123, 160–61, 163

Gong (Kung), Prince, 16n22, 60, 63, 161
Guang Xuehui (Kuang Hsüeh Hui). *See* Society for the Diffusion of Christian and General Knowledge among the Chinese (SDK)
Guangxu (Kuang/Kwang Hsü), Emperor, 69, 94

Hanbury, Thomas, 53n7, 55, 56n13, 87
Hanlin, 40, 59–61, 107–8
Hart, Sir Robert, 27–28, 47, 51, 56, 57, 75, 88, 113n4, 160, 162
Haverfordwest Theological College, 9, 159
Hayes, W. M., 73, 95, 97n20
Higher Learning Society (Jiang Xuehui). *See* Reform Society/Club
Home Mission Committee, 17n28, 28
honorary doctorates, 112
Hsien Feng. *See* Xian Feng, Emperor
Hundred Days' Reform, 68, 69n44, 76, 79–80, 91, 115, 162

Imperial Chinese Customs. *See* Chinese Imperial Maritime Customs
Imperial University of Peking, 2, 67, 70, 80, 107
Imperial University of Shansi, ix, 4–5, 19n33, 33, 59n19, 83n90–91, 84n92, 89–111, 113, 125, 128–29, 131, 153, 162–63, 169

indemnity, x, 27, 56, 57, 78n76, 79, 83n90, 90–91, 93n11, 97, 99, 122, 162
Islam (Muslim), 13–15, 116–17, 159
Ito, Prince, 124, 163

Japan, 2, 13n15, 15, 22n40, 38n18, 41, 43n31, 45–46, 49, 52, 53n6, 57–58, 59n21, 65, 67, 71, 77–78, 81–82, 84–85, 87–88, 92n8, 95, 97n20, 99n25, 104, 108, 113, 121–125, 160, 161–64
Jiang Xuehui (Higher Learning Society). *See* Reform Society/Club
Jinan, 25–26, 39, 42n27, 44, 68n41, 73n58, 159–60
Jinshi, (degree equivalent to PhD) 84
Jones, A. G., 16n22, 17, 25, 39, 41, 74n64, 97, 160, 166, 168
Juren, (degree equivalent to MA) 53n8, 84, 102

Kang Youwei (K'ang Yu-wei), 28n52, 59–60, 64, 66, 69–71, 91n8, 124–25, 161
Korea, 14–15, 68, 163
Kuang Fuzhuo (Fong F. Sec), 87, 108n41
Kuang Hsüeh Hui (Guang Xuehui). *See* Christian Literature Society
Kuang/Kwang Hsü. *See* Guangxu, Emperor
Kung, Prince. *See* Gong, Prince

League of Nations, 124
Legge, James, 15, 120
Li Hongzhang (Li Hung-chang), Viceroy, 5, 13, 14n17, 18, 21, 27, 40, 43–45, 49, 59, 61, 63–65, 67n39, 68, 75n67, 87, 90, 93–94, 98, 101, 105, 107, 129, 159, 161–62, 167
Liang Qichao (Liang Ch'i-ch'ao), 59, 60, 64, 66, 69–71, 124–25, 164
Liu Kunyi (Liu K'un-i), 95
Lucerne Peace Conference, 123, 163

MacGillivray, Donald, 76n70
Mackenzie, Robert, 52, 55, 58, 63, 65, 67, 161, 167

192

Martin, W. A. P., 38n16, 119
Mateer, Calvin, 12, 73–74, 80n82
Missionary Memorial, 60n23, 62
Missionary Review, The, 52, 55, 64, 67, 76
model province, 110
Moffett, Samuel, 120
Muslim. *See* Islam

Nevius, John L., 12, 13n14
Nystrom, Erik, 97n22, 98n22, 105n37, 108, 109, 110n44

Order of the Double Dragon, 113, 163
orphanage, 15–16, 20, 82n88
Overseas Missionary Fellowship (OMF). *See* China Inland Mission

Parliament of Man, 123
Peace Plenipotentiaries, 90, 92–94, 96, 162
Peace Societies, 123–24
Peking Gazette, 11, 60n22, 98n24, 162
Peking Oriental Society, 39
Pethick, William, 59
Potts, F. L. H., 66n38, 73, 74n64

Qing, Prince (Ch'ing), 90, 94, 98, 101n30, 162, 169
Qinghua University (Ts'inghua), 2, 99n25

red button, 105n38, 113, 163
Red Cross, 84, 92n8, 113, 123, 163
Rees, J. Lambert, 57–58
Reform Society/Club, 59–60, 61n25, 62, 69, 71, 161–62
Reid, Gilbert, 28n52, 59, 61n25, 74n62, 74n64
Religious Tract Society, 18, 34n8, 82n88
Review of the Times, 24n44, 51, 52, 55, 60, 64–65, 67–68, 84
Ricci, Matteo, 20, 117, 166
Richard, Mary (Mary Martin), 20, 22n40, 25n45–46, 26n49, 27n50, 31n1, 33n5, 34n7, 36n12, 37, 38n18, 39–40, 42, 44n33–34,
46n37–39, 56, 64, 66, 84, 117, 128, 159, 163, 166–67
Russo-Japanese War (1904–1905), 84, 92n8, 113, 123

School and Textbook Series Committee, 71–72
scientific lectures, 21
Second General Missionary Conference, 43, 161
seeking the worthy, 13, 15n20, 116
Self Strengthening Movement, 49
Shandong Provincial College, 100
Sheffield, D. Z., 73, 74n64
Shen Dunhe (Tunho), 83n91, 91, 92n8
Sheng Xuanhuai, 65, 66n36, 67n39, 68
Shi Bao (Shih Pao; The Times), 4, 44–47, 64, 120, 161
Sino-Japanese War (1894–1895), 2, 52, 58, 67
Society for the Diffusion of Christian and General Knowledge among the Chinese (SDK, Guang Xuehui), xiii, 4, 12n14, 46, 47n41, 48, 50, 55n11, 58n18, 72, 74n64, 114, 161. *See also* Christian Literature Society (CLS)
Soothill, William E., x, 12n14, 13n15, 14n18, 23n41, 42n26, 46n39, 56n13, 62n27, 63n30, 69n43, 84n92, 88n99, 91n7, 97n22, 98n23, 100, 102n31–32, 104, 105n38, 106n39, 108, 110n44, 110n46, 113n3, 122n9
Sun Jia'nai, 52, 59, 63

Taiping Rebellion, 11, 19, 27, 160
Taylor, J. Hudson, 10n9, 13n16, 35n10, 87, 119, 120
Tianjin (T'ientsin), 13n16, 21, 37, 40–42, 44, 49, 52n6, 53n7, 67n39, 104, 120, 159–61
Tls. (Tael), xiii, 33, 38, 40, 50, 53n7, 55, 56n13, 57, 66n38, 93, 97, 103–4, 106–7
Tribe, Dr. Ethel, 122, 164
Triennial Meeting of the Educational Association of China, 71–73,

Index

74n63–64, 75, 80n82–83, 84, 87n98
Ts'ai Er-kang. *See* Cai Ergang
Ts'en Ch'un-hsüan. *See* Cen Chunxuan
Tseng Kuo-ch'üan. *See* Zeng Guochuan
Tseng Kuo-fan. *See* Zeng Guofan
Ts'inghua University. *See* Qinghua University
Tso Tsung-t'ang. *See* Zuo Zongtang

Wales: as country, 4, 7–9, 48, 108n42, 113, 116, 154, 156, 159; National Library of, xiii, 154; University of, 112–13, 154–55, 164; Bible College of, 155
Walshe, W. G., 76, 168
Wang Tao, 125
Wangguo gongbao/Wan-kuo kung-pao. *See Review of the Times*
Weifang (Ch'ing-chow), 14–15, 25, 26n47
Weng Tonghe (Weng T'ung-ho), 59, 60n21, 61, 62, 161
Western Department, ix, xi, 98–103, 108n42, 153, 162
Western learning, xi, 3–4, 6, 16, 19, 25n44, 26, 29–33, 36n11, 38, 42n28, 49–50, 52, 56, 61, 66–68, 69n43, 73, 74n64, 75, 80–82, 89–90, 92n10, 93–94, 96, 99, 106, 110, 114, 117–18, 160, 162, 167
Whitewright, John S., 25–26
Williams, N. T., 98n22, 104, 108n42, 109, 110n44
Williamson, Alexander G., 12, 18n31, 20n36, 47, 50–51

World Baptist Conference, 123, 163
World Missionary Conference, 123, 163
Wuhan (Wuchang), 19n31, 25, 43, 46, 57–58, 67n39, 68n41, 89

Xian Feng, Emperor (Hsien Feng), 61
Xiucai (degree equivalent to BA), 61, 84, 102

YMCA (Young Men's Christian Association), 57n16, 100
Yu Xian (Yu Hsien), 77
Yuan Shikai (Yuen Shih-k'ai), 60n23, 72, 83, 85, 95, 104n36

Zeng Guochuan (Tseng Kuo-ch'üan), 19, 89
Zeng Guofan (Tseng Kuo-fan), 19, 40, 160
Zeng Jize (Tseng Chi-tse), Marquis, 19, 28n52, 34, 40, 160, 167
Zhang Baixi (Chang Pai-hsi), 80
Zhang Yinhuan (Chang Yin-huan), 59n21, 161
Zhang Zhidong (Chang Chih-tung), Viceroy, 24–25, 38n16, 43, 46n38, 49, 50n1, 57–58, 59n19, 59n21, 61n25, 66, 67n39, 68, 83, 88–89, 94–95, 129, 160–61
Zhou Fu, 75n67, 83, 163
Zongli Yamen. *See* Foreign Affairs Office
Zuo Zongtang (Tso Tsung-t'ang), 24, 160

www.ingramcontent.com/pod-product-compliance
Lightning Source LLC
Chambersburg PA
CBHW051738230426
43670CB00012B/2070